Retuarã Syntax
Studies in the Languages of Colombia 3

Summer Institute of Linguistics and
The University of Texas at Arlington
Publications in Linguistics

Publication 112

Editors

Donald A. Burquest
University of Texas
at Arlington

William R. Merrifield
Summer Institute of
Linguistics

Series Editor

Paul Frank

Assistant Editors

Rhonda L. Hartell

Marilyn A. Mayers

Consulting Editors

Doris A. Bartholomew
Pamela M. Bendor-Samuel
Desmond C. Derbyshire
Robert A. Dooley
Jerold A. Edmondson

Austin Hale
Robert E. Longacre
Eugene E. Loos
Kenneth L. Pike
Viola G. Waterhouse

Retuarã Syntax
Studies in the Languages of Colombia 3

by Clay Strom

A Publication of
The Summer Institute of Linguistics
and
The University of Texas at Arlington
1992

©1992 by the Summer Institute of Linguistics, Inc.
Library of Congress Catalog No.: 92–85042
ISBN: 0-88312-181-6
ISSN: 1040-0850

All Rights Reserved

No part of this publication may be reproduced, stored in a retrieval system, or transmitted in any form or by any means—electronic, mechanical, photocopy, recording, or otherwise—without the express permission of the Summer Institute of Linguistics, with the exception of brief excerpts in journal articles or reviews.

Cover sketch and design by Hazel Shorey

Copies of this and other publications of the Summer Institute of Linguistics may be obtained from

International Academic Bookstore
Summer Institute of Linguistics
7500 W. Camp Wisdom Road
Dallas, TX 75236

Contents

Abbreviations xi
Acknowledgments xiii
1. Introduction 1
    1.1–1.10 Word order constituents
    1.1. Basic word order 2
    1.2. Adpositions 4
    1.3. Descriptive modifiers 4
    1.4. Genitives 5
    1.5. Affixation 5
    1.6. Relative clauses 6
    1.7. Comparatives 6
    1.8. Negation 6
    1.9. Questions 7
    1.10. Word order summary 7
    1.11–1.14 Distinguishing major syntactic functions
    1.11. Word order 7
    1.12. Subject expression 8
    1.13. Nominalization 10
    1.14. Categorization of nouns 10

1.15–1.20 Phonology sketch

- 1.15. Phonemic inventory 11
- 1.16. Phonological rules 12
- 1.17. Stress 13
- 1.18. Nasalization 19
- 1.19. Word and syllable structure 21
- 1.20. Morphophonology 21

2. Parts of Speech 23

- 2.1. Nouns and adjectives 23

2.2–2.8 Verbs

- 2.2. Copular verb 28
- 2.3. Spatial relators 29
- 2.4. Intransitive verbs 31
- 2.5. Transitive verbs 31
- 2.6. Ditransitive verbs 32
- 2.7. Verbs with sentential objects 32
- 2.8. Compound verbs 33
- 2.9. Adverbs 33

2.10–2.12 Pronouns and other pro-forms

- 2.10. Personal pronouns 34
- 2.11. Demonstratives 36
- 2.12. Dummy pronoun 36

2.13–2.15 Noun adjuncts

- 2.13. Case markers 37
- 2.14. Quantifiers 37
- 2.15. Classifiers 37

2.16–2.22 Verb adjuncts

- 2.16. Auxiliary verb 38
- 2.17. Tense 38
- 2.18. Aspect 38
- 2.19. Mood 38
- 2.20. Intensifiers 39
- 2.21. Evidentials 39
- 2.22. Subordinating suffixes 39
- 2.23. Coordinating conjunctions 39
- 2.24. Subordinating conjunctions 40
- 2.25. Negators 40

Contents

    2.26–2.29 Derivational affixes

    2.26. Nominalization by number/gender suffixes 41
    2.27. Deverbalizer 41
    2.28. Adverbializer 43
    2.29. Causatives 43

3. Noun Phrase 45
    3.1. Noun classes 45
    3.2. Genitives 47
    3.3. Relative clause 48
    3.4. Quantifiers 48
    3.5. Numerals 50
    3.6. Adjectives 51
    3.7. Demonstratives 51
    3.8. Relative order of elements in noun phrase 53
    3.9. Case 53
    3.10. Classifiers and concord in the noun phrase 54

4. Case 59
    4.1. Term 59
    4.2. General locative 61
    4.3. Specific locative 62
    4.4. Ablative 62
    4.5. Instrument 63
    4.6. Comitative 64
    4.7. Benefactive 65
    4.8. Possessive 66
    4.9. Case combinations 67

5. Verb Phrase 69
    5.1. Order of verb affixes 69
    5.2. Agreement 71
    5.3. Auxiliary verb 72

    5.4–5.9 Tense

    5.4. Present 72
    5.5. Immediate past 73
    5.6. Recent past 73
    5.7. Remote past 74
    5.8. General past 74
    5.9. Future 75

    5.10–5.15 Aspect

    5.10. Habitual 77

5.11. Imperfective	77
5.12. Continuative	78
5.13. Perfect	78
5.14. Impersonal	79
5.15. Punctual	80

5.16–5.19 Mood

5.16. Intention	81
5.17. Possibility	81
5.18. Consequence	82
5.19. Contra-expectation	82

5.20–5.24. Other verbal affixes

5.20. Stativizer	84
5.21. The functions of *-i* (stativizer) and *-eʔka* (general past)	85
5.22. Directionals	88
5.23. Intensifiers	89
5.24. Evidentials	90
5.25. Compound verbs	91

5.26–5.28 Causatives

5.26. Volitional causation	93
5.27. Nonvolitional causation	94
5.28. Lexicalized causatives	96
5.29. Reciprocals	99
5.30. Incorporation	100

6. Adverbs	103
6.1. Manner	103
6.2. Time	104
6.3. Location	104
6.4. Speaker attitude adverbs	105
6.5. Mood/aspect adverbs	106
6.6. Derived adverbs	107

7. Sentence Structure	111
7.1. Intransitive	112
7.2. Transitive	114
7.3. Ditransitive	118
7.4. Copular sentences	123
7.5. Existential	124

7.6–7.8 Locationals

7.6. Locative/existential	126
7.7. Predicate nominal and possessive 'to be'	129

7.8.	Possessive 'to have'	131
7.9.	Reflexives	133
7.10.	Subordinate clauses	134

8. Imperatives 135

8.1.	Second-person imperatives	135
8.2.	Indirect imperative	136
8.3.	Negative imperative	137
8.4.	Hortatory	137
8.5.	Third-person imperatives	138
8.6.	Responses to imperatives	139

9. Questions 141

9.1.	Yes/no questions	141
9.2.	Content questions	142
9.3.	Alternate questions	143
9.4.	Indirect questions	143
9.5.	Courtesy in question-asking	144
9.6.	Answers to questions	144

10. Negation 145

10.1.	Sentential negation	145
10.2.	Negative verb	147

11. Subordination 151

11.1–11.2 Relative clauses

11.1.	Internally headed classification	151
11.2.	Relativization into different syntactic positions	156

11.3–11.7 Complementation

11.3.	Modality verbs	159
11.4.	Manipulative verbs	161
11.5.	Cognition/utterance/sensory verbs	162
11.6.	Motion verbs with purpose complements	164
11.7.	Preventative constructions	165

11.8–11.17 Adverbial clauses formed by suffixes

11.8.	Time: after	168
11.9.	Time: simultaneous	169
11.10.	Purpose	169
11.11.	Intention	170
11.12.	Contingency	170
11.13.	Negative purpose	172
11.14.	Condition/grounds	172

11.15. Reason (different subject)	173
11.16. Reason (same subject)	174
11.17. Contra-expectation	175

11.18–11.22 Adverbial clauses formed by conjunctions

11.18. Time: when	176
11.19. Time: prior	176
11.20. Comparison: like	177
11.21. Condition: if	177
11.22. Continue: still/yet	178
12. Elements of Discourse	179

12.1–12.5 Participant reference

12.1. Participant reference rules	181
12.2. Introduction of participants	181
12.3. Further participant reference	183
12.4. Reintroduction of participants	186
12.5. Exceptions to rules	188
12.6. Stative versus active	191
12.7. Backgrounding	195
12.8. Agentiveness reduction strategy	198
12.9. Thematic development	201
Appendix	209
References	221

Abbreviations

ABL	ablative	DO	direct object
ADJ	adjective	DVBL	deverbalizer
ADVLZR	adverbializer	EMPH	emphatic
ASRT	assertative	EP	epenthetic syllable
ASSM	assumption evidential	EXTENT	extent
AUD	auditory evidential	f	feminine
AUX	auxiliary	FUT	future
AWAY	directional (away)	HAB	habitual
BEN	benefactive	IMP	imperative
C	consonant	IMPF	imperfective
CAUS	causative	IMPRS	impersonal
CLAS	classifier	INDEF	indefinite
CMP	complement	IND.IMP	indirect imperative
CMPR	comparison	INSTR	instrument
CNTGN	contingency	INT	intentional (intention)
COM	comitative	INT.FRUS	frustrated intent
COND	condition	INT.IMM	immediate intention
CONJ	conjunction	INTRG	interrogative
CONSQ	consequence	INTS	intensive
CONT	continuative	IO	indirect object
CONTRA	contra-expectation	LOC	location (general)
DIM	diminutive	LOC.SPEC	locative specific
DIMEN	dimensional	m	masculine

MAN	manner	RECPR	reciprocal
MAT	matrix/main	RPT	reportative evidential
n	neuter (3rd person)	s	singular
NEG	negative	SIM	simultaneous
NEG.IMP	negative imperative	STAT	stative
NEG.PUR	negative purpose	S/SUBJ	subject
NOM	nominalizer	SUBOR	subordinator
O/OBJ	object	SUP	supposition
OBL	oblique	TERM	human (SUBJ, DO, IO)
OPT	optative	TWRD	directional (toward)
p	plural	V	verb
PERF	perfect	VERT	directional (vertical)
PNCT	punctual	Y/N	yes/no question
POSS	possession	*	ill-formed/ungrammatical
POSSD	possessed	?	unknown or marginal
POSSR	possessor	1p	first person plural exclusive
PRES	present		
PRSUB	pronominal subjects	12	first person plural inclusive
PSBL	possibility		
PST	past	1	first person
PURP	purposive	2	second person
PX	pronominal prefix	3	third person
REAS.DS	reason/different subject	1DIMEN	1 dimensional classifier
REAS.SS	reason/same subject	2DIMEN	2 dimensional classifier
REC	recipient	3DIMEN	3 dimensional classifier

Acknowledgment

The study of the grammar of Retuarã has been and continues to be a challenge. I owe much to the following people for their encouragement and help in starting and continuing the study:

Dave Weber's teaching and advice at the beginning of this project sparked in me an appreciation for the wonder of language, not just linguistics. He balanced his high expectations with the freedom to ask any question no matter how basic. His help in organizing and accessing data made the continuing study of the language manageable.

Paul Frank offered much needed advice and insight into the analysis. Taking my rough observations, he organized and summarized them in a concise manner. Often he saw the overall implications of how they fit into the system of the grammar before I did. His help, humor, and friendship throughout the project lightened my burden greatly.

Stephen Levinsohn opened up the study of discourse to me in a way that no textbook ever did. He is both patient and eager to teach a subject he loves. I owe my newfound interest in this subject to him and am grateful for his insights and careful editing of the sections dealing with discourse studies.

1
Introduction

The Retuarã and Tanimuca,[1] located in southeast Colombia, consider themselves separate groups yet speak the same language which is a member of the central branch of Tucanoan. There are slight lexical differences between the two groups, the extent of which has not yet been determined. Also, because of the wide distribution of villages and the resulting contact with other languages (both Tucanoan and Arawakan) there are some grammatical variations. For these reasons, this paper and its examples will henceforth refer to the dialect spoken by the Retuarã on the lower Apaporis.

Both Key (1979:120) and Ruhlen (1987:372) have classified Tanimuca as a member of the western branch of Tucanoan, but recent work by Malone (to appear) more correctly places Tanimuca and Retuarã in the central branch. Although Retuarã is Tucanoan, it does not reflect as many of the features common to the family as other Tucanoan languages and seems to have been influenced by contact with Yucuna, a neighboring Arawakan language.

Both groups (Tanimuca and Retuarã) number about 300 all together. The people live along five rivers in the Amazon Basin: lower Apaporis, Popeyaca, Guacaya, Oiyaca, and Mirití. The people hunt and fish, cultivate several crops (principally manioc), and gather various fruits when in season. The Retuarã and Tanimuca have had some contact with the national culture due to Catholic mission schools, the rubber boom at the turn of the century, and more recently the coca leaf trade. As a result,

---

[1]The Retuarã have also been referred to as the Letuama. Likewise, the names Ũpairã or Umfaina occur as alternatives to Tanimuca.

there is some culture change as new ideas, values, and material goods are received. The process, however, is slow due primarily to the relative inaccessability of the region.

The material contained in this sketch has been obtained from transcribed oral texts, written texts, conversations, and translated materials. Texts include narratives, folktales, procedural texts, hortatory texts and dialogues. Some material has been elicited in cases of infrequently occuring constructions. I have been involved with a group of Retuarã on the lower Apaporis since November, 1982 and have made frequent visits (though not of long duration) to a village location. The linguistic investigation has been conducted under the auspices of the Colombian Ministry of Government. Language material has been obtained through a variety of language assistants outside of the village. Published materials have also been useful (e.g., the work of students from the University of the Andes; see Gaviria and Azcárate 1979, Robayo 1981).

1.1–1.10 Word order constituents

The following is a brief typological summary of Retuarã. It will show that Retuarã has the major correlates of an SOV language.

1.1. Basic word order. In main declarative clauses, the usual word order is subject-object-verb (SOV). The following clauses illustrate the word order. The suffix -re, glossed (term) in (1), is a case marker for subjects, objects, and recipients, and for proper names.

(1)   S   O   V
      kle-re   yiha-re   eʔe-waʔ-rape
      Clay-TERM 1p-TERM get-AWAY-PST
      Clay took us to Puerto Lleras.

In the above example, a full NP (a proper name) was used to illustrate the basic word order. Full NPs, however, do not occur frequently in discourses. Since subject pronoun clitics are prefixed to the verb as in (2), a much more common pattern is O S-V.

Subject pronoun clitics do not take -re (term) case marking. Usually subject pronouns are cliticized prefixes on the verb as in (2).[2] They also

---

[2] There are infrequent examples in my corpus of free pronouns marked as subject or object with term case marking. The construction is used to indicate deixis. The free pronouns have a different form than the clitic pronouns. For further information see §1.17.

Introduction

commonly occur clause finally as full pronouns in negated clauses when a number/gender suffix which agrees with the subject in number and gender is used. In (2), the number/gender suffix *-ka* (masculine singular) agrees with the subject *yiʔi* (first-person singular) The subject pronoun is not marked with *-re* (term). Thus any clitic pronoun with *-re* case marking can only be an object or recipient. The OVS word order in (2) is typical of negative declarative sentences, but not of other common constructions.

(2)   O   V   S
      ki-re   *ĩã-be-yu-ka*   *yiʔi*
      3ms-TERM see-NEG-PRES-ms 1s
      I don't see him.

Word order is rigid only for the subject which, apart from negative declaratives, occurs before other major constituents. Time and locative obliques may precede the subject. The preference is for the verb to be clause final, but it is not unusual to find an object or locative in clause final position. The reordering of the elements does not seem to change the meaning but may affect focus, though sometimes word order is affected by noun incorporation in the verb. In the following example, the instrument *bũa* 'salt' is incorporated into the verb. Normally an instrument would be on the periphery.

(3)   *supatirã bã-re*   *ki-bũa-koa-rãyũ*
      then   12-TERM 3ms-salt-cure-FUT
      Then he will cure us (with) salt.

Other constituents of the clause such as benefactive, time, locative, recipient, instrument, etc. can vary in their ordering throughout the clause as in (4) and (5). The ordering between objects and recipients as in (6) is also acceptable. It should be noted that recipients are the only constituents that can occur between the verb and object.

(4)   TIME   LOC
      dõʔõka   *yiha-aʔ-rape baya-rã*
      yesterday 1p-go-PST   dance-LOC
      Yesterday we went to the dance.

(5) S   O   REC   V
     paulina-re   waʔia yi-re īhī-koʔo
     Paulina-TERM fish   1s-TERM give-PST
     Paulina gave me fish.

(6) S   O   V   REC
     anita-re   baʔarika   īhī-koʔo betania-re
     Anita-TERM   food   give-PST Bethanie-TERM
     Anita gave the food to Bethanie(recipient).

1.2. Adpositions. Retuarã has postpositions, which is typical of OV languages. For example, *-pi* (instrument), *-rã* (location), and *-ka* (comitative) follow their respective heads (upriver and uncle) in (7).

(7) *apapuri   waye-rã   ãʔã-ka   yiha-tu-rape*
     Apaporis upriver-LOC   uncle-COM   1p-travel-PST
     We traveled up the Apaporis river with my uncle.

1.3. Descriptive modifiers. The modifier generally precedes the head in a noun phrase. In (8) and (9), modifiers of number and quality precede their heads.

(8) *īʔrãpitaraka-pãũ   pãũã*
     five-CLAS^hammock   hammock
     five hammocks

(9) *hi-iʔtaka   saya*
     pretty-very   dress
     very pretty dress

Modifier-head order is not absolute; there are occasional cases of head-modifier order, and some modifiers such as *-hīka* 'small' always follow their head. In (11), the color modifier *hīʔbīã* 'green, blue' follows the head. Modifiers also follow the head in noun phrases where the head of a genitive construction is being modified as in (12).

(10) *pusi-hīka*
     hill-small
     small hill

Introduction

(11) *wehepebā hīʔbīā*
    sky   blue
    blue sky

(12) *gloria saya hūʔāka be-ri-koʔo-a*
    Gloria dress red   rip-EP-PST-n
    Gloria's red dress ripped.

It is usual for only one modifier to precede the head of a NP, with the rest following the head (§3.8).

Although there are exceptions to the order of modifier-head, the majority of examples support this ordering. Thus the position of the descriptive modifiers in the noun phrase is typical also of an OV language.[3]

1.4. Genitives. The genitive construction is genitive-head, as shown in (12). Because the order of genitive-head is typical of OV languages, it further supports an OV typology of Retuarã.

1.5. Affixation. Affixation is overwhelmingly done by suffix. The only prefixes in the language are cliticized subject pronouns and one non-human object pronoun. In some constructions subject agreement is achieved with number/gender suffixes. Tense, aspect, modals, negation, etc. are all verb suffixes as well as derivational morphemes, e.g., causative suffix. In (13), *bī-* (second-person singular) is prefixed, but the modal *-hī* (possibility) and tense marker *-yū* (present) are suffixed. Example (14) has negation *-be*, tense *-yu*, and the number/gender suffix *-ka* which agrees with the subject, suffixed to the verb. The dominant suffixing of Retuarã is consistent with its analysis as an OV language.

(13) *bī-baʔa-hī-yū*
    2s-eat-PSBL-PRES
    You could/should eat.

(14) *sokoa yapa-be-yu-ka   yiʔi*
    soup like-NEG-PRES-ms 1s
    I don't like the soup.

---

[3]Derbyshire (1986:474), however, claims that either order of the modifier and head is typical of Amazonian OV languages. Thus for Tucanoan languages, this particular feature may not be helpful for a typological classification.

1.6. Relative clauses. The head of relative clauses occurs with no overt expression in the main clause. In (15), the head *bēʔrī* 'child' occurs internally in the restrictive clause 'the child that the snake bit'.

(15) [*āyāka **bēʔrī**-te kuku-koʔo]-ki-roʔsi iʔka īkoa ībē*
     snake child-TERM bite-PST-ms-BEN   this medicine be
     This medicine is for the child that the snake bit.

Typically OV languages have prenominal relative clauses (the restricting clause precedes the head nominal). It has also been noted, however, that internally headed relative clauses occur only in OV languages (Keenan 1985). Thus the relativization strategy of Retuarā is further support for an OV classification.

1.7. Comparatives. In a comparative construction, there are three elements involved: the standard against which something is compared, the marker (or pivot) which indicates that a comparison is being made, and the adjective of comparison. Typically, in OV languages the standard element precedes the adjective. In Retuarā, the order is standard-adjective. The following example has the the order: *yi-* (first-person singular) (standard), *kūpāhī* 'little' (adjective), and *bahi* (comparison). This order is typical of an OV language.

(16) *yi-re kūpāhī-bahi ki-rika-yu*
     1s-TERM little-CMPR 3ms-have-PRES
     He has less than me.

1.8. Negation. There are three types of negation in Retuarā. Two involve suffixes and one involves a negative verb:

1. The sentential scope affix *-be* (negative) is suffixed to the verb root and precedes the tense, aspect, and mood, as in (17).
2. The negative imperative marker *-aʔsi* is word final, as in (18).
3. The negative verb *bā* is often deverbalized by *-ri* and indicates the lack or absence of something, as in (19).

The use of negative suffixes is typical of OV languages.

(17) *rū-rī-**be**-yu-ko iʔko*
     tired-EP-NEG-PRES-fs 3fs
     She's not tired.

(18) bī-wape-aʔsi
      2s-bark-NEG.IMP
      Don't bark!

(19) hia   bā-rī-ā
      good   not^be-DVBL-n
      no good, bad

1.9. Questions. Retuarã marks yes/no questions with the clause-initial morpheme *yahe* 'yes/no'. This position of the yes/no question marker is more typical of VO languages than of OV languages where the question marker generally follows the verb. Content question markers also occur clause initially as in (21). Such fronting of content question markers is widely attested in both VO and OV languages.

(20) yahe   bī-hī-yū
      Y/N   2s-sick-PRES
      Are you sick?

(21) bārāpate   ki-iʔta-rāyū
      when   3ms-come-FUT
      When will he come?

1.10. Word order summary. Seven of the nine categories of constituents were consistent with an OV language which indicates that Returã is at least an OV language, and possibly an SOV language. One category (descriptive modifiers) was inconclusive, as Amazonian OV languages may show either modifier-head or head-modifier order. Only one category, the position of the yes/no question marker, was characteristic of VO rather than OV languages.

1.11–1.14 Distinguishing major syntactic functions

Several major syntactic functions will be discussed briefly including the use of word order to distinguish subject from object in Retuarã. The various ways that the subject can be expressed plays a part in distinguishing subjects from objects as well as communicating information about the subject in the discourse. The widespread use of nominalization, and the categorization of nouns according to animacy, number, gender, and person are also significant.

1.11. Word order. In Retuarã, word order is important for distinguishing the subject and object. Normally the subject occupies the position of the first major constituent in the clause relative to the verb and objects, though occasionally, due to right dislocations, a subject NP will occur clause finally. Thus subjects and objects are distinguished in potentially ambiguous clauses such as (22) in which both arguments precede the verb.

(22) arturu-te   andre-te   heyobaa-rape
     Arturo-TERM Andrés-TERM help-PST
     Arturo helped Andrés.

The suffix -te on *Arturo* marks (term) which includes subjects, objects, and recipients that are either human or animate with a proper name.[4] In (22), the case marking does not distinguish the subject from the object, so the first argument in the clause is interpreted as the subject. An alternate ordering that resolves potential ambiguity shifts the object nominal to a post-verbal position. Thus an SVO order can also distinguish two nominals as in (23), which has the same meaning as (22).

(23) arturu-te   heyobaa-rape andre-te
     Arturo-TERM help-PST   Andrés-TERM
     Arturo helped Andrés.

Except for the subject, word order is not rigid, and in cases where the speaker wants to avoid ambiguity, he or she will use word order to clarify the roles of the arguments. In sentences such as (24) and (25) where the roles of object (fish) and recipient (me) are not easily confused, the subject is first, but the recipient and object may vary their position in the clause. The order of object-recipient is most common, though to have an object follow the verb, as in (25), is not unusual.

(24) andre-te   waʔia yi-re   īhī-koʔo
     Andrés-TERM fish 1s-TERM give-PST
     Andrés gave me fish.

(25) andre-te   yi-re   īhī-koʔo waʔia
     Andrés-TERM 1s-TERM give-PST fish
     Andrés gave me fish.

1.12. Subject expression. The subject of a Retuarã clause is influenced by discourse constraints and can be expressed in a variety of ways. In the

---

[4] -*te* and -*re* are variants of the term marker. To date, no functional or semantic difference between them has been established.

Introduction

following list, two ways of expressing subject occur in active, foregrounded material in which the subject is agentive. They are shown in (26) and (27). The other two methods of expressing the subject occur in inactive, backgrounded material with de-emphasis on the subject as agent. These two ways are shown in (28)–(30).

1. A subject NP (or very infrequently a third-person pronoun) is case-marked by *-re/-te* (term). In (26), the subject NP 'Ernesto' is case-marked with *-te*.
2. Most commonly the subject of a sentence is expressed as a personal pronoun clitic that is prefixed to the verb, marking number and person (and gender in third-person singular). Because no other free subject NP or pronoun occurs with it they cannot be mistaken for the subject. Subject expression by prefix generally occurs with active constructions. In (27), the subject pronouns in both the main and embedded questions are clitic prefixes.
3. Bare subject NPs (28) or pronouns (29) without term case marking can occur. In such cases there is a number/gender suffix on the verb to show subject agreement.
4. There can be clauses with no expression of the subject. Such clauses include subordinate clauses in which switch reference makes clear the identity of the subject. Also verbs with number/gender suffixes often occur without an overt expression of the subject as in (30).

For further discussion of subject agreement see §5.2.

(26) *bikitoho ernesto-te   eta-rãyũ*
     morning Ernesto-TERM arrive-FUT
     Ernesto will arrive in the morning.

(27) *yahe bĩ-õ-yũ   dõʔõ-rã   ko-aʔ-ri-koʔo*
     Y/N   2s-know-PRES where-LOC 3fs-go-EP-PST
     Do you know where she went?

(28) *fernando baʔirĩhia kõke-reʔka-ki*
     Fernando things   carry-PST-ms
     Fernando was the cargo carrier.

(29) *boha-be-sa-rã-ki   iʔki*
     tell-NEG-EP-FUT-ms 3ms
     He will not tell/will be a not-teller.

(30) a?-ri-be-ri-ko?o-rã
 go-EP-NEG-EP-PST-p
 (They) did not go.

1.13. Nominalization. Nominalization is often used to create opposition between active and nonactive constructions. The usage is motivated by the discourse to signal background information or to remove the focus from the subject (see §§12.2 and 12.4). In addition, relative clauses, dependent clauses, and nearly every noun is marked as a nominal with a number/gender suffix (see §§11.1, 7.10, and 2.1).

1.14. Categorization of nouns. Nouns are categorized according to animacy, number, and gender. The parameters that apply in the categorization of the noun vary in different areas of the grammar.[5]

Terms. NPs in the grammatical roles of subject, object, or recipient which are either human or a proper name are categorized together and are eligible for term case marking. Nonhuman subjects, objects, and recipients are categorized separately, and can not be case-marked as terms. Thus, the subject of (31) 'boy' and the object of (32) (first-person singular) are categorized as terms. The subject 'dog' is not categorized as a term and is thus unmarked.

(31) bē?rī-te   o-yu   ba?a-ērã
 boy-TERM cry-PRES eat-PURP
 The boy cries to eat.

(32) yaiwēkoa yi-re   kuku-rape
 dog   1s-TERM bite-PST
 The dog bit me.

Noun classes. Noun classes are relevant to subject agreement on nominalized verb constructions. The parameters of number, gender, and animacy combine to create the following four classes:

- neuter (nonhuman or inanimate)
- human masculine singular
- human feminine singular
- human plural

---

[5]The relevant parameters are distinctive to Retuarã; other Tucanoan languages make slightly different distinctions.

Example (33) illustrates the agreement between the feminine singular noun and the number/gender suffix agreement marker -*ko* (feminine singular) on the verb. For further discussion see §3.1.

(33) *pakia-ko   kā-rī-ti-i-ko*
　　　old^person-fs sleep-EP-PERF-STAT-fs
　　　The old woman is already asleep.

Predicate adjectives. The categorization of predicate adjectives is similar to that of the noun classes, but includes the additional category of human feminine plural (see §2.26). Example (34) illustrates the predicate adjective 'short' with the feminine singular suffix -*ko*.

(34) *ye?e-ko i?ko*
　　　short-fs 3fs
　　　She is short.

Classifiers. Whereas noun class and predicate adjective categorization have relevance outside the NP, classifiers categorize nouns within the NP according to gender, number, animacy, and shape/function. The six classes include:

- masculine and animate singuluar
- feminine singular
- masculine and animate dual
- masculine and animate plural
- feminine plural
- inanimate

The first five classes are relatively small, while the sixth class is large and varied including all the subclasses of shape and function.

1.15–1.20 Phonology sketch

A brief overview of the phonology of Retuarã is provided in this section. It may be useful to those who want to compare the systems of Tucanoan languages.

1.15. Phonemic inventory. The phonemic inventory of the consonants followed by the vowels is charted in (35).

(35)

	labial	alveolar	palatal	velar	glottal
stop –vd	p	t		k	ʔ
stop +vd	b	d	dy		
fricative		s			h
resonant		r			
semi-vowel	w				

	front	central	back
high	i ī		u ū
mid	e ē		o ō
low		a ā	

The phonemes will be represented in this paper as they appear in (35) except that /dy/ will be written y. For example:

(36) dōʔō-rā   bī-re   sa-dyiʔaʔ-dyu
     dōʔō-rā   bī-re   sa-yiʔaʔ-yu
     where-LOC 2s-TERM 3ns-hurt-PRES
     Where does it hurt you?

Nasalization on vowels will be represented as ã, ẽ, etc. Stress is also phonemic but it will not be written in this paper. Vowel length is phonemic and will be indicated by two vowels in succession, i.e., aa, ee, etc.

Finally, for easier reading of examples, morphemes will be represented in their underlying form. There are not many differences between the underlying forms and the surface forms, but in certain environments nasal spreading or vowel deletion can occur. The underlying form is written to maintain a single form for every morpheme.

1.16. Phonological rules. Some rules of the phonology are as follows:
1. Voiced stops /b d dy/ change to nasal consonants [m n ñ] when they precede a nasal vowel. The nasalization of the vowel is weakened as it spreads regressively to the consonant. For example /būyūa/ 'piranha' is pronounced [muñua], in which the u's are only weakly nasalized.
2. /r/ is realized as a flap [ň] when it precedes a nasal vowel. Thus /riakarā/ 'at the river' becomes [riakaňā].
3. /s/ is affricated to [ᵗs] when preceded by a glottal stop, e.g., /-roʔsi/ (benefactive) becomes [-roʔᵗsi].
4. Prenasalization occurs on obstruents (including [ts]) when preceded by a nasal vowel that has not been weakened by the nasalization rule

Introduction

(rule 1). The nasal consonant has the same point of articulation as the obstruent that it precedes.

(37)   V   + C_1 →   V   C C_1
      [+nas]   [+obs]   [+nas]   [+nas]   [+obs]
                                                    [α pt. art]   [α pt. art]

For example /ũʔpua/ 'foot' becomes [ũʔᵐpua], but in /yĩka/ 'leg', the ĩ is weakened by rule 1 and no prenasalization occurs before the *k*. Thus it becomes [ñika], not *[ñĩⁿka]. (This rule has some exceptions. See §1.18).

5. [ř] and [l̆] vary freely word initially as in [řomõ] ~ [l̆omõ] 'woman'.
6. /w/ becomes a voiceless rounded fricative before front vowels. For example /wiʔia/ 'house' is produced with tighter lips and some resulting friction on the *w*.

1.17. Stress. Stress is phonemic as the following minimal pairs demonstrate.

(38)   āʔá   áʔā   yũʔtáka   yũʔtaká
       uncle   yes   thread   soft
       uncle vs. yes   thread vs. soft

There are many examples in which stress distinguishes verb roots.

(39)   aʔte   bī-báe-be   aʔte   bī-baé-be
       again   2s-serve-IMP   again   2s-cut-IMP
       Serve (yourself) again.   Cut (with machete) again.

Stressed syllables often occur with raised pitch. If only the first of two consecutive vowels is stressed, the pitch will start high but often fall on the second vowel. A rising pitch contour occurs when just the second vowel is stressed. A level pitch contour results when both vowels are stressed (high level), or both are unstressed (low level). Stress also tends to lengthen a vowel. As a result it is often difficult to determine if a vowel is phonemically long, or just long as a result of stress.

Deixis and stress. Stress can also indicate deixis on personal pronouns (in third person). Stress occurs on the first syllable of the pronoun when the referent is relatively far away from the speaker; when the referent is close, the stress occurs on the final syllable. Thus, the question 'Which one is your sister?' may be answered simply with a pronoun, *i'ko* (feminine singular), but the stress will indicate the general location of the referent as in (40) and (41).

(40) i?kó
    2fs
    her (the close one)

(41) í?ko
    2fs
    her (the one far away)

In the same way, stress distinguishes proximity for the third plural pronoun: ĩ?rá (third-person plural, close) and ĩ́?rã (third-person plural, far). The third singular masculine, however, has two forms that do not require stress to make the distinction: ĩ?ĩ (masculine singular, close), and i?ki (masculine singular, far).

Usually personal pronouns take a clitic form when they have term case marking as an object or recipient as in (42). The clitic form does not indicate deixis.[6]

(42) dã-re   yi-yoi-yu
    3p-TERM   1s-watch-PRES
    I watch them.

However, when the speaker wishes to indicate proximity, the full pronoun form with the term case marker is used.[7] Again stress occurs on the first syllable of the pronoun when the referent is relatively far away from the speaker as in (43), and on the final syllable and the case marker -re (term) when the referent is close, as in (44).

(43) ĩ́?rã-re   yi-yoi-yu
    3p-TERM   1s-watch-PRES
    I watch them (those far away).

---

[6]The clitic form of the third plural pronoun dã- does not appear at first glance to be derived from the full pronoun form, ĩ?rã (third-person plural). However, /dã-/ is pronounced [na] while /ĩrã/ is pronounced [iña]. It is likely that the form of the pronoun was once *ĩ?dã, but a sound change has replaced all word medial /dṼ/ with /rṼ/.

[7]This is the only environment in which full pronouns occur with term case marking. All other occurrences of pronominal objects and recipients are clitic forms. Most pronominal subjects are clitics, but full subject pronouns without case marking also occur with verbs that show subject agreement with a number/gender suffix. Thus, most pronominal subjects are prefixed to the verb while all objects and recipients receive -re (term) case marking. See (881) in the Appendix.

Introduction

(44) ĩʔrã-ré   yi-yoi-yu
    3p-TERM 1s-watch-PRES
    I watch them (the close ones).

The singular pronouns *iʔki* (first masculine singular) and *iʔko* (first feminine singular) follow the same pattern when they have *-re* (term) case marking. The pronoun *ĩʔĩ* (first masculine singular, close)' does not occur with term case marking. Instead *iʔki-ré* (third masculine singular-term) is used to indicate closeness to speaker.

Stress pattern in the VP and affix -ri. The rules for assigning stress in the verb phrase are still under study. Part of the pattern involves the epenthetic syllable *-ri* which can be stressed or unstressed and is epenthesized in order to conform to one or more rules of the stress pattern. It is also semantically empty. The typical verb stem contains one or two syllables, though there appears to be pressure in the language to have an even number of syllables in the stem. Verb stems that are just one syllable (no long vowels), such as *aʔ* 'go', fill the second 'slot' with *-ri* (epenthetic syllable) when the following morpheme is unstressed. No epenthesis occurs for one-syllable stems that contain a long vowel. There are a few verb roots of three and four syllables. Roots of three syllables fill the fourth slot with *-ri* in the same way as one syllable roots fill the second slot. The affix *-ri* is not epenthesized in roots of an even number of syllables. The suffixes *-yu* (present) and *-rape* (past) usually begin with a stressed syllable, so *-ri* is not epenthesized as shown in (53a). and (53d).

Rule 7. This rule applies to just the verb root and epenthesizes the affix *-ri* as the second (or fourth) syllable. Stress is assigned to *-ri* if the first (or third) syllable of the root is unstressed.

(45) 0   → -ri   /   ((C)V (C)V)   (C)V   ———— #[8] (C)V
         [αstress]   [βstress]   [–stress]
                                           [–length]

Examples of rule 7 illustrate that *-ri* is epenthesized in (46) because the roots of one and three syllables respectively are followed by an unstressed syllable. In the following two examples, there is no epenthesis because the following syllable is stressed in (47), and because the vowel in the root 'burn' is long (48).

---

[8]The notation of a single # indicates a morpheme boundary.

(46) yi-aʔ-rí-koʔó
   1s-go-EP-PST
   I went.

(47) yi-tu-rápe
   1s-travel-PST
   I traveled.

(48) yi-oo-koʔó
   1s-burn-PST
   I burned myself.

Rule 8. Rule 8 applies to the VP and only assigns stress to the first syllable of the final two syllables of a VP if both syllables are stressed. The phonetic realization in (50) shows the result when a stressed root precedes a stressed tense suffix. The same result is obtained when a morphophonemic rule deletes the stressed vowel of some prefixes prior to the single vowel of the verb root: the stress is retained and falls on the root vowel. If the tense suffix is stressed, the VP will end with two stressed syllables as illustrated in (51).

(49) (C) V́ (C) V́ ##⁹ → (C) V́ (C) V ##

(50) ki-ó-yú   [kióñū]
   3ms-know-PRES [phonetic realization]
   He knows.

(51) yí-aʔ-yú   [yáʔyu]
   1s-go-PRES   [phonetic realization]
   I go.

The affix *-ri* also occurs outside the verb root in association with affixes such as *-be* (negative) and *-waʔ* (directional away) which are never stressed.[10] This rule also accounts for the unstressed suffix *-yu* in the affirmative column of (53a).

It seems likely that this rule is part of a larger pattern of stress which further study will reveal.

---

[9] The notation ## indicates word boundary.

[10] Another affix, *-hī* (possibility) is never stressed, yet does not occur with *-ri*. This is not surprising since in the order of affixes in the VP it is only followed by stressed affixes.

Introduction

Rule 9. Rule 9 epenthesizes *-rí* after the affixes *-be* (negative) and *-waʔ* (directional away) when the following morpheme is unstressed.

(52)   0 → *-rí* /   { *-be* } ——   (C) V
                    -waʔ   [–stress]

In the negation of the future in (53b), *-be* (negative) is followed by *-sa* which is the form of the epenthetic syllable (equivalent to *-rí*) for future negations. For further examples see §5.9. Syllable breaks are indicated on the first line of each example since the vowel *i* of the person marker prefix *ki-* and the vowel *a* of the verb stem fuse to form a single syllable rather than two. Thus, for example, (53a) contains three morphemes, but just two syllables and has the phonetic form: [keʔ/-dyu].

(53)   Affirmative   Negative

   a. [kéʔ/dyu]   [keʔ/rí/be/dyú]
       ki-áʔ-yu   *ki-aʔ-rí-be-yú*
       3ms-go-PRES   3ms-go-EP-NEG-PRES
       He goes.   He does not go.

   b. [keʔ/rí/ña/ñú]   [keʔ/rí/be/sá/ña/ñú]
       ki-aʔ-rí-rãyú   *ki-aʔ-rí-be-sá-rãyú*
       3ms-go-EP-FUT   3ms-go-EP-NEG-EP-FUT
       He will go.   He will not go.

   c. [keʔ/rí/koʔ/ó]   [keʔ/rí/be/rí/koʔ/ó]
       ki-aʔ-rí-koʔó   *ki-aʔ-rí-be-rí-koʔó*
       3ms-go-EP-PST   3ms-go-EP-NEG-EP-PST
       He went.   He did not go.

   d. [keʔ/rá/pé]   [keʔ/rí/be/rá/pé]
       ki-aʔ-rápé   *ki-aʔ-rí-be-rápé*
       3ms-go-PST   3ms-go-EP-NEG-PST
       He went.   He did not go.

   e. [keʔ/rí/reʔ/ká]   [keʔ/rí/be/rí/reʔ/ká]
       ki-aʔ-rí-reʔká   *ki-aʔ-rí-be-rí-reʔká*
       3ms-go-EP-PST   3ms-go-EP-NEG-EP-PST
       He went.   He did not go.

f. [ke?/rí/hī/ñú]   [ke?/rí/be/rí/hī/ñú]
    ki-a?-rí-hī-yṹ   *ki-a?-rí-be-rí-hī-yṹ*
    3ms-go-EP-PSBL-PRES   3ms-go-EP-NEG-EP-PSBL-PRES
    He could go.   He could not go.

The pattern of usage for *-ri* is different with verb stems of two syllables. In (54), there is no syllable slot for *-ri* to fill in the stem of the two syllable verb *e?e* 'get'. Instead, it only occurs in the specified environments with the affixes *-be* (negative) and *-wa?* (directional away).

(54)   Affirmative   Negative

   a. [dyé?/e/dyú]   [dyé?/e/be/dyú]
       yi-é?e-yú   *yi-é?e-be-yú*
       1s-get-PRES   1s-get-NEG-PRES
       I get   I do not get

   b. [dyé?/e/wa?/dyú]   [dyé?/e/wa?/rí/be/dyú]
       yi-é?e-wa?-yú   *yi-é?e-wa?-rí-be-yú*
       1s-get-AWAY-PRES   1s-get-AWAY-EP-NEG-PRES
       I take (it) away.   I do not take (it) away.

   c. [dyé?/e/ko?/ó]   [dyé?/e/be/rí/ko?/ó]
       yi-é?e-ko?ó   *yi-é?e-be-rí-ko?ó*
       1s-get-PST   1s-get-NEG-EP-PST
       I got   I did not get

   d. [dyé?/e/wa?/rí/ko?ó]   [dyé?/e/wa?/rí/be/rí/ko?ó]
       yi-é?e-wa?-rí-ko?ó   *yi-é?e-wa?-rí-be-rí-ko?ó*
       1s-get-AWAY-EP-PST   1s-get-AWAY-EP-NEG-EP-PST
       I took (it) away.   I did not take (it) away.

   e. [dyé?/e/ra/pé]   [dyé?/e/be/rá/pé]
       yi-é?e-rapé   *yi-é?e-be-rápé*
       1s-get-PST   1s-get-NEG-PST
       I got   I did not get

   f. [dyé?/e/wa?/rá/pé]   [dyé?/e/wa?/rí/be/rá/pé]
       yi-é?e-wa?-rápé   *yi-é?e-wa?-rí-be-rápé*
       1s-get-AWAY-PST   1s-get-AWAY-EP-NEG-PST
       I took (it) away.   I did not take (it) away.

Introduction

    g. [dyé?/e/hī/ñú]   [dyé?/e/be/rí/hī/ñú]
        yi-é?e-hī-yū́   *yi-é?e-be-rí-hī-yū́*
        1s-get-PSBL-PRES   1s-get-NEG-EP-PSBL-PRES
        I could get   I could not get

Stress shifts. The stress pattern in the VP is still under study. The following examples illustrate some of the stress pattern shifts that can occur. In (55), the normally stressed root *kā* 'sleep' is unstressed when *-ka* (masculine singular) is suffixed to the VP. In (56), although it is the same type of construction, it has a different stress pattern with the verb *ko* 'try, test' which is normally stressed.

(55) *bāki kā-yū́-ka*
     who sleep-PRES-ms
     Who is the one sleeping?

(56) *bāki kó-yu-ká*
     who try-PRES-ms
     Who is the one who tried (it)?

Stress can also vary between syllables of the verb root depending on what is prefixed to it.

(57) *yi-é?e-wa?-yú*   *[dyé?/e/wa?/yú]*
     1s-get-AWAY-PRES [phonetic realization]
     I take (it) away.

(58) *yihá-e?é-wa?-yú*   *[dyi/há/e?/é/wa?/yú]*
     1p-get-AWAY-PRES [phonetic realization]
     We take (it) away.

1.18. Nasalization. Nasalization is phonemic as illustrated by the minimal pair in the following examples.

(59) *yi-popo-yu*
     1s-vomit-PRES
     I vomit.

(60) *saya yi-põpo-yu*
     dress 1s-dry-PRES
     I dry the dress.

In a limited way, nasalization spreads both progressively and regressively. Regressive nasalization is limited to the person prefixes. In (61), the prefix *yi-* (first-person singular) is realized as [ñ-] (*i* drops before morphemes that begin with vowels, thus the rule (rule 1) of the nasalization of voiced stops predicts /y/ will be realized as [ñ]).

(61) *yi-õ-yū*   *[ñõñū]*
  1s-know-PRES [phonetic realization]
  I know.

Nasalization also spreads progressively as shown by the comparison of (62) and (63). In (62), the present tense suffix *-yu* is not nasalized, but when the nasalized modal *-hī* is affixed to the same construction the suffix is realized as *-yū* (63).

(62) *ko-re   ki-hai-yu*   *[kihaidyu]*
  3fs-TERM 3ms-talk-PRES [phonetic realization]
  He talks to her.

(63) *ko-re   ki-hai-hī-yū*   *[kihaihīñū]*
  3fs-TERM 3ms-talk-PSBL-PRES [phonetic realization]
  He could talk to her.

Nasal spreading is blocked by obstruents (except /dy/). In (64), the suffix *-yu* (present) is nasalized by the progressive spread of the the nasalization from *õ* 'know', but in (65) it is not nasalized because the obstruent of *-be* (negative) prevents the spreading.

(64) *yi-õ-yū*   *[ñõñū]*
  1s-know-PRES
  I know.

(65) *yĩ-õ-rĩ-be-yu*   *[ñõñĩbedyu]*
  1s-know-EP-NEG-PRES
  I don't know.

The progressive spread of nasalization is inconsistent, however, and occasionally creates exceptions to the rule of voiced stop nasalization. It may be that the language is in the process of change in the area of nasal spreading. For example, the term case marker *-re* is realized with some speakers as [ñẽ] in *dā-re* (third-person plural) and *bī-re* (second-person singular) due to a progressive spread of the nasalization. The rule predicts that the regressive nasalization

Introduction

that changes /dā/ to [nā] sufficiently weakens the nasalization on the vowel to prevent any progressive nasalization. A further example illustrates this inconsistent pattern. When (66) and (67) are compared it is found that regressive and progressive nasal spreading has taken place in (66), but only regressive in (67). Both examples have similar environments for nasal spreading, yet they have different results. Perhaps verb classes that allow or disallow nasal spread will need to be proposed.[11]

(66) yi-ã-yu   [ñãñũ]
    1s-say-PRES (/-yu/ changes to [ñũ])
    I say.

(67) yi-ĩã-yu   [ñĩãdyu]
    1s-see-PRES (/-yu/ does not change)
    I see.

1.19. Word and syllable structure. The Retuarã syllable conforms to the pattern: (C)V(V)(V). Neither consonant clusters nor closed syllables are permitted except that a glottal stop may occur following any vowel. For example, aʔte 'again' has the sequence of a glottal stop before a consonant rather than a vowel unlike all other consonants. A word (other than a conjugated verb) may have as many as six syllables, but three or four is most common. Verb constructions with a variety of affixes may have seven or eight syllables, but more commonly they have three to six. There are very few words with just one syllable.

1.20. Morphophonology. There are very few morphophonemic changes in the language. The person prefixes display most of these changes. In the examples contained in this paper, the underlying form of each prefix is written for ease of reading. Table (68) shows the morphophonemic changes that occur with each prefix when affixed to a vowel-initial morpheme. The same changes occur when affixing to nasalized vowels, except that the result is also nasalized. For example yi- + u becomes [dyu-] while yi- + ũ becomes [ñũ-]. When the person prefixes are affixed to a consonant-initial morpheme, there is no change; they are realized as written in the column under 'Person prefixes'.

---

[11]Since nasalization is not predictable for the present tense morpheme -yu, it will be written -yũ in this sketch when it is nasalized. Other morphemes that are predictable in their nasalization such as yi- (first-person singular) will be represented in the examples in just their oral form. In the same way, morphophonemic changes are nearly always predictable for subject and object prefixes (see (68)) and will be represented in just their underlying form.

(68) Morphophonemic changes with prefixes

Person prefixes		a	e	i	o	u
1s	yi-	ya	ye	yi	yo	yu
2s	bī-	bīa/bē	bē	bī	bīo	bīu
3ms	ki-	kia/ke	ke	ki	kio	kiu
3fs	ko-	koa/ko	koe	koi	ko	ko/ku
3n	sa-	sa	se	si	so	su
1p	yiha-	yiha	yihae	yihai	yihao/yiho	yihau
12	bā-	bā	bāe	bāi	bō	bū
2p	bīhā-	bīhā	bīhāe	bīhāi	bīhāo/bīho	bīhāu
3p	dā-	dā	dē	dī	dō	dū

Examples (69) and (70) illustrate some of the morphophonemic changes with the prefix *ki-* (masculine singular)

(69) *ki-eta-yu*   *[ketadyu]*
      3ms-arrive-PRES [phonetic realization]
      He arrives.

(70) *ki-aʔ-yu*   *[keʔdyu]*
      3ms-go-PRES [phonetic realization]
      He goes.

In general, there is a somewhat consistent pattern of assimilation when the vowels of the prefix and stem-initial vowels are both front or back in their points of articulation. There are exceptions to this such as *yi-* (first-person singular), *sa-* (neuter), and *dā* (third-person plural) which drop the prefix vowel before any stem vowel. Also when the stem begins with the [–back] [–front] vowel *a*, there is more variation in the assimilation pattern.

2
Parts of Speech

The two largest categories of parts of speech are nouns and verbs. Smaller categories include: adverbs, adjectives, noun adjuncts, verb adjuncts, pronouns, demonstratives, conjunctions, postpositions, and evidentials.

2.1. Nouns and adjectives. It is difficult to divide nouns and adjectives into two separate categories because they share many of the same morphosyntactic markers. The following points of similarity illustrate this difficulty. For ease of discussion, the terms 'noun' and 'adjective' will be used. The basis of the distinction at this point in the discussion is semantic or notional; that is, prototypical things/substances are called nouns while prototypical attributes are called adjectives.

1. The great majority of both adjectives and nouns end with the neuter noun class suffixes -*a* or -*ka*. The two suffixes act like nominalizers and occur on any nonhuman noun or adjective when it is either in a nonmodifier role, (i.e., head of a noun phrase or complement to a copula) or modifying an indefinite head.[12] In (71) both nouns and adjectives can be modifiers in a noun phrase. Each example in the

---

[12]Nonderived human nouns do not drop their noun class marking when in a modifier role. For example, *paki* 'father' cannot be reduced to **pak*. For further information see §3.1.

second column is one phonological word. Notice also that the endings -*ka* and -*a* do not appear when in a modifier role of a definite head.[13]

(71) Noun/adjective modifiers in NP

	Components		NP [+definite]
N + N	wiʔia + bota house + post	→	wiʔibota housepost
	kubūa + teriā canoe + support	→	kubūteriā canoe seat
ADJ + N	hoʔbaka + bota big + post	→	hoʔbabota big post
	hiyia + bota hard + post	→	hiyibota hard post

A modifier may end with -*ka* or -*a*, but this indicates that the head is indefinite. In (72), the modifier *hoʔbaka* 'big' ends with -*ka* indicating that the head *kūbuyapua* 'canoe tree' is indefinite. In (73) the referents are specific and the modifier 'big' is not marked with -*ka*.

(72) hoʔbaka kubū-yapua dā-bōʔa-yu
    big   canoe-tree 3p-search-PRES
    They are searching for a big canoe tree (tree for making a canoe).

(73) īʔrā-bi   yapua hoʔba-bi   bīhā-eʔe-waʔ-pe
    one-1DIMEN tree   big-1DIMEN 2p-get-AWAY-IND.IMP
    You take the one big (canoe) tree.

Some nouns which end with -*a* such as *pota* 'thorn', *saya* 'dress, cloth', and *bota* 'post' have a simple CVCV syllable pattern that does not allow the final -*a* or -*ka* to drop if used in a modifier role. The reason is phonological since consonant clusters are not allowed in the CV pattern.

2. Both adjectives and nouns can be marked for case. In (74) the adjective *hiyia* 'hard' is marked as the instrument with the case marker -*pi*.

---

[13]Some may object that we are confusing adjective-noun modification as in 'big post' with the formation of compound nouns as in 'house post'. To date we know of no basis on which to distinguish them in Retuarā.

It is acting as a nominal, thus it retains its final -*a* form with case marking.

(74) *sa-ki-pi?pe-re?ka hiyia-pi*
 3ns-3ms-tie-PST   hard-INSTR
 He tied it with hard (vine).

Although other examples could be cited showing the same with locative and source, case-marked adjectives are rare. The reason for their rarity may be semantic, but the grammar does allow it.

3. Modifiers that are typically used with one category can be used to modify the other. For example, the diminuitive -*hīka* is usually used with nouns as in (75), but can also be found on predicate adjectives as in (76). Most likely -*hī* is the diminuitive and -*ka* a nominalizer. It could therefore be argued that -*hī* must be used with a nominal but there are no examples of free adjectives without -*ka* or -*a* to test this.

(75) *wi?i-hī-ka*
 house-DIM-n
 little house

(76) *hāhī-hī-ka   sa-ībē*
 strong-DIM-n 3ns-be
 It is a little bit strong (i.e., river current).

Another example of this interchange of modifiers is the suffix -*i?taka* (intensive) which is common on adjectives as in (77), but which also is occasionally found on nouns as well as in (78).

(77) *ba?i-i?taka yi-re   bī-baa-yu*
 bad-INTS   1s-TERM 2s-do-PRES
 You treat me very badly.

(78) *sa-ki-tawe?ata-re?ka sa-pebā-i?taka-rā*
 3ns-3ms-dump-PST   3ns-face-INTS-LOC
 He dumped it (right/directly) in its face.

4. Finally, both adjectives and nouns can be the complement of a copula as in (79) and (80).

(79) *ho?baka sa-ībē*
 big   3ns-be
 It is big.

(80) *wi?ia sa-ībē*
 house   3ns-be
 It is a house.

There are, however, some other areas where nouns and adjective are not interchangeable. Most notably, adjectives do not make good heads of noun phrases. Example (81) with *ho?baka* 'big' as the head is judged to be marginal or ungrammatical depending on the speaker. To make it acceptable, a specific classifier must be suffixed to *ho?baka* which causes it to become a modifier to the classifier. Notice that final *-ka* drops in (82).

(81) **hībī-ho?baka*
 blue-big
 *the blue big (one)

(82) *hībī-ho?ba-ri-o*
 blue-big-INDEF-3DIMEN
 some big blue ones

Further, only adjectives occur as the adjective of comparison in a comparative construction. In (83) the adjective of comparison is *ho?ba* 'big'.

(83) *yi-re   ho?ba-bahi ki-ībē*
 1s-TERM big-CMPR   3ms-be
 He is bigger than I am.

Although the reasons listed in this section suggest that nouns and adjectives are very closely related, they probably should not be considered so indistinguishable as to form a single category.

Hopper and Thompson (1984:703), in discussing the categories of noun and verb, state:

> We find that the grammars of languages tend to label the categories N [noun] and V [verb] with morpho-syntactic markers which are iconically characteristic of these categories to the degree that a given instance of N or V approaches its prototypical function. In other words, the closer a form is to signaling this prime function, the more the language tends to recognize its function

through morphemes typical of the category—e.g., deictic markers for N, tense markers for V. We conclude by suggesting that categoriality itself is another fundamental property of grammars which may be directly derived from discourse function.

Extending this line of reasoning to the distinction between noun and adjectives one should expect that prototypical nouns and prototypical adjectives should contrast in the morphosyntactic form they exhibit. The amount of contrast will depend on the degree to which they signal their prime function. Concerning the contrast between categories, Hopper and Thompson continue:

> A form which is prototypical of its category will tend to display all those characteristics which are representative of the category, and none which are representative of another. This means that prototypical instances of categories are maximally distinct from one another. (p.709)

An examination of prototypical nouns and adjectives in Retuarã does reveal some areas in which they differ in their morphosyntactic form.

According to Hopper and Thompson, prototypical nouns "... function to introduce participants and 'props' and to deploy them. To the extent that a linguistic form is carrying out this prototypical function, it will be coded as N, and will manifest the full range of nominal trappings conventional in the language."(p.710)

For nouns in Retuarã, the distinctive characteristics that prototypical nouns will manifest (either actually or potentially) are the following:

1. marked as belonging to one of the four noun classes,
2. take case marking where appropriate, and
3. take modifiers such as adjectives or genitives.

Schachter (1985:13) in discussing the definition of adjectives states that "... even in notionally based grammars, adjectives have usually been defined at least in part in functional terms, as words which modify nouns." Based on the above definition of prototypical nouns it would seem reasonable to posit that prototypical adjectives function to modify a reference to a participant or prop. To the degree they perform that function they manifest (actually or potentially) the following characteristics:

1. occur proximate to the head of a noun phrases. With definite noun phrases (which occur without noun class marking) they are bound to the head, and
2. can take classifier suffixes.

Thus, the fairly frequent instances where nouns and adjectives resemble each other are examples of non-prototypical usage of one of the categories. One will expect a noun in a modifier role to lose its noun class marking and be bound to the head of a noun phrase, or to take a classifier suffix. Adjectives take noun class markers and occasionally case markers when they function like a noun. The contrast between the categories is reduced the less they function in a prototypical way.

2.2–2.8 Verbs

The typical Retuarã verb refers to an action, process, or state. It is commonly inflected for person, number, and tense. Other less common inflections include mood, aspect, directionals, intensifiers, and evidentials.

2.2. Copular verb. The verb *ībā* 'to be'[14] is the copula in Retuarã. It can form a verb phrase with an adjectival, nominal, or locational complement, as in (84).

(84) ADJECTIVAL

    ho?baka   sa-ībē
    big   3ns-be
    It is big.

    NOMINAL

    āyāka   sa-ībē
    snake   3ns-be
    It is a snake.

    LOCATIONAL

    riaka-rā   ki-ībā-ko?o
    river-LOC   3ms-be-PST
    He was at the river.

In addition, the copula is often omitted, as in (85) and (86).

(85) *ho?ba-ki (ki-ībē)*
      big-ms   (3ms-be)
      He (is) big.

---

[14]It often has the alternate form *ībē* in present tense.

(86) ho?ba-ka yi?i
 big-ms   1s
 I'm big.

2.3. Spatial relators. Spatial relators are special forms derived from verb roots that locate things or beings in space. They function as stative verbs that are inflected for person, but not for tense. Spatial relators seem to primarily predicate present position or state and also, but optionally, location. The construction is formed by replacing the last vowel of a verb root with -*e* (or -*ẽ* if the final vowel was nasalized), or -*bẽ*. Some forms do not replace the final vowel before the suffix -*bẽ*.[15] In (87), *rupe* (derived from *rupa* 'sit') indicates a position on the ground. The sentence can also be rendered using a locative construction as in (88), although the use of spatial relators is more common. There is some difference in meaning since (87) is more specific about position of the object.

(87) balon yepa-rã   sa-rupe
 ball ground-LOC 3ns-be/sit
 The ball is on the ground.

(88) balon yepa-rã   ĩbã
 ball ground-LOC be
 The ball is on the ground.

Further examples show that different locations of the same object determines what spatial relator is used. In both examples, the copula *ĩbã* 'to be' could be used in a more general way to express the location.

(89) balon riaka-reka   sa-yũbẽ
 ball river-LOC.SPEC 3ns-be/float
 The ball is/floats in the river.

(90) balon yapu-rĩpia-reka   sa-rope
 ball tree-branch-LOC.SPEC 3ns-be/mount
 The ball is in the tree branches.

The spatial relator *rope* 'be on, mounted on' in (90) always has the meaning of being placed on or in something. The object is supported above the ground.

---

[15] Occasionally the construction will include an intensifier. When this happens it is the last vowel of the intensifier that is affected rather than that of the verb root.

The subject of a spatial relator can also be animate as in (91). They can also be compounded with other verbs as in (92). (Notice that the spatial relator suffix -bē does not replace the final vowel of the verb root rīka 'to stand'.)

(91) ruparikubūā-rā ki-rupe
bench-LOC   3ms-be/sit
He is/sits on the bench.

(92) ko-pupahoa-rīkabē
3fs-think-stand
She stands thinking.

Occasionally spatial relators are used to indicate a general state of action. This usage is descriptive rather than active as in (93), where the vowel change occurs in the intensifier -tapa 'everywhere' rather than the verb root.

(93) ki-tu-ri-tape
3ms-travel-EP-everywhere
He's traveling around.

Spatial relators differ from locatives in that they often indicate something about the location or position of something in a sentence that does not contain an overt locative. For example in (94) the spatial relator hīʔbē 'hang' implies a vertical location, such as a wall.

(94) aiya herāka hīʔbē
sun measure hang
The clock hangs (on the wall).

Similarly, in (95), the hearer will know that the location involves water, whereas a similar construction using the copula without a locative NP says nothing about a location and would be interpreted as a predicate nominal.

(95) balon yūbē
ball be/float
The ball is/floats (in the/some water).

The form of spatial relators varies depending on the speaker of the language. Occassionally speakers will use a form ending with *a* rather than *e* when the subject is indefinite or inanimate. This -a/-e variation may correspond to the variation of the irregular verb *ībā* 'to be' which often has the form *ībē*.

2.4. Intransitive verbs. Intransitive verbs include verbs which describe states, involuntary processes (e.g., *grow, flow, die*), and voluntary actions. Example (96) illustrates a verb that expresses a state or quality.

(96) *ko-wehabi-yu*
      3fs-crazy-PRES
      She is crazy.

Verbs describing involuntary processes have patient subjects, (i.e., the subject undergoes the effect of the verb), but are not morphosyntactically distinguished from voluntary action verbs.

(97) *riaka yu-yu-a*
      river flow^downriver-PRES-n
      The river flows.

The other verbs in this class are ones which describe voluntary activity, e.g., *dance, talk, cook, bathe*, etc. The subject can be both agent and patient as in (98).

(98) *lui-re   bayatāā-reʔka*
      Lui-TERM dance-PST
      Lui danced.

Some intransitive verbs are the product of object incorporation which reduces the valence of transitive verbs. In (99), the object *tāʔāpi*, 'coca' combines with the verb *hāā́* 'put' to create the compound 'chew coca'.

(99) *dā-tāʔāpi-hāā́-reʔka*
      3p-coca-put-PST
      They chewed coca.

Other intransitive verbs have transitive counterparts that are very similar in form such as intransitive *hihi* 'to cool' and transitive *hihe* 'to cool'. These are discussed in §5.28.

2.5. Transitive verbs. The class of transitive verbs is large. Typically the subject is agent. When a proper or human noun is the subject, object, or recipient of the action, it is often marked by -re/-te (term).[16] Note that -re in (101) marks Lui as the object, but the object 'fish' in (100) is not marked since it is neither human nor a proper name.

(100) waʔia yi-baʔa-koʔo
 fish 1s-eat-PST
 I ate the fish.

(101) lui-re   yi-īā-yu
 Lui-TERM 1s-see-PRES
 I see Lui.

Several transitive verbs incorporate instruments as in (102) in which *peka* 'shotgun' is incorporated to give the meaning 'to shoot'.

(102) yaia ki-peka-hāā-rape
 tiger 3ms-shotgun-kill-PST
 He shot the tiger.

2.6. Ditransitive verbs. Retuarã has a class of verbs which take two objects, one of which is understood semantically to be the recipient. The two objects are not distinguished grammatically. Both recipients and objects vary between themselves in word order. Word order, however, can be more rigid when the speaker wants to clearly distinguish the object from the recipient in potentially ambiguous sentences. Example (103) illustrates the most common order. For further discussion see §7.3.

(103) OBJ   REC   S-VERB
 sara   ki-re   yi-peata-rape
 machete 3ms-TERM 1s-return-PST
 I returned the machete to him.

Other less frequent orders include: OBJ   S-VERB   REC
                                      REC   S-VERB   OBJ
                                      REC   OBJ   S-VERB

2.7. Verbs with sentential objects. Retuarã allows sentential objects with verb categories such as modality, manipulative, sensory, purpose (with

---

[16]A subject that is human or a proper noun can also be unmarked as a term. When this occurs, the verb takes a number/gender suffix that agrees with the subject (see §5.2.).

motion) and preventative. The object complement in most of the categories is bound to the main clause as illustrated in the example of a modality verb in (104) where, because the subject of the object complement is coreferential with that of the main clause, the subject of the complement is deleted. Complementation is discussed in §§11.3–11.7.

(104) aʔ-ri-ri-ka   yi-pupahoa-yu
      go-EP-DVBL-n 1s-plan-PRES
      I plan to go.

2.8. Compound verbs. Verbs may be added to another verb to form a compound verb. For example, the verbs *wea* 'to finish', *tiyi* 'to end', and *ūʔbū* 'to begin' may be suffixed to the main verb to indicate a phase of a process. In (105), the beginning of a process, that of fish entering a stream, is indicated by the combination of 'enter' and 'begin'. Many other types of compounding are possible and are illustrated in §5.25.

(105) la cinco   rōʔōhirā sa-wa-ūʔbū-yu
      five^p.m. at   3np-enter-begin-PRES
      At 5 p.m. they (fish) begin to enter (a stream).

2.9. Adverbs. Adverbs express time, location (or direction), and manner as in (106).

(106) TIME   MANNER
      bāē   yiha-iʔta-reʔka   hāhīā
      now   1p-come-PST   fast
      Now we came fast.

Many adverbs (particularly manner) are derived from other classes. In (107), *-hV* (adverbializer) is used to derive a manner adverb from a nominalized verb. The vowel of the suffix is derived by a harmony rule which copies the features of the preceding vowel.

(107) hai-be-ka-ha   yiha-tu-rape
      talk-NEG-n-ADVLZR   1p-travel-PST
      We travelled quietly/without talking.

The category of adverbs also includes speaker attitude adverbs and mood/aspect adverbs. Attitude or opinion may be indicated by the adverbs *heʔe* (supposition) and *ruku* (assertion). Adverbs that express mood and aspect include *koiʔtēhe* 'almost', *kopakaha* 'already', and *aʔte* 'again'. For further examples see §6.4 and §6.5.

(108) *wapahārīa sa-ībē heʔe*
      expensive 3ns-be SUP
      It's probably expensive.

2.10.–2.12 Pronouns and other pro-forms

Retuarã has personal, demonstrative, and dummy pronouns.

2.10. Personal pronouns. Personal pronouns encode person, number, and gender as shown in (109)[17]. This free form of the pronoun generally occurs as an abbreviated answer to a question, or when it is the subject of certain types of clauses. In all other uses they occur in a cliticized form, as discussed below, that is prefixed to the verb as subject or case-marked in any other case role.

(109) *yiʔi*   (first-person singular)
      yiha   (first-person plural exclusive)
      bārā   (first-person plural inclusive)
      bīʔī   (second-person singular)
      bīhā   (second-person plural)
      iʔki   (third-person singular masculine)
      iʔko   (third-person singular feminine)
      iʔka   (third-person singular neuter)
      iʔrā   (third-person plural)

The personal pronouns are not frequently used, perhaps because the person marker prefixes are preferred. When a free personal pronoun occurs as subject, a number/gender suffix that agrees with it is also present on the verb. For a fuller discussion of agreement see §5.2. Occassionally just the number/gender suffix is present with the free pronominal being implied. Personal pronouns, however, are frequently used in negated declaratives where often a number/gender suffix is followed by the corresponding personal pronoun. In (110), the number/gender suffix *-ka* (masculine singular) is followed by the free person pronoun *yiʔi* (first-person singular)

---

[17]The second-person plural pronoun, *bīhā*, also occurs as *bīha*. The pronunciation varies between speakers.

Parts of Speech

(110) *ki-re   īā-be-yu-ka   yiʔi*
      3ms-TERM see-NEG-PRES-ms 1s
      I don't see him.

Subject agreement is usually accomplished by means of person marker prefixes (see (114); also §5.2), but even in positive clauses, a free pronoun may occur (with a number/gender suffix on the verb that agrees with the subject in gender and number) to give emphasis, as in (111).

(111) *yiʔi ā-yū-ka   bī-ībā-be*
      1s say-PRES-ms 2s-be/live-IMP
      I say, "Live (with him)!"

The set of number/gender suffixes for subject agreement are displayed in (112). This set reflects the same parameters, and very nearly the same forms as that of the four noun classes (see §3.1).

(112) -*ka*/-*ki*   (masculine singular)
      -*ko*   (feminine singular)
      -*rā*   (masculine/feminine plural)
      -*ka*/-*a*   (neuter singular/plural)

Two other sets of suffixes, animate classifers and number/gender suffixes for adjectives, have a different distribution, but the same function as the suffixes listed in (112) (see (113) and (136) in §2.26). The slight differences in form between the three sets make it impossible to combine them into one chart, but they should probably be considered one category nonetheless. They all have the function of indicating number and gender, and nominalizing the construction.

(113) -*ika*   (singular masculine or animate)
      -*ko*   (singular feminine)
      -*rā*   (dual masculine or animate)
      -*bāki* (plural masculine or animate)
      -*korā* (dual/plural feminine)

The person marker prefixes are the only prefixes of the language. They can mark subject on a verb phrase or possessor in a genitive construction, and are used in conjunction with postposition case markers. (*sa-* third-person (neuter) can also refer to an object, as well as a subject.) A comparison with the person pronouns in (109) strongly suggests that they were once free pronouns that have become clitics.

(114) *yi-*   (first-person singular)
   yiha-   (first-person plural exclusive)
   bã-   (first-person plural inclusive)
   bī-   (second-person singular)
   bīhã-   (second-person plural)
   ki-   (third-person singular masculine)
   ko-   (third-person singular feminine)
   dã-   (third-person masculine/feminine plural)
   sa-   (third-person neuter singular/plural)

The forms displayed in (114) are as they occur prefixed to a verb root that begins with a consonant. Before a vowel, the last vowel of the prefix may be deleted or assimilated to the following vowel. The rules differ somewhat for each morpheme (see §1.20).

2.11. Demonstratives. There are demonstratives but no definite or indefinite articles in Retuarã. They may head a noun phrase or they may precede a noun as a modifier. The most common forms of the demonstratives are *iʔi* 'this person', *iʔka* 'this (neuter)', and *iʔsia* 'that (neuter)'. For further discussion see §3.7.

2.12. Dummy pronoun. The pronoun clitic *sa-* (third-person neuter) may be used to fill a subject slot when no particular subject is intended. Similar to the English 'it' in 'it is cold', Retuarã fills the subject slot with *sa*, as in (115). The pronoun *sa-* also serves as an object prefix as in (116).

(115) *hihia sa-baa-yu*
   cold   3ns-make-PRES
   It is cold.

(116) *sa-bã-ko-ri-ērã*
   3ns-12-try-EP-PURP
   Let's try it.

2.13–2.15 Noun adjuncts

Noun adjuncts typically form constituents with nouns. Case markers, quantifiers, and classifiers are discussed in the following sections. Adjectives, genitives, and numerals are discussed in chapter 3.

Parts of Speech

2.13. Case markers. Retuarã marks case with postpositions. There are eight case markers listed in (117). The locative case marker *-rã* is illustrated in (118).

(117) *-re/-te* 'TERM'
 -rã 'LOC'
 -reka 'LOC.SPEC'
 -ka-gender/number 'ABL'
 -pi 'INSTR'
 -ka 'COM'
 -roʔsi 'BEN'
 -ri-gender/number 'POSS'

(118) *wiʔia-rã   yi-aʔ-yu*
 house-LOC 1s-go-PRES
 I go to the house.

2.14. Quantifiers. Quantifiers modify head nouns in quantity. They include the distinctions in (119). Also included in quantifiers is the adverbial *upati* 'every, all' which is used with the verb *ĩbã* 'be' as in (120).

(119) *rĩkibã* 'many' (mass nouns)
 kũpahĩ 'few'
 ritaha 'all'

(120) *dã-ĩbã-upati-hi   sa-ĩbã-upatihi*
 3p-be-all-ADVLZR 3ns-be-all
 everyone everything

2.15. Classifiers. The system of classifiers is less extensive in Retuarã than other Tucanoan languages (see Barnes 1990). While they are obligatory on numerals, they generally classify a noun according to some parameter such as shape, unit of measure, animacy, etc. There are three general shape classifiers which distinguish objects on the basis of the number of their most salient dimensions. They are: *-bi* (1 dimensional), *-to* (2 dimensional), and *-o* (3 dimensional). There are also specific classifiers such as *-pãũ* 'hammock', *kũbũ* 'canoe, or any hollowed out container', etc. Examples (121) and (122) illustrate their use. Classifiers are further illustrated in §3.10.

(121) *ĩʔrã-bi   yapua*
 one-1DIMEN tree
 one tree

(122) *ĩʔrã-pãũ*   *pãũã*
    one-CLAS^hammock hammock
    one hammock

2.16–2.22 Verb adjuncts

In addition to the main verb, subject markers (prefix and suffix), object marker (prefix), negative and causative affixes, the verb phrase also includes the adjuncts listed below.

2.16. Auxiliary verb. The auxiliary verb *baa* 'do, make' is used to create a construction that indicates imminence. The auxiliary takes the tense suffix while the content verb takes the subject prefix if it occurs. The subordinator *-ērā* (purpose) is suffixed to the content verb.

(123) *karaka yi-baʔa-ērā baa-yu*
    chicken 1s-eat-PURP do-PRES
    I am going to eat the chicken.

2.17. Tense. Tense is marked by a suffix that usually occurs last on the verb phrase, except for constructions containing number/gender suffixes. There is one present tense, one future, and four past tenses. Past tenses distinguish immediate past (today), recent past (yesterday and before), remote past (distant past), and general past (nonspecified) (see §§5.4–5.9).

2.18. Aspect. There are seven aspect suffixes that occur immediately following the verb root (see §5.10–5.15). The aspectual distinctions are in (124).

(124) *-wai* 'HAB'
    -rūki 'IMPRS'
    -royi 'IMPF'
    -yūhū 'CONT'
    -riha 'CONT'
    -ti 'PERF'
    -ta 'PNCT'

2.19. Mood. There are four modal suffixes that, like the aspect suffixes, immediately follow the verb root. (Mood and aspect suffixes do not occur together in the verb phrase (see §§5.16–5.19).

Parts of Speech

(125) -korī 'INT'
      -hī 'PSBL'
      -kope 'CONTRA'
      -hã 'CONSQ'

2.20. Intensifiers. Verb adjuncts of range and intensity are used to extend the effect of the action of the verb. They are suffixed to the verb root and include -pata 'all, completely', -tapa 'everywhere', and -tiya (intensive).

(126) bī-baʔa-*pata*-be
      2s-eat-all-IMP
      Eat it all.

(127) yi-rū-rī-*tiya*-yu
      1s-tired-EP-INTS-PRES
      I am really tired.

2.21. Evidentials. The three evidential markers are optional and encode information acquired by auditory clues, assumption, and second hand reports. Evidentials are discussed in §5.24.

2.22. Subordinating suffixes. Subordinating suffixes create subordinated clauses in areas such as time, logic, intention, contraexpectation, etc. In (128), the subordination suffix *-tirā* indicates that the main clause occurs after the event of the subordinated clause. Subordinating suffixes are discussed further in §§11.8–11.17.

(128) baʔa-tirā ki-aʔ-ri-koʔo
      eat-after 3ms-go-EP-PST
      After eating, he went.

2.23. Coordinating conjunctions. The coordinating conjunction *oka* conjoins two clauses, or noun phrases and has the sense of 'or, either, also'. The conjunction follows the second clause or noun phrase (when both occur). Usually much of the context is left implicit as illustrated in (129) and (130).

(129) āūā   ki-baʔa-koʔo waʔia oka
      casava 3ms-eat-PST   fish also
      He ate casava (and) fish also.

(130) *iʔsupaka īparibārā-re ā-pakāʔā   dā-ā-rī-be-ri-hī-ka   **oka***
like^that chiefs-TERM say-REAS.DS 3p-say-EP-NEG-EP-PSBL-n also

   bārā ībā-be-yu-a   yi-re
   how be-NEG-PRES-n 1s-TERM
   If the chiefs say like that, or don't say like that also, it doesn't matter to me.

2.24. Subordinating conjunctions. Subordinating conjunctions are one means of forming adverbial clauses. They always occur clause finally. Examples (131) and (132) illustrate some adverbial clauses formed with subordinating conjunctions. Subordination by conjunction is discussed further in §§11.18–11.22.

(131) *bī-re   yi-piʔpe-royi-i-ka   **upaka-ha**   bī-re   yi-piʔpe-yu*
   2s-TERM 1s-tie-IMPF-STAT-n like-ADVLZR 2s-TERM 1s-tie-PRES
   I'm tying you just like I always tie you.

(132) *wiʔia-rā   ki-eta-reʔka   **potohī** ki-re   ko-īāwarū-reʔka*
   house-LOC 3ms-arrive-PST when 3ms-TERM 3fs-recognize-PST
   When he arrived at the house, she recognized him.

2.25. Negators. There are three strategies for negation. In declarative or interrogative sentences, the suffix *-be* negates the clause and follows the verb root. Its scope is the whole sentence. Negation of imperatives is accomplished by suffixing *-aʔsi* to the verb root, and constituents are negated by the negative verb *bā*.

(133) *ō-rī-**be**-yu-ka   yiʔi*
   know-EP-NEG-PRES-ms 1s
   I don't know.

(134) *ki-re   bī-boha-aʔsi*
   3ms-TERM 2s-tell-NEG.IMP
   Don't tell him.

(135) *hia-**bā**-rī-a   iʔsia*
   good-not^be-DVBL-n that
   That's no good.

Parts of Speech   41

2.26–2.29 Derivational affixes

Nouns, adjectives, and adverbs can be derived by affixation. In addition, causative suffixes can be used to derive transitive and ditransitive verbs.

2.26. Nominalization by number/gender suffixes. The set of suffixes in (136) is used to nominalize adjectives as well as indicate the number and gender of the referent.[18]

(136) -ki/-ika (masculine singular)
      -ko   (feminine singular)
      -ka/-a   (neuter singular and plural)
      -rã   (masculine plural)
      -korã   (feminine plural)

Example (137) illustrates derivations using these suffixes. Notice that the masculine plural suffix is also used for general plural when the group referred to is of mixed gender.

(137) aʔpe-a   other-n   'another one'
      aʔpe-ika   other-ms   'another male'
      aʔpe-ko   other-fs   'another female'
      aʔpe-rã   other-p   'other ones (males or mixed gender)'
      aʔpe-korã   other-fp   'other ones (females)'

2.27. Deverbalizer. The affix -ri occurs after a verb root and has the function of deverbalization.[19] The resulting construction does not report a discourse event (as one would expect a verb to do), but rather modifies the following suffix, or if there is no following suffix, it functions as a participial. Not surprisingly, the verb root does not exhibit any morphology typical of verbs (such as tense, aspect, mood etc.). Instead it resembles a prototypical noun with noun class marking. This is consistent with Hopper and Thompson (1984) who state that nouns and verbs tend to display the full range of attributes characteristic of nouns and verbs when they occur

---

[18] Although this set of number/gender suffixes is slightly different than those that are used for subject agreement (see (112) or those that occur on animate classifiers (113)), they have the same functions as nominalizers and indicators of number and gender.

[19] The root always contains two or four syllables so that the epenthetic syllable discussed in §1.17 fills the second or fourth syllable slot for roots of one or three syllables. Thus, two homophonous morphemes -ri (epenthetic syllable) and -ri (deverbalizer) may occur together but should not be confused.

in their typical environments. Accordingly, in environments where a verb reports a discourse event or a noun introduces a participant in the discourse, the contrast between nouns and verbs will be greatest. Conversely, in non-prototypical environments, the contrast between them tends to be neutralized.

In (138), the neuter number/gender suffix -*ka* follows -*ri* creating an abstract noun or infinitive.

(138) *hie-ri-ka*
    fix-DVBL-n
    to fix

When the suffix following -*ri* is animate, the animate number/gender suffixes are not used but rather suffixes such as -*bāhī* 'man', -*bāhō* 'woman', or -*bāhā* 'people'.

(139) *wārō-ri-bāhā*
    teach-DVBL-people
    teachers

There are a few cases in which a deverbalized verb root modifies a classifier as in (140).

(140) *weā-ri-pāīā*
    to^paddle-DVBL-CLAS^blade
    paddle (noun)

When no suffix follows the affix -*ri*, the construction functions like a participial and is more verb-like with the potential to display some morphology typical of verbs. In (141), the continuative aspect suffix -*riha* is present on the participial verb. Example (142) further illustrates the participial sense that -*ri* can produce. In the example it has the form -*rĩ* due to nasal spreading.

(141) *supa   baa-riha-ri   dīyērū   dā-re   ki-ẽʔbā-rape*
    like^that do-CONT-DVBL money 3p-TERM 3ms-take-PST
    Doing like that, he took their money.

(142) *āʔbīhīā-bua-be-yu-rā   ībā-rĩ   hia   dā-heyobaa-bua-yu*
    hate-RECPR-NEG-PRES-p be-DVBL good 3p-help-RECPR-PRES
    Being those that do not hate each other, they help each other well.

Parts of Speech

2.28. Adverbializer. The suffix *-hV* is used to derive adverbs from nominalizations. In (143) the resulting adverb expresses manner. The adverbializer *-hV* is further discussed in §6.6.

(143) *baʔa-be-ka-ha   yi-baʔirabe-rape*
 eat-NEG-n-ADVLZR 1s-work-PST
 I worked without eating.

2.29. Causatives. There are two causative suffixes, both of which increase the valence of a verb by one. Thus the intransitive verb *ya* 'to extinguish' in (144) becomes transitive in (145) with the addition of the causitive suffix *-ta*.[20] The causative suffix *-ta* is used for nonvolitional causees (i.e., 'candle' in (144)). The other causative, *-rōhe*, is used with volitional causees.

(144) *tūparāperia ya-yu-a*
 candle   extinguish-PRES-n
 The candle went out.

(145) *tūparāperia bī-ya-ta-be*
 candle   2s-extinguish-CAUS-IMP
 Put the candle out.

In the following examples, with the addition of the causative *-rōhe*, the valence of the transitive verb 'eat' is increased from one object in (146) to two in (147).

(146) *āūā   ko-baʔa-koʔo*
 casava 3fs-eat-PST
 She ate casava.

(147) *āūā   ko-re   ki-baʔa-rōhe-koʔo*
 casava 3fs-TERM 3ms-eat-CAUS-PST
 He made/ordered her to eat casava.

---

[20]The suffix *-ta* is very likely borrowed from Yucuna, an Arawakan neighboring language.

3
Noun Phrase

The noun phrase (NP) is made up of a noun, pronoun, or nominalized adjective as head, and zero or more modifiers. Modifiers can be genitives, relative clauses, quantifiers, numerals, adjectives, or demonstratives. The following sections discuss noun classes, the parts of the noun phrase and their ordering and concord within the noun phrase.

3.1. Noun classes. There are four noun classes in Retuarã.

Class 1   neuter nouns (inanimate or nonhuman)
Class 2   human singular masculine nouns
Class 3   human singular feminine nouns
Class 4   human plural nouns

Dixon (1982:160, 163) cites the following three criteria for distinguishing noun classes: "We can say that the category of noun classes is (1) a grouping of all the nouns of a language into a smallish number of classes, (2) so that there is some overt indication of the class of a noun within any sentence in which it occurs with one of a certain set of syntactic functions, (3) and this indication is not entirely within the noun word."

The grouping of all the nouns of the language into four classes meets criterion one. The second and third criteria are met in that the subject agreement suffixes on verbs, agreement suffixes on predicate nominals/adjectives, and the agreement with the head of a relative clause are based on the same categorization (and form of the suffixes) as the noun classes.

Class 1 includes all neuter nouns (inanimate or nonhuman animate). It is the largest class and all of its members can be distinguished by -*ka* or -*a* word final.[21] For the purpose of distinguishing noun classes, we will simply say that all members of class 1 are -*a* final. Class 1 nouns are not marked for number; they can be singular or plural according to the context. The class includes words such as *wiʔia* 'house', *yaiwĕkoa* 'dog', and *aiyaka* 'sun'. The agreement within the sentence for animate, nonhuman members of class 1 is generally neuter (-*a*/ or -*ka*). In cases where the gender and number is known or in focus from the context, agreement will be reflected in predicate nominals or adjectives, indicative sentences or numbers.

Class 2 includes all human singular masculine nouns. The majority of nouns in this class are distinguished by word final -*i* (either -*ki* or -*hĩ*)[22] as in *ībīrīhī* 'male', *pōʔībāhī* 'man', *iʔki* 'he' and *paki* 'father'. The class contains nouns that have masculine humanity projected onto them such as *yābīkaki* 'moon' (lit. man of the night). This class also includes some of the masculine kinship terms, and some human masculine referents that have no distinguishing marking (-*ki* or -*hĩ*), but their inclusion in class 2 is based on their semantic content and their agreement with -*ki* 'singular masculine' on verbs and predicated nominals or adjectives. Examples of the kinship terms are *āʔā* 'paternal uncle' and *yaʔya* 'maternal uncle'.

Class 3 includes all human singular feminine nouns. The majority are distinguished by word final -*o* (-*o* or -*ko*). Included in this class are words like *rōbō* 'woman', *bāko* 'daughter', and *aʔko* 'grandmother'. The class also includes feminine kinship terms that are not marked -*o* word finally. Again they are included in class 3 based on their semantic content and their agreement with -*ko* 'singular feminine' on verbs and predicate nominals or adjectives. They include direct address kinship terms such as *bāʔī* 'mother'. Other such kinship terms include *bēʔē* 'paternal aunt' and *bāʔbīrubū* 'wife of older brother'.

Class 4 includes all human plural nouns. They are marked by word final -*rā* or -*hā*/-*ha*[23] as in *bākarā* 'children' and *bīhā* (second-person plural). This class also includes group nouns such as *surararāka* 'soldiers', and

---

[21] It is possible that the variation was once -*ka* ~ -*ga*. Malone (to appear) points out that /g*/ was unstable and has disappeared in some Tucanoan languages.

[22] The nasal *i* in -*hĩ* may be due to nasal spreading. The few environments in which -*hĩ* occurs are all nasal.

[23] The plural affix -*hā*/-*ha* varies in nasality between speakers. It has been included here in its nasal form since this fits well with the analysis of -*ā* marking a noun class. Throughout this paper, the variation of the form reflects the most common pronunciation of a word.

Noun Phrase

ehersitarāka 'army' (both borrowed from Spanish). (The suffix *-ka* (neuter) seems to group a plural noun into one entity.)

Dixon (1982:166) states that "In some languages the noun classes are mutually exclusive—each noun belongs to one and only one class. In other languages there are some nouns—usually only a fairly small number—that can occur with markers from more than one class." It is possible to assign a small number of words to multiple classes in Retuarā. For example, the words for father and mother are *paki* and *pako* respectively. It could be argued that the noun is *pa-* 'parent' and that it has no class until it is nominalized by *-ki* (masculine), or *-ko* (feminine). Thus it is a member of both class 2 and 3. Other examples include *aʔki/aʔko* 'grandfather/ grandmother', *bāki/bāko* 'son/daughter', and *pakiaki/ pakiako* 'old man/old woman'. The kinship term *hū* 'younger relative' can also be assigned to class 2 or 3 since it can agree with *-ki* or *-ko* depending on the sex of the referent.

Another problem arises when one considers derived nouns. As was discussed previously (see §2.1) it is difficult to distinguish nouns from adjectives. Both nouns and adjectives are alike in form and ending with the nominalizers *-a* or *-ka*. There is a rather large group of nouns derived from adjective-like words that take the noun class suffixes as illustrated by *yeʔe-* 'short'.

(148) *yeʔe-a* 'short thing (inanimate)'
    yeʔe-ki 'short person (masculine)'
    yeʔe-ko 'short person (feminine)'
    yeʔe-rā 'short persons, animals (plural)'

Although adjective-like words such as *yeʔe-* 'short' or *hoʔba-* 'big' usually are found as nominalizations, they probably should not be considered part of the noun class system since they are a fairly large group that could potentially belong to any of the four classes depending on its derivation. They differ from words like *paki* 'father' in that, (1) semantically they are modifiers, and (2) they do not have the same referential strength as a noun in a noun phrase. For example, *hīʔbīā* 'blue' is acceptable as a modifier in *hīʔbī-oʔorika* 'blue flower', but as the head of a noun phrase in **?hoʔba-hīʔbīā* 'big blue (one)', it is marginal.

3.2. Genitives. The genitive construction is formed by a possessor plus the head. The construction can have either an animate or inanimate possessor. Example (149) illustrates an animate noun phrase possessor (Roberto) and (150) illustrates an inanimate possessor.

(149) *roberto rūbū iʔko*
Roberto woman 3fs
She is Roberto's woman.

(150) *piʔi-rihea*
basket-lip/border
lip of the basket

It is very common that the genitive be expressed simply by a person pronoun prefix on the possessed object, as in (151).

(151) *ki-wiʔia*
3ms-house
his house

3.3. Relative clause. Relative clauses in Retuarā are internally-headed; the head occurs within the restricting clause that modifies it. In (152), the head is *bēʔrī* 'boy'. The restricting clause, 'boy burned himself in the fire', is set off by brackets. The relative clause is case-marked with the benefactive *-roʔsi* rather than the term marker *-te* (which would indicate its role as an object in the main clause). The benefactive case marking gives the sense that the medicine was given for the boy (indirectly). For further discussion of relative clauses see §§11.1–11.2.

(152) *[bēʔrī-te peka ōtoa-rā oo-rapa]-ki-roʔsi īkoa   yi-īhī-rape*
boy-TERM fire site-LOC burn-PST-ms-BEN medicine 1s-give-PST
I gave medicine for the boy who burned himself in the fire.

3.4. Quantifiers. Quantifiers in the noun phrase generally precede the head as in (153). An exception to the order of quantifier-head is *rita* 'all' in (154).

(153) *rīkibā-iʔtaka baʔarika ībē*
much-very food be
There is a lot of food.

(154) *pōʔībāhā-rita dā-ībā-reʔka*
people-all 3p-be-PST
All the people were there.

The quantifier *-rita* always follows the head. The most common order of quantifiers and heads in the language is actually not easy to establish since

Noun Phrase

quantifiers often occur in an adverbial role without their heads. The context or topic of conversation makes the head implicit as in (155). The quantifier *kũpahĩ* 'little' can take a classifier, but the other quantifiers do not.

(155) *ĩbã kũpahĩ*
   be little
   There is a little (e.g., food).

Related to the discussion of quantity is the affix *-ri* (indefinite) that occurs between classifiers and adjectives or demonstratives.[24] Generally it seems to indicate an indefinite amount or some quantity more than one. In (156), it is used with *aʔpe* 'other'.

(156) *aʔpe-ri-kuri*
   other-INDEF-time
   sometimes

The sense of 'some' is particularly common when used with the number one as in (157). The affix *-ri* does not occur with other numbers.

(157) *ĩʔrã-ri-bãki*
   one-INDEF-p
   some people

Although the number *ĩʔrã* 'one' can occur with or without the affix (with a change in meaning), some combinations of a modifier and a classifier will allow just one construction. There are cases like (158) in which the affix *-ri* is required and (159) where it must be omitted. In such cases, the context or shared information between speaker and hearer must determine if the construction means 'one' or 'some'.

(158) *hoʔba-iʔta-ri-bi   dã-eʔe-rape*
   big-INTS-various-1DIMEN 3p-get-PST
   They got one/some very big one(s). (i.e. sticks)

(159) *kũpahĩ-bi   dã-eʔe-rape*
   little-1DIMEN 3p-get-PST
   They got one/some small one(s).

---

[24]This is not the same morpheme as discussed in §1.17 since it is not semantically empty.

More study of this particular usage of -*ri* is needed. It seems that there also may be some usages of -*ri* in which the sense is 'one by one' or 'each' rather than strictly plural.

3.5. Numerals. The number system is base five until the number twenty. After twenty, counting is by increments of twenty. The system groups the digits of the hands and feet. Thus 'one hand and two' is the number seven, 'two hands and a foot' is the number fifteen, etc. 'One person' is twenty; 'two people' is forty. The numbers are apparently frozen forms that have not changed as other parts of the language changed. It is thus difficult to establish the literal translation of some constructions.[25] The number constructions are long and cumbersome, even for native speakers so that young men may consult older men about accurate pronunciation of numbers between eleven and twenty. As a result, Spanish numbers are beginning to replace the Retuarā number system though the Retuarā numbers one through ten, are still widely used.

(160) *bāēka-raka-o-ū?pua-rā-teyāri-raka-bāki*
 three-number-3DIMEN-foot-LOC-?-number-p
 thirteen people

Numerals precede the head and have an obligatory classifier following the numeral. In (160), the final classifier is -*bāki* (plural).

The animate classifiers on numerals indicate singular, dual (masculine) and plural (more than two). The masculine classifiers -*ika* (singular), -*rā* (dual), and -*bāki* (plural) are also used for general animacy (or mixed gender). Thus, for example, *īpa-rā* (two-dual) can mean two men, two people, or any two animate beings (see (113) in §2.10.). Examples (161)–(163) illustrate the use of animate classifiers on numerals.

(161) *ī?rā-ika yaiwēkoa*
 one-ms dog
 one dog

(162) *īpa-rā yaiwēkoa*
 two-p dog
 two dogs

---

[25]It may be that *teyāri* (found in the numbers 6–9 and 11–14) was once a compound verb made up of 'go' and 'cross over'. It has become phonologically fused and shortened. Thus the number thirteen may have the literal translation 'go cross over to three on the foot.'

Noun Phrase

(163) *īpa-korā rōbīha*
 two-fp   women
 two women

The numeral never follows the head except in cases where it occurs with a possessive or a demonstrative. The numeral and classifier can often occur without an explicit head depending on whether the head has been previously mentioned.

3.6. Adjectives. The adjective generally precedes the head in Retuarã.

(164) *ho?baka saya ko-wapahī-rape*
   big   dress 3fs-buy-PST
 She bought a big dress.

Adjectives may follow the noun, however, and such phrases in isolation may be interpreted as a noun phrase or as a descriptive clause with a predicate adjective and an implicit copula as in (165).

(165) *ki-pisadāka boia*
   3ms-cat   white
 his white cat *or* His cat is white.

There are very few examples where more than one adjective is used in a noun phrase. When examples are elicited, one modifier precedes the head, and the rest follow. In (166), the number *-īpa* 'two' precedes the head while *ho?baka* 'big' and *hūsipoa* 'yellow' follow. It is also possible to find examples of two modifiers preceding the head but this is very rare.

(166) *īpa-o   ō?ōrika ho?baka, hūsipoa ībā*
 two-3DIMEN flower big   yellow be
 There are two big, yellow flowers.

There may also be some constraints on the ordering of adjectives. Generally adjectives of size precede adjectives of color, but preference for this order over the other is only slight.

3.7. Demonstratives. There are demonstratives but no definite or indefinite articles in Retuarã. The most common forms of the demonstratives are *i?ka* 'this (neuter)', *i?sia* 'that (neuter)', and *ī?ī* 'this one (singular, animate)'.[26] As modifiers they precede the head in a noun phrase (167), but (like adjectives) they follow the head noun when used as a predicate (168).

(167) *bī-rika iʔka radio*
    2s-POSS this radio
    This radio is yours.

(168) *radio iʔsia*
    radio that
    That's a radio.

Demonstratives can take classifiers as illustrated by (169) and can occur alone without a head, as a demonstrative pronoun (170).

(169) *iʔsi-to   yi-re   bī-īhī-be*
    that-2DIMEN 1s-TERM 2s-give-IMP
    Give me that (flat thing, i.e., a piece of cloth).

(170) *iʔka-pi   ki-re   ko-hãā-rape*
    this-INSTR 3ms-TERM 3fs-kill-PST
    With this she killed him.

The locative pronouns *ōʔō-* 'here', *ito-/to-* 'there' and *rōʔō-* 'place' can function as the head of a locative phrase but they can not be modified like other heads. They are always marked for case as in (171) and (172).

(171) *ito-hi-rā*
    there-EXTENT-LOC
    up to there

(172) *to-pi*
    there-INSTR
    from there

The difference between *ito-* and *to-* is that *to-* refers to a location already mentioned in the discourse, whereas *ito-* introduces a new location. In (173) the narrative has already mentioned the location of the first character when a second character arrives and speaks to the first so *torā* 'there' is used.

---

[26]Deixis can also be indicated on free person pronouns by stress (see §1.17.).

(173) to-rã   ki-re   ki-ã-rĩ-re?ka
      there-LOC 3ms-TERM 3ms-say-EP-PST
      He spoke to him there.

3.8. Relative order of elements in noun phrase. In a noun phrase with only one modifier, whether possessor, quantifier, numeral, adjective, or demonstrative, the modifier usually precedes the head.[27] For the infrequent occurence of two or more modifiers, one modifier precedes the head and the rest follow. For example, in (174) the numeral precedes the head *pisadãka* and the color follows.

(174) *bãēkaraka-bãki pisadãka boia*
      three-p   cat   white
      three white cats

When the same noun phrase is expanded by adding a possessor, the possessor precedes and the number follows the head.

(175) *ki-pisadãka bãēkaraka-bãki boia*
      3ms-cat   three-p   white
      his three white cats

When a demonstrative and an adjective occur in the same phrase, the demonstrative appears before the head noun as in (176).

(176) *i?si pisadãka ho?baka boia po?i-i-ka   boebaka sa-ībē*
      that cat   big   white body-STAT-n mean   3ns-be
      That big, white-bodied cat is mean.

The ordering of at least some of the modifiers in the noun phrase then appears to be: [possessor] [demonstrative] [number] [size, color]. Of the occurring modifiers, the highest in the hierarchy will precede the head while the rest will follow in descending order.

3.9. Case. Noun phrases may be case-marked by postposition suffixes attached to the last word in the phrase. For example, the locative *-rã* is suffixed to *wi?ia* 'house' in (177).

---

[27]In relative clauses, the head is expressed internally, so they are not relevant to this discussion.

(177) wiʔia-rã   ki-eta-rape
house-LOC 3ms-arrive-PST
He arrived at the house.

The case marker follows the classifier when they occur together on the head of a noun phrase. In (178), -pi (instrument) follows the classifier *pāīā* 'strip'. Where a modifier such as -iʔtaka (intensifier) follows the head, the case marking is suffixed to the modifier as in (179). Case is covered in more detail in chapter 4.

(178) jūā-re   tūā-rape   kubū-pāīā-pi
Juan-TERM pound-PST canoe-CLAS^(strip)-INSTR
John pounded with the board.

(179) ãta   hoʔba-iʔtaka-pi   dā-tāte-reʔka
rock big-INTS-INSTR   3p-cover-PST
They covered it with a very big rock.

3.10. Classifiers and concord in the noun phrase. Classifiers occur obligatorily bound to numerals and optionally to adjectives and demonstratives. They agree with the head in shape or classification. The table in (180) illustrates some common classifiers. The list of classifiers is more extensive than those cited in the table, yet Retuarã seems to have fewer classifiers than other Tucanoan languages (i.e., Barasano, Cubeo, Tuyuca and others).

(180) General shape   Specific shape
    -bi '1 dimensional'   -tai   'pole'
    -to '2 dimensional'   -tāko   'coil, hoop'
    -o '3 dimensional'   -pāīā   'strip, blade'
                              -kubū   'long, hollowed'
    Botanical   -koʔa   'bowl, container'
    -hãʔã 'plant'   -kope   'hole'
    -hūkia 'tree'   -ti   'string'
                              -taʔi   'cylindrical'

    Time span   Animate
    -rībī 'day'   -ika   'masculine singular'
    -kuri 'occurence'   -ko   'feminine singular'
                              -rã   'masculine, dual'

Noun Phrase

Measure/unit		-korā	'feminine plural'
-hoto	'potful'	-bāki	'masculine, plural'
-piʔi	'basketful'		
-taʔia	'remnant'	Specific	
-burua	'small remnant'	-pāū	'hammock'
-waho	'bagful'	-wiʔi	'house'
-boka	'bundle'	-roka	'message, word'

In some cases, the head of the noun phrase appears to be copied onto the modifier to create the classifier. For example in (181), the head *pāūā* 'hammock' is copied to the numeral as a classifier, but drops the nominalizer -*a*. The absence of -*a* indicates the classifier's role as a modifier along with the numeral.

(181) *ĩʔrā-pāū   pāūā*
     one-CLAS^(hammock) hammock
     one hammock

There are three general classifiers which distinguish referents on the basis of the number of salient dimensions they possess. Thus, for example, a stick is primarily one dimensional, a piece of cloth is two dimensional, and a rock is three dimensional. The three general classifiers are: -*bi* (1 dimensional), -*to* (2 dimensional), and -*o* (3 dimensional).

(182) *bāēkaraka-bi rīpia*
     three-1DIMEN branch
     three branches

(183) *bāēkaraka-to puyūā*
     three-2DIMEN leaf
     three leaves

(184) *bāēkaraka-o āta*
     three-3DIMEN stone
     three stones

The classifiers are bound to the modifier and immediately precede the head in the noun phrase. Classifiers can also occur without a head. Thus they can have refential capability like the head of a noun phrase. In such cases the concordance is with an implicit head. In (185) the classifier -*bi* (1 dimensional) is suffixed to the adjective *piyi* 'last' creating a nominalization.

(185) *piyi-bi   yi-wapahī-koʔo*
last-1DIMEN 1s-buy-PST
I bought the last one (flashlight).

Some classifiers such as *-rībī* 'day' occur on demonstratives as in (186).

(186) *iʔsi-rībī   yiha-peʔ-rape*
that-day 1p-return-PST
That day we returned.

Adjectives can also take classifiers. When they do, the classifier becomes the head of the noun phrase as illustrated by *-bi* (1 dimensional) and *-piʔi* 'basketful' below. The affixation of a classifier onto an adjective may also require the affix *-ri* (indefinite) following the adjective.

(187) *hīʔbī-ri-bi   dā-eʔe-rape*
green-INDEF-1DIMEN 3p-get-PST
They got (a) green one(s) (sticks).

(188) *rīkibā-iʔta-ri-piʔi   dā-eʔe-rape*
many-INTS-INDEF-CLAS^(basketful) 3p-get-PST
They got many basketfuls.

When the head of the NP is animate, the classifier agrees in number and gender. As mentioned in §3.5, animate classifiers on numerals distinguish between singular, plural (two beings), and plural (three or more). This agreement is illustrated in the examples of singular heads in (189) and (190). The masculine/animate singular agreement marker for numbers, *-ika*, does not vary as it does with the sets of number/gender suffixes that occur with verbs or adjectives. It is always *-ika*, rather than *-ka/-ki* or *-ika/-ki*.

(189) *īʔrā-ko rōbō*
one-fs woman
one woman

(190) *īʔrā-ika pōʔībā-hī*
one-ms man-ms
one man

There are three animate plural markers for numbers. The plural suffix *-rā* is used for two (masculine or general plural/mixed gender) as in (191). More than two (masculine or general plural) is marked *-bāki* as in (192).

Noun Phrase

The feminine plural marker is *-korā* and is used for two or more as in (193).

(191) *īpa-rā pōʔībā-hā*
two-p person-p
two people

(192) *bāēkaraka-bāki pōʔībā-hā*
three-p   person-p
three people

(193) *īpa-korā rōbī-hā*
two-fp   woman-p
two women

For animate nonhuman heads of noun phrases (for which the gender is unknown or not in focus), the classifier will indicate number employing one of the three masculine gender suffixes even though there is no overt marking of gender or number on the head as in *wāhūā* 'worm(s)' in (194) and (195).

(194) *īʔrā-ika wāhūā*
one-ms worm
one worm

(195) *īpa-rā wāhūā*
two-p worm
two worms

When the feminine gender of an animate, nonhuman head is known or in focus, a feminine classifier can reflect this focus.

(196) *īʔrā-ko yaiwēkoa*
one-fs dog
one (female) dog

(197) *īpa-korā yaiwēkoa*
two-fp dog
two (female) dogs)

4
Case

Case markers indicate the relationship of a noun phrase to the verb of a clause. It also marks the relationship between two noun phrases in the same clause in the case of accompaniment. The case markers are postposition clitics on the last word in the noun phrase. When case markers cliticize to pronouns, the prefix form of the pronouns in chart (114) are used.

4.1. Term. The suffix -re marks subjects or objects which are human or referred to by a proper name.[28] ('Term' is used here to refer to both the subject or the object whether semantically agent, recipient, or patient.) Therefore terms that are proper names are marked with -re[29] regardless of whether they are human or not as in (198). The form -re also has the variant form -te with no apparent difference in meaning between the two forms. It may be that the choice of forms resulted from an ancient morphophonemic variation of (t~d, d* > r).[30] The two forms are still under study to determine if there is any functional distinction between them.

---

[28]Not all subjects and objects eligible for term case marking are so marked. See §5.2 for discussion.

[29]In other Tucanoan languages the same form, -re, often marks objects or focus. It is never used, however, on a subject as it is in Retuarã. Apparently language change has brought about a redefinition of the role of the term case marker in Retuarã.

[30]For further study see Malone (to appear).

(198) *moka-re   waʔia baʔa-koʔo*
　　　 mocha-TERM fish   eat-PST
　　　 Mocha (a dog) ate the fish.

Terms which refer to humans, such as *baīpo* 'owner' and *põʔībāhā* 'people' are also marked by *-re*. In (199), *baīpo* is marked by *-te* and *põʔībāhā* is marked by *-re* to indicate their roles as terms.

(199) *bāē sa-baīpo-te   ā-yū   sa-bā-bia-ērā   põʔībāhā-re*
　　　 now 3ns-owner-TERM   say-PRES 3ns-12-plant-PURP   people-TERM
　　　 Now it's (garden) owner says, "Let's plant it", to the people.

Person pronoun prefixes can take term case marking when they are the object, as *ki-* (masculine singular) in (200), but not when they are in the subject role. Subject person prefixes always occur prefixed to the verb as in (201).

(200) *ki-re   aʔbīti-ri-tirā   dā-iyo-pi-ri-koʔo*
　　　 3ms-TERM hear-EP-AFTER   3p-shame-feel-EP-PST
　　　 After hearing him, they were ashamed.

(201) *iʔsia aʔbīti-ri-tirā   ki-iyo-pi-ri-koʔo*
　　　 that hear-EP-after   3ms-shame-feel-EP-PST
　　　 After hearing that he was ashamed.

Terms must usually be human to be marked with *-re*, as shown by comparing the objects *sa-* (third-person neuter) in (202), with *ki-* (masculine singular) in (203). It is unlikely that *-re* is marking definiteness since the tree in (202) is definite.

(202) *sa-yi-īā-yu*
　　　 3ns-1s-see-PRES
　　　 I see it (e.g., a tree).

(203) *ki-re   yi-īā-yu*
　　　 3ms-TERM 1s-see-PRES
　　　 I see him.

In a text in which the characteristics of game animals are described, an animal is referred to with the person prefix *ki-* (masculine singular) instead of *sa-* (third-person neuter). In that context, *ki-* is marked with *-re* when it is an object or recipient. When it is a subject it is prefixed to the verb without case marking. In (204) *ki-* (masculine singular) refers to a fox-like animal and is marked with *-re* (term) because it is the object. Thus, under certain circumstances, a nonhuman object or recipient can be marked as a term at the choice of the speaker because it is the topic of the discourse.

(204) *ki-re   puri   dã-baʔa-wai*
      3ms-TERM as^for   3p-eat-HAB
      As for him, they (people) eat him (animal).

Occasionally a nonhuman subject or object will have case term marking. This occurs particularly in myths in which nonhuman characters display human characteristics such as speech and logical thought. It can also be used as a special focus or topic marker as in (205).

(205) *ōterikia-re   ki-jai-eʔka*
      fruit^tree-TERM   3ms-talk-PST
      He talked to the fruit tree.

4.2. General locative. Location is marked in different ways depending on the specific role of the noun phrase and the type of action or event indicated by the verb. The locative marker *-rã* indicates general location, goal, and location in time. Example (206) illustrates *-rã* as marking general location. When there is motion to a location, the location or goal is also marked by *-rã* as in (207). The *-rã* of location in time is illustrated in (208).

(206) *pusi-pebã-rã   dã-ībã-reʔka*
      hill-top-LOC   3p-live-PST
      They lived on the hilltop.

(207) *riaka-rã   yi-aʔ-yu*
      river-LOC   1s-go-PRES
      I'm going to the river.

(208) *la cuatro   rōʔō-hi-rã   ki-eta-rape*
      four^o'clock   place-EXTENT-LOC   3ms-arrive-PST
      He arrived at four o'clock.

Example (209) suggests a source for the connection between location and time; the time of day is traditionally indicated by points in the sun's movement.

(209) *dõʔõ-hi-rã*   *aiyaka eya-waʔ-yu*
where-EXTENT-LOC sun   reach-AWAY-PRES
What time is it? (Up to what point has the sun reached?)

4.3. Specific locative. A second locative case marker, *-reka*, is used in a more specific manner. It indicates that the object or action is contained in a certain location. The location has boundaries so that it usually has the meaning 'in' as in (210) (rather than 'at' as in (211).)

(210) *wiʔia-reka*   *ki-ībē*
house-LOC.SPEC 3ms-be
He is in the house.

(211) *riaka-rã ki-ībē*
river-LOC 3ms-be
He is at the river.

The case marker *-reka* is also used to indicate perspective or point of view as illustrated in (212) and (213).

(212) *dika*   *bīhā-reka aʔpe upaka ībā*
where/which 2p-LOC.SPEC other like be
Which are the differences for you (from your perspective)?

(213) *dã-ibā-upati-hi-reka*   *baʔirata-rã yiha-ībē*
3p-be-all-ADVLZR-LOC.SPEC bad-p   1p-be
From everyones' perspective, we are bad.

4.4. Ablative. The ablative *-ka* marks the origin of something. It frequently indicates a location as in (214), but can also indicate any origin such as the material from which something is made. The ablative is different from most of the other case markers in that it always takes a number or gender suffix that agrees with the noun phrase whose origins are being described. In (214) the ablative is neuter and agrees with 'lion'.

(214) *afrika-ka-ka iʔka leon ihi-rõʔõ-ka-ka*
Africa-ABL-n this lion hot-place-ABL-n
This lion is from Africa; (he is) from where it is hot.

In (215) *-kaka* indicates the material (wood) from which a club is made.

(215) *warupeka yapua-**ka-ka** ki-baa-i-ka   hi-i?taka   sa-ībē*
club   wood-ABL-n 3ms-make-STAT-n pretty-very 3ns-be
The wood he made the club from is very pretty.

The ablative can also indicate a group as an origin. In (216), the group 'first ones' is the origin of the subset 'one, some'.

(216) *bābārī-**ka-ka** yi-e?e-rape*
first-ABL-n   1s-get-PST
I got (one, some) of the first ones.

Examples (217)–(219) illustrate the masculine, feminine, and plural forms of the ablative case marker.

(217) *yābī-**ka-ki***
night-ABL-ms
moon (lit. man of the night)

(218) *apapuria-**ka-ko**   yi?i*
Apaporis-ABL-fs 1s
I (feminine) (am) from Apaporis.

(219) *yiha-wi?ia-rā bogota-**ka-rā**-re   eta-rape*
1p-house-LOC Bogotá-ABL-p-TERM arrive-PST
People from Bogotá arrived at our house.

4.5. Instrument. The case marker *-pi* indicates instrument and, less frequently, source and path. The instrument can be a concrete object such as a spear (220), or something intangible as in (221), where *wābēā* 'name' is the instrument.

(220) *bī-re   yi-hāā-a?si   yi-behoa-**pi***
2s-TERM 1s-kill-NEG.IMP 1s-spear-INSTR
(Be careful) lest I kill you with my spear.

(221) *ko-wābēā-**pi**   ko-re   ki-heyē-re?ka*
3fs-name-INSTR 3fs-TERM 3ms-greet-PST
He greeted her by her name.

-pi can indicate the source of some motion or predication as well as the source or beginning point of a nonmotion verb. The source of motion is

contrasted with *-rā* which marks the goal in (222). Example (223) illustrates the source of a nonmotion verb.

(222) *kaketa-pi   sa-iʔta-yu   bīriti-rā*
Caquetá-INSTR 3ns-come-PRES Mirití-LOC
From the Caquetá (river) it comes to the Mirití (river).

(223) *yoe-pi   ki-īā-eʔka*
far-INSTR 3ms-see-PST
He saw from afar.

Path, like source, is marked by *-pi*. Path differs semantically from source in that it refers to motion along a route, not the source and goal endpoints. In (224), *bāʔā* 'road, path' is not an endpoint, but rather the specification of the route.

(224) *ki-tu-ri-royi-reʔka   bāʔā-pi   īpa-rā põʔībāhā-ka*
3ms-travel-EP-IMPF-PST road-INSTR two-p people-COM
He was traveling along the road with two people.

The case marker *-pi* can also indicate that two things are mixed or intermingled. In (225) *-pi* marks *yukira* 'salt' as intermingled with *waʔia* 'fish'.

(225) *waʔia bī-baʔa-be yukira-pi*
fish 2s-eat-IMP salt-INSTR
Eat fish with salt.

4.6. Comitative. The case marker *-ka* which I have called comitative, indicates both coparticipant and conjunction. When *-ka* conjoins two subject noun phrases, one noun takes *-ka*, the other takes *-re* (term). The formula for conjoined subject noun phrases is:

(226) [NP-**ka** + NP]-**re**

In (227) the noun phrases 'Anita' and 'Gloria' are both subject. They are conjoined with *-ka,* and *-re* (term) applies to the conjoined term.

(227) *[anita-ka   gloria]-re   wiʔi-ērā baa-yu*
Anita-COM Gloria-TERM wet-PURP do-PRES
Anita and Gloria are going to get wet.

Case

A coparticipant refers to someone who participates in the action along with the subject of the clause and may also be indicated by -*ka*. In such a case, the coparticipant is an oblique constituent rather than a second subject. When the subject is a full noun phrase, as *júã* in (228), it is marked with -*re*/-*te* (term). If the subject is pronominal, as *ki*- in (229), it is indicated by a subject prefix on the verb.

(228) *júã-re   tu-ri-koʔo   paki-ka*
Juan-TERM travel-EP-PST father-COM
Juan traveled with his father.

(229) *yẽko-ka   waʔia ki-eʔe-yu*
grandmother-COM fish 3ms-get-PRES
He catches fish with his grandmother.

Examples (230) and (231) contrast the use of -*ka* as coparticipant and as conjunction. In (230) 'father' is a coparticipant and -*yi* (first-person singular) is the subject. In (231) the subject is the conjoined noun phrase 'father and I'.

(230) *peta-rã   yi-tu-ri-koʔo   aʔbi-ka*
downriver-LOC 1s-travel-EP-PST father-COM
I traveled downriver with my father.

(231) *[yi-ka aʔbi]-re   tu-ri-koʔo   peta-rã*
1s-COM father-TERM travel-EP-PST downriver
Father and I traveled downriver.

4.7. Benefactive. The case marker -*roʔsi* marks benefactive, purpose, change of state, and the idea of 'also'. Noun phrases which receive the benefit of the action of the verb are marked with -*roʔsi*, e.g., *bã-roʔsi* 'for us' in (232). Occassionally -*roʔsi* can have a malefactive sense as in (233). However, it is not frequently used since it occurs with few verbs that are punitive. Other verbs of this class such as 'hit', 'kill', 'betray', etc. mark the recipient of the action with -*re* (term).

(232) *baʔa-ri-ka bã-roʔsi yi-bõʔã-aʔ-ri-korĩ*
eat-DVBL-n 12-BEN 1s-search-go-EP-INT
I'm going to look for food for us.

(233) ko-*ro?si* ki-kareba?a-ko?o
     3fs-BEN 3ms-steal-PST
     He stole (it) from her.

A noun phrase that is the goal of a purpose or intention is also marked with *-ro?si*. This notion is illustrated in (234).

(234) *a?pe-rībī a?pea-ro?si e?e-rī ki-a?-yu*
     other-day other-BEN get-PURP 3ms-go-PRES
     Another day he goes to get some more.

The case marker *-ro?si* may also indicate the changed state of something (or final state of a change). In (235) it is used when wood changes to stone.

(235) *yapua āta-ro?si sa-wehabi-yu*
     wood stone-BEN 3ns-change-PRES
     The wood changes to stone.

Occasionally *-ro?si* has the meaning of 'also' as illustrated in (236).

(236) *rioa-rā ko-a?-pakā?ā ō-rī-tirā ki-ro?si*
     field-LOC 3fs-go-REAS.DS know-EP-after 3ms-BEN

    rioa-rā ki-a?-ri-ko?o
    field-LOC 3ms-go-EP-PST
    When he found out that she went to the field, he also went to the field.

4.8. Possessive. The case marker *-rika* (possessive) comes from the verb *rika* 'to have' and marks a normally human noun phrase as a possessor or owner. In (237), *-rika* is suffixed to a proper name and in (238), it is suffixed to the person prefixes *yi-* (first-person singular) and *bī-* (second-person singular).

(237) *hūā-rika i?ka yaiwēkoa*
     Juan-POSS this dog
     This dog is Juan's.

(238) *bī-rika pu-ri-rā-ka   potohī yi-rika bā-ba?a-rāyū*
     2s-POSS run^out-EP-FUT-n when 1s-POSS 12-eat-FUT
     When yours runs out, we will eat mine.

The possessive case marker agrees in gender and number with the possessed object. Usually the object is inanimate so the form -*rika* is most common. Animate possessions (such as one's daughter) in (239) require number and gender agreement on the case marker.

(239) *marco-ri-ko   ko-ībẽ*
Marco-POSS-fs 3fs-be
She is Marco's.

4.9. Case combinations. Although it is not common, case markers can also be suffixed to each other as illustrated in (240)–(242).

(240) *riho-ka-ka-pi   sa-ki-papa-ko?o*
mouth-ABL-n-INSTR 3ns-3ms-glue-PST
He glued it with spit.

(241) *bogota-ka-ki-ka   ki-tu-ri-ko?o*
Bogotá-ABL-ms-COM 3ms-travel-EP-PST
He traveled with the one from Bogotá.

(242) *benito-rika-pi   yaiwēkoa dā-hi?a-rape*
Benito-POSS-INSTR dog   3p-feed-PST
They fed the dog with Benito's (food).

5
Verb Phrase

The topics covered in the discussion of the verb phrase in Retuarã include affix order, agreement, auxiliary verbs, tense, aspect, mood, other verbal affixes, verb compounding, causatives, reciprocals, and incorporation.

5.1. Order of verb affixes. The general order of the affixes of the verb phrase is illustrated in (243)–(245). The majority of the affixes are discussed in this section. Other discussions include: verb prefixes (§§2.10–2.12), sentential negation (§10.1), and imperatives (chapter 8).

(243) Order of verb prefixes

Object		Subject	
sa-	'it'	yi-	'I'
		bī-	'you'
		ki-	'he'
		ko-	'she'
		sa-	'it'
		yiha-	'we'
		bā-	'we'
		bīhā-	'you pl.'
		dā-	'they'

(244) Order within the verb stem

Incorporated element	Verb root	Compound verb root Directionals
object instrument		-ta 'VERT' -wa? 'AWAY' -ra?a 'TWRD'

(245) Order of verb suffixes

Reciprocal Cause Stativizer	Negative Evidential	Intensifier	Mood Aspect	Tense Imperative	Number/ gender Evidential
-bua 'RECPR' -ta 'CAUS' -rõhe 'CAUS' -a 'CAUS'	-be 'NEG' -rihi 'ASSM' -ko 'AUD'	-tiya 'INTS' -tapa 'INTS' -pata 'INTS'	-hī 'PSBL' -hā 'CONSQ' -kope 'CONTRA' -korī 'INT.IMM' -royi 'IMPF' -yūhū 'CONT' -riha 'CONT' -ti 'PERF' -ta 'PUNC'	-yu 'PRES' -ko?o 'PST' -rape 'PST' -re?ka 'PST' -e?ka 'PST' -rāyū 'FUT'	-a 'n' -ka 'n' -ki 'ms' -ko 'fs' -rã 'p' -re 'RPT'
-i 'STAT'	―[31]	―			
	―		-rūki 'IMPRS' -wai 'HAB'		
	―			-be 'IMP' -pe 'IND.IMP' -a?si 'NEG.IMP' -rū 'OPT' -ērā 'PURP' -ye?e 'CNTGN' -a?ri 'GO'	

In an independent indicative clause, the subject, the verb root, and either tense, aspect, or marking as a spatial relator (see §2.3) are obligatory.

---

[31]Dashes indicate no affix could be added from that column.

Verb Phrase

5.2. Agreement. Subject agreement is marked on the verb by the number/gender suffixes (see (112)) only when there is no expressed subject (noun phrase or pronoun), or when there is a bare subject noun phrase or pronoun (i.e., not marked by -*re* (term); see §1.12). The choice of suffix is determined by the noun class of the subject (see §3.1). Example (246) illustrates a sentence with a bare subject noun phrase (chief) not marked by -*re* (term); note that the verb takes the number/gender suffix -*ki* (masculine singular). In example (247), the number/gender suffix -*ko* (feminine singular) agrees with the free subject pronoun *yiʔi*. Negated clauses typically take number/gender suffixes that agree with a postverbal subject.

(246) *dã-ipabáki dã-re hãʔbẽ-eʔka-ki*
     3p-chief   3p-TERM order-PST-ms
     Their chief (was the one who) ordered them.

(247) *bãẽ ko-yiʔ-yu   õ-rĩ-be-yu-ko   yiʔi*
     now 3fs-answer-PRES know-EP-NEG-PRES-fs 1s
     Now she answers, "I don't know." (or: Now she answers, "I'm a not-knower.")

Example (248) further illustrates agreement with a free subject pronoun in a positive clause.

(248) *yiʔi ã-yū-ka   bĩ-ĩbã-be*
     I   say-PRES-ms 2s-live-IMP
     I say, "Live (with him)!"

There exists some variation in the use of the number/gender suffixes. Usually singular, masculine speech-act participants (first- and second-person) take the suffix -*ka* as in (249), but occasionally -*ki* is used instead, as in (250).

(249) *ãʔã yiʔi-aka ãʔbĩti-ri-koʔo-ka*
     yes 1s-also   hear-EP-PST-ms
     Yes, I also heard (it).

(250) *reya-be-sa-rã-ki   yiʔi*
     die-NEG-EP-FUT-ms 1s
     I won't die.

Occassionally the suffix -*ka* can also occur on verbs to mark third-person singular as in (251).

(251) iʔki baʔa-koʔo-ka
      3ms eat-PST-ms
      He ate.

It may be that the variation in the agreement suffix system is due to incomplete change from an earlier stage more typical of the majority of Tucanoan languages (where the person marker suffixes only distinguish third- and non-third-person). In Barasana, for example, the suffix system marks speech-act participants (first- and second-person) with only one suffix, regardless of gender. This pattern is typical of many Tucanoan languages. That the language should be changing away from a typical Tucanoan pattern is not surprising since there is substantial influence from a neighboring Arawakan language.[32]

For further illustrations see Appendix Text 4 which summarizes the various ways agreement is marked (or not marked) in chart form.

5.3. Auxiliary verb. The verb *baa* 'do, make' is used as an auxiliary verb to form a construction that indicates imminence or intent. The formula for the construction is: [subject]-VERB-*ērā baa*-[tense]. The content verb is subordinated with the suffix -*ērā* (purpose) and inflected with a subject prefix, and the auxiliary is marked for tense as illustrated in (252) and (253).

(252) bāharoka yi-oʔo-ērā   baa-yu bāē
      story   1s-write-PURP do-PRES now
      I am going to write a story now.

(253) ki-re   sa-yīʔā-ērā   baa-reʔka potohī
      3ms-TERM 3ns-capture-PURP do-PST   when
      When it was going to capture him...

5.4–5.9 Tense

Tense markers are suffixed to the verb and, except in cases where number/gender suffixes occur, are the final elements in verb constructions. There are present, past, and future tenses.

5.4. Present. Retuarã marks present tense with the suffix -*yu*. Constructions marked with -*yu* are active, as opposed to descriptive, and occur on

---

[32]See Strom (to appear) for further information on language change in Retuarã and the Tucanoan family.

Verb Phrase

the event line in the discourse.[33] Following certain nasalized affixes or verb stems, the suffix becomes nasalized also and has the phonetic form [-ñũ] as shown in (255).

(254) baẽ uʔya-rī   yi-aʔ-yu
      now bathe-PURP 1s-go-PRES
      Now I go to bathe.

(255) ko-kā-yũ   [kokāñũ]
      3fs-sleep-PRES [phonetic realization]
      She sleeps.

5.5. Immediate past. Immediate past -koʔo is used for any past event within one day of the time of the speech act. When -koʔo occurs on a nominalized clause, as in (257), it takes -a (neuter) marking and is realized phonetically as [koʔa]. For further discussion see §12.8.

(256) hia   yi-kā-rī-koʔo
      good 1s-sleep-EP-PST
      I slept well.

(257) bī-ā-rī-koʔo-a   āʔbīti-ri-tirā   yi-iʔta-koʔo
      you-say-EP-PST-n   hear-EP-after   1s-come-PST
      After hearing what you said, I came.

5.6. Recent past. The recent past tense suffix is -rape. It extends from yesterday to any previous event considered recent (or nonremote) by the speaker. The limit depends on the speaker's subjective opinion of remoteness. Example (258) refers explicitly to one day prior to the time of speaking by the use of 'yesterday'. Example (259), however, refers to a hunting trip which took place one month before the story was told.

(258) dōʔōka   waʔia yiha-baʔa-rape
      yesterday   fish   1p-eat-PST
      Yesterday we ate fish.

(259) arturo-te   hēkaperaka hāā-rape īpa-rā
      Arturo-TERM   wild^pig   kill-PST two-p
      Arthur killed wild pigs, two (of them).

---

[33]Other present tense constructions that are descriptive/stative or subordinated are marked with the stativizer -i which is discussed in §5.21.

When the recent past occurs with a number/gender suffix, it always has the variant form *-rapa*. When there is no other subject indicated (i.e., subject pronominal prefix or full noun phrase with term case marking), the number/gender suffixes agree in number and gender with the subject. With an explicit subject, the number/gender suffix *-ka* can occur with *-rapa* to nominalize or subordinate the verb phrase. Other tenses use verb final *-a* for nominalization. Example (260) illustrates a nominalized verb phrase with *-rapa-ka* in a subordinated clause.

(260) *ki-eya-**rapa-ka** potohī ki-re dā-yīʔā-rape*
   3ms-arrive-PST-n when 3ms-TERM 3p-capture-PST
   When he arrived they captured him.

Example (261) illustrates agreement (by the suffix *-ko*) with a female subject. The choice of this construction over one in which the subject is marked as a term (and thus without a number/gender suffix) is likely influenced by discourse considerations.

(261) *paulina yi-re   hēyē-**rapa-ko***
   Paulina 1s-TERM greet-PST-fs
   Paulina greeted me.

5.7. Remote past. The remote past suffix *-reʔka* is used for events considered to have occured a long time ago.[34] In my data, this occasionally includes events that occured as recently as three months ago, but most often it is used for recounting legends or myths. Example (262) is from a trip that was taken about six months before it was related and (263) is from a myth.

(262) *bāē yiha-bīā-**reʔka**   apapuri*
   now 1p-go^upriver-PST Apaporis
   Now we went up the Apaporis (river).

(263) *aʔte ki-poʔirā   sa-wi-ri-**reʔka***
   again 3ms-toward 3ns-appear-EP-PST
   Again it appeared to him.

5.8. General past. The past tense suffix *-eʔka* (past) expresses a general past without specifying distance of time from the point of speaking. It seems to parallel the present constructions that are suffixed with *-i-ka* (stative-neuter). Like them, it contrasts with the other past tense suffixes

---
[34]Some younger speakers use the form *-rika*.

Verb Phrase

in that it is often used for background information, embedded clauses, and past participles. For further discussion see §5.21.

5.9. Future. Future tense is indicated by the suffix *-rāyū*.[35] Unlike the past tenses, there are no distinctions that depend on the proximity of the projected event to the moment of speaking. The following examples illustrate the lack of disctinction between a future the same day and two months hence.

(264) *wāhītēhī aiya yi-eta-rāyū*
straight sun 1s-arrive-FUT
I will arrive at mid day.

(265) *īpa-rā aiya beʔerōʔō yi-eta-rāyū*
two-p moon after 1s-arrive-FUT
I will arrive after two months.

Like the other tenses, the future tense has a nominalized form that is used for future descriptions or conditions. The variant form is composed of *-rā* (future) plus a number/gender suffix.[36] It is most often used in subordinate clauses as illustrated in (266) though occasionally, *-rā-ka* is found in an independent clause as in (267).

(266) *bī-rika pu-ri-rā-ka   potohī yi-rika bā-baʔa-rāyū*
2s-POSS run^out-EP-FUT-n when 1s-POSS 12-eat-FUT
When yours runs out, we will eat mine.

(267) *waʔua bā-baʔa-rā-ka rupu*
monkey 12-eat-FUT-n yet
We could still/yet eat monkey.

When the subject is a free pronoun or human noun phrase not marked by the term case marker (*-te/-re*), the future tense will be indicated with the nominalized form to show agreement with the subject. Again, the choice of this type of construction may be motivated by the discourse. In (268), the suffix *-ki* (masculine singular) agrees with the pronoun *yiʔi* (first-person singular) and the suffix *-ko* (feminine singular) agrees with 'Paulina' in (269).

---

[35] In some geographical areas the future tense suffix has the form *-rūyū*.

[36] It may be that *-rāyū* (future) should be analyzed as *-rā* + *-yu* where *-yu* expresses events or actions like the present tense marker and *-rā* is simply future. Then *-rā* + *-ka/-ki/-ko* would express a future state or description rather than an action.

(268) *yiʔi   sa-kaʔsia   baʔa-rā-ki*
     1s   3ns-liver   eat-FUT-ms
     I will be the eater of its liver.

(269) *paulina   yoʔa-rā-ko*
     Paulina   cook-FUT-fs
     Paulina will be the cook.

One might expect a future plural form such as *-rā-rā* in addition to the *-rā-ki* (masculine singular) and *-rā-ko* (feminine singular) forms, but this form does not exist. Rather the (active) future tense form *-rāyū* takes the *-rā* (plural) number/gender suffix resulting in the form: *-rāyū-rā*. A negation of a future tense construction always contains the affix *-sa* following the negative affix *-be*. It has the same function as *-ri* (epenthetic syllable) in the other tenses of simply filling a syllable slot without having any meaning. For further discussion see §1.17.

(270) *waeroka   ki-aʔ-ri-be-sa-rāyū*
     tomorrow   3ms-go-EP-NEG-EP-FUT
     He will not go tomorrow.

The (future) tense markers might be seen as including the suffix *-ērā* which occasionally seems to indicate immediate future. *-ērā* is more correctly regarded as expressing intention or purpose (with a subordinating function as well) and is therefore not directly contrasted with tense. Example (271) illustrates the properties of *-ērā* (purpose). Notice that the example is in the past tense which would indicate that *-ērā* is outside of the tense system.

(271) *ki-re   dā-hāā-ērā   baa-reʔka*
     3ms-TERM   3p-kill-PURP   do-PST
     They were intending to kill him.

5.10–5.15 Aspect

Aspectual concepts can be expressed using aspect suffixes, adverbs, or compound verbs. Examples of aspect, as phasal 'begin' or 'end', expressed by verb compounding can be found in §2.8 and aspect expressed by adverbs is discussed in §6.5. The aspectual affixes discussed below occur between the verb root and the tense marker.

Verb Phrase

5.10. Habitual. The habitual aspect suffix *-wai* does not indicate an event as occurring at a specific time but rather as characteristic of all time. For example, the questions of how a certain word is expressed or how to make a basket are characteristic of any time and are marked with *-wai* (habitual). This suffix does not occur with a tense marker, perhaps because time is irrelevant to a habitual event. The habitual suffix occurs with the suffix *-ya* when the verb root is either a single syllable with a short vowel, or three syllables. Like the epenthetic syllables *-ri* and *-sa*, the suffix *-ya* fills the second or fourth syllable slot and is semantically empty. The form *-yāwai* arises from progressive nasalization.

(272) *bārākā?ā dā-ā-yā-wai (x)*
    how   3p-say-EP-HAB (x)
    How do they say ... x?

(273) *bārākā?ā pi?ia dā-baa-wai*
    how   basket 3p-do-HAB
    How do they make baskets?

5.11. Imperfective. The affix *-royi* (imperfective) describes an action in process, often of some duration. In (274), imperfective aspect is used to express a time period of sickness. The time period is not specified except by the context. The period can thus be quite long which makes 'always' an appropriate or possible translation in (275).

(274) *yi-hī-rī-royi-re?ka*
    1s-sick-EP-IMPF-PST
    I was sick (for a fairly long time).

(275) *rīkibā-i?taka bāē bī-e?e-royi*
    much-INTS now 2s-get-IMPF
    You always catch lots (of fish). *or* You are/have been catching lots (of fish) now.

The tense is optionally omitted when *-royi* has the sense of 'always', as in (275). The example differs from a habitual in that *-royi* (imperfective) describes actual, specific events rather than a general procedure. Often a long time-span is not intended when *-royi* is used as illustrated in (276).

(276) *ko-o-ri-royi-re?ka dīyērū dā-kare?e-yu ārīwa?ri*
    3fs-cry-EP-IMPF-PST money 3p-steal-PRES because
    She was crying because they stole the money.

An iterative sense may be implied with punctual verbs like 'hit' or 'laugh'.

(277) ki-re   dā-pahe-royi-reʔka
      3ms-TERM 3p-hit-IMPF-PST
      They were hitting him.

The imperfective suffix is also used at a higher level in the discourse to background a sentence. This is discussed and illustrated in §12.7.

5.12. Continuative. Continuative aspect is indicated by the suffixes -yūhū and -riha. For animate subjects -yūhū expresses a sense of persistence in some action as in (278). When the subject is not volitional as in (279), the sense is simply the continuation of some state or condition.

(278) hī-yū-upaka   bī-īāʔbā-yūhū-yu
      sick-PRES-like   2s-groan-CONT-PRES
      You keep on groaning like you are sick.

(279) arusu ībā-yūhū-a
      rice   be-CONT-n
      There's still some rice (to eat).

For actions that are continuous or characteristic over a long period of time, the suffix -riha (continuative) is used.

(280) rīkibāka dīyērū   bīhā-hie-riha-yu
      much   money   2p-save-CONT-PRES
      You continue to save lots of money.

(281) hia-ha   sa-bā-baa-riha-ri-rāyū
      good-ADVLZR   3ns-12-do-CONT-EP-FUT
      Slowly one continues to do it. *or* Little by little one/we will do it.

5.13. Perfect. The affix -ti (perfect) indicates a completed action with present consequence or significance. It often has the meaning 'now' or 'already'.

(282) īʔrā-kuri-bā-ñ-a   bī-re   yi-boha-ti-yu
      one-time-notˆbe-DVBL-n   2s-TERM   1s-tell-PERF-PRES
      I have already told you more than once (not one time).

Verb Phrase

The affix -*ti* frequently occurs with the adverb *kopakaha*, which also means 'now' or 'already' as in example (283). Notice that the completed action is that of 'falling asleep', not that the subject has finished sleeping.

(283) *aʔpe-ika kopakaha kā-rī-ti-i-ki*
 other-ms now sleep-EP-PERF-STAT-ms
 Now another one is already asleep.

The perfect can have the sense of 'finish' depending on the type of action the verb expresses and particularly when used in a dependent clause such as 'when x, (then) y'.

(284) *ki-koa-ti-bāka   ko-uʔya-hī-yū*
 3ms-cure-PERF-COND 3fs-bathe-PSBL-PRES
 When he (shaman) has cured/finished curing, she may bathe.

In (284), the perfect is used even though the event is future. -*ti* (perfect) is used in the subordinate clause, not to indicate (past), but to indicate completed action. A further illustration of this completed action or 'finish' is (285). The example is past tense and occurs with *kopakaha* 'now'.

(285) *kopakaha dā-tāʔāpihāā-ti-koʔo*
 now   3p-chew^coca-PERF-PST
 Now they have finished chewing coca.

The basic meaning of (285) is the same without *kopakaha* 'now'. It apparently lends emphasis to the perfect aspect.

5.14. Impersonal. The aspect suffix *rūki* (impersonal) indicates an impersonal subject as illustrated in (286). Like the habitual aspect, a specific instance is not in focus but rather a description of a general procedure.

(286) *kopea tāte-rūki sa-po-ri-koreka*
 hole seal-IMPRS 3ns-leave-EP-NEG.PUR
 One seals the hole so that it does not get out.

Often -*rūki* (impersonal) is nominalized with -*a* to indicate function or purpose. Example (287) is the answer to the question: "What is this (rope) for?" It often has the meaning 'thing' (and its function). Example (288) illustrates -*rūki-a* with the meaning 'thing'.

(287) *wapahī-rūki-a*
    buy-IMPRS-n
    It is what one buys. *or* (It is) for sale.

(288) *taʔapi-tūā-rūki-a*
    coca-pound-IMPRS-n
    coca pounding thing/stick (what one pounds coca with)

Occasionally the impersonal aspect -*rūki* and the habitual -*yawai* seem to overlap in their usage. For example, (289) and (290) are judged by speakers to have about the same meaning.

(289) *bārākāʔā baʔa-rūki bāeruka*
    how   eat-IMPRS pineapple
    How does one eat pineapple?

(290) *bārākāʔā bāeruka dā-baʔa-wai*
    how   pineapple 3p-eat-HAB
    How do they eat pineapple?

5.15. Punctual. The affix -*ta* (punctual) describes an action of brief duration. This is illustrated in the following examples in which (291) and (292) contrast in punctuality.

(291) *bī-pīpi-be*
    you-close^eyes-IMP
    Close your eyes!

(292) *bī-pīpi-ta-be*
    you-close^eyes-PNCT-IMP
    Blink your eyes!

The aspectual affix -*ta* (punctual) and the directional affix -*ta* (vertical) are homophonous. Since they also occur immediately following the verb root they must be distinguished by the intended meaning of the verb phrase.

5.16–5.20 Mood

There are four modal suffixes which indicate non-actual (irrealis) events. The categories are: intention, possibility, consequence, and contra-expectation.

Verb Phrase

5.16. Intention. The suffix -*korī* indicates intent. The following examples illustrate its usage in independent clauses. It is also possible to use -*korī* in an imperative construction (see §8.1) and as a subordinator (see §11.11).

(293) *waʔiroʔsia bā-roʔsi yi-bōʔā-aʔ-ri-korī*
game   12-BEN   1s-search-go-EP-INT
I am going to search for game for us.

(294) *bī-re   yi-bea-korī*
2s-TERM 1s-show-INT
I'm going to show you.

5.17. Possibility. The modal suffix -*hī* indicates obligation ('ought, should'), possibility ('might, could'), and permission ('may'). The modal -*hī* (possibility) always indicates irrealis; the proposition is not asserted to be actual, only possible.

(295) *bāe dā-baʔa-hī-yū*
now   3p-eat-PSBL-PRES
Now they may eat.

(296) *bārākāʔā bā-baa-be-ri-hī-i-ka   ki-re   sa-ībā-reʔka*
how   12-do-NEG-EP-PSBL-STAT-n 3ms-TERM 3ns-be-PST
There wasn't anything he could do. ((Like when) one isn't able to do anything it was for him.)

The modal -*hī* has the sense of permission or possibility in (297). The proposition does not have a realis sense, only potential. Note that the question also includes the adverb *heʔe* (supposition).

(297) *yahe bī-baa-hī-yū   heʔe*
Y/N   2s-do-PSBL-PRES SUP
Could you do (it) perhaps?

Example (298) is a further illustration of supposition marked by -*hī* (possibility). In the dependent clause, the first supposition (a taboo of the culture) is 'if children were to see' and the probable result (also supposition) is the 'it (a canoe) could split'.

(298) *bērāka īā-hī-i-ka   sa-si-rī-hī-yū*
children see-PSBL-STAT-n   3ns-split-EP-PSBL-PRES
(If) children were to see, it could split.

This example appears to be very similar to a conditional formed with -rā-ka (future (condition)). -hī (possibility) differs from -rā-ka (future (condition)) in the tense of the main (consequent) clause. The consequent of a -hī clause always has nonfuture tense, as in (298). It expresses a general possibility or situation that is in the domain of irrealis. The consequent following a -rā-ka clause always has future tense and expresses a specific situation which is likely to occur.

The conjunction *reka* 'if' also occurs with -hī. Note the common construction in (299) in which both clauses contain -hī.

(299) *dīyērū yi-re   ībā-hī-i-ka   reka motoro yi-wapahī-hī-yū*
    money 1s-TERM be-PSBL-STAT-n if   motor 1s-buy-PSBL-PRES
    If I had money, I could buy a motor.

5.18. Consequence. The suffix -hā indicates the consequence of a hypothetical situation. It expresses the notion of 'would'.

(300) *bārākāʔā dā-baa-hā-eʔka*
    what/how 3p-do-CONSQ-PST
    What would they have done?

When the consequence suffix -hā occurs on the independent verb of a compound construction, it expresses the nonactual consequence. The dependent verb of the antecedent to the consequence often occurs in infinitival form (i.e., it ends with -ri-ka) and expresses a nonactual condition or circumstance.

(301) *juanita-re   reya-ri-ka reka aʔpe-ko-te*
    Juanita-TERM die-DVBL-n if   other-fs-TERM

   yi-pitayīā-be-ri-hā-eʔka
   1s-marry-NEG-EP-CONSQ-PST
   If Juanita had died, I would not marry another woman.

(302) *karebārīa kēsia   yi-hī-rī-ērā   baa-hī-i-ka   bīhā-re*
    even   hunger 1s-die-EP-PURP do-PSBL-STAT-n 2p-TERM

   yi-heyē-be-ri-hā-eʔka
   1s-ask-NEG-EP-CONSQ-PST
   Even if I were about to die of hunger, I would not ask of you.

5.19. Contra-expectation. The modal -*kope* (contra-expectation) indicates a situation where the expected result of some proposition is

Verb Phrase

frustrated and does not occur.[37] In (303) the expected result of going to buy hooks is to obtain them. Because that expectation is not met, *-kope* marks the reversal in expectation.

(303) *pota   wapahī-rī   yi-tu-ri-kope-rape*
   hooks buy-PURP 1s-travel-EP-CONTRA-PST
   I went to buy hooks (but there were none).

This frustrated expectation is further illustrated in the following examples where the proposition of the first part of the sentence is not concluded as expected.

(304) *a?-ri-ri-ka   yi-pupahoa-kope-yu*
   go-EP-DVBL-n 1s-plan-CONTRA-PRES
   I plan to go (but ...)

(305) *okoa ha-ri-hī-yu̅   ībā-kope-yu*
   rain become-EP-PSBL-PRES be-CONTRA-PRES
   It needs to rain. *or* It would be good if it rained.

Contra-expectation is also indicated by the subordinating suffix *-kobā?kaha* (contra-expectation) as illustrated in (306). See §11.17 for more examples.

(306) *bī-yapa-be-ri-kobā?kaha bī-ībā-rāyū*
   2s-like-NEG-EP-CONTRA   2s-live-FUT
   Even though you don't like (him), you will live (with him)!

With the subordinator *-kobā?kaha*, contra-expectation arises from the conjunction of two incompatible clauses. With *-kope*, it is a single proposition that is not concluded as expected.

5.20–24. Other verbal affixes

Besides affixes of tense, aspect, and mood, the verb phrase includes affixes labeled as: stativizer, directional, intensifier, negator, reciprocal, imperative, evidential, and causative. This section will discuss stativizer, directionals, intensifiers, and evidentials. (For discussion of negation see

---

[37]Other studies in the Tucanoan language family have labeled the equivalent form the 'frustrative'.

§10.1; causative see §5.26–5.28; imperative see §8; and reciprocals see §5.29).

5.20. Stativizer. The affix *-i* (stativizer) occurs immediately following the verb root. It always occurs with a classifier or a number/gender suffix with the effect of creating a nonfinite stative construction or a nominalization. Most commonly it takes the neuter number/gender suffix *-ka* as in (307). In such cases the construction is a description of a general setting, situation, or state.[38]

(307) *okoa   iʔta-i-ka*
     water/rain come-STAT-n
     Rain is coming.

As mentioned previously (see §5.2) the number/gender suffixes (*-ki/-ko/-a/-ka/-rã*) can occur with *-yu* (present) marking agreement with the subject. In a somewhat similar way, *-i* plus a number/gender suffix can show number and gender, but have no tense marking and are nonfinite in nature. The answer in (308) illustrates the use of *-i* (stativizer) with the masculine singular number/gender suffix *-ki*. (309) further illustrates the nominal environment in which *-i* typically occurs.

(308) *Q. yahe kape   bī-yapa-yu*
       Y/N coffee 2s-want-PRES
     Do you want coffee?

     A. yapa-i-ki
        want-STAT-MS
     (Yes), I'm one who wants (coffee).

(309) *beʔi-rã-ka oaka baʔa-i-rã*
     rat-p-n   corn eat-STAT-p
     Rats are corn eaters.

The *-i* (stativizer) with classifiers in (310) and (311) clearly illustrate that nominalization has occurred. In (310), the verb phrase 'wind blows' modifies the classifier *-rõʔõ* 'place' which is the head of the noun phrase.

---

[38]In some preliminary investigations, the suffix *-ika* has been glossed as present tense. Thus, this discussion contrasts its usage with the present tense marker *-yu* in support of the proposed classification of *-i* as a stativizer. A similar suffix *-i* (stativizer) also occurs in Cubeo (Central Tucanoan) with some differences in usage. See Maxwell and Morse (to appear) for further information.

Verb Phrase

(310) *wīrōa bae-i-rõʔõ-rā*
wind blow-STAT-place-LOC
place where the wind blows

(311) *ernesto-te baa-ūʔbū-i-wiʔi*
Ernesto-TERM build-begin-STAT-CLAS^house
the house Ernesto begins to build

5.21. The functions of *-i* (stativizer) and *-eʔka* (general past). The stativizer *-i* and general past *-eʔka* have similar functions and typically occur in three environments. They mark verbs off the event line, they mark verbs in dependent clauses, and they create past participles.

Background information. In the present tense the stativizer *-i* is used for background information while the present tense suffix *-yu* is usually used with verbs on the event line of a discourse. This is particularly clear in procedural discourses where each step of the process has the main verb marked with *-yu*. (See Appendix Text 1 'Canoe story' for an example of part of a procedural discourse contrasting *-yu* and *-i*).

In another text describing the order of events in preparing for a dance, *-i* is used with the verb *wea* 'finish' to mark endpoints of steps in the discourse. Specific action verbs are all marked with *-yu*. (See Appendix Text 2 'Dance story').

Background information in the past is marked with *-eʔka* as opposed to the other tense suffixes which occur on the event line. This is illustrated in (312) where a group of people are bringing someone to see a chief who has not been introduced previously in the story. The background information concerning the chief's identity is marked by *-eʔka*.

(312) ... *ki-re dā-eʔe-waʔ-ri-ērā bēhabī poʔirā wehea*
3ms-TERM 3p-get-AWAY-EP-PURP Benjamin toward land

ipabāki ki-ībā-eʔka
chief 3ms-be-PST
... in order that they take him to Benjamin. He was the chief of the land.

The suffix *-eʔka*, however, does occasionally occur on the event line, and the other past tense suffixes can occur in background information. It may be that it is used on the event line when the speaker does not know or chooses to indicate the remoteness in time of the event.

Embedded clauses. Dependent clauses in the present tense are marked with *-i*. In (313) and (314) *-i* occurs in the dependent clauses while the main clause is marked with present tense *-yu*.

(313) *yi-re   dā-itakare-i-ka   yi-kārūrū-yū*
　　　1s-TERM 3p-disembowel-STAT-n 1s-dream-PRES
　　　I dreamt of their disemboweling me.

(314) *ki-koa-wea-i-ka   ko-re   ki-īhī-yu   būbū-ka?ia*
　　　3ms-cure-finish-STAT-n 3fs-TERM 3ms-give-PRES bee-dirt
　　　(When) he finishes curing, he gives her bee dirt (food).

In the same manner, embedded clauses in the past are marked by *-e?ka* as illustrated by the embedded clause 'because I burned his face ... ' in (315).

(315) *ki-pebā yi-hoe-e?ka wapa   yi-re   ki-riata-kope-yu*
　　　3ms-face 1s-burn-PST payment 1s-TERM 3ms-kill-CONTRA-PRES
　　　(Because) I burned his face, he almost killed me. *or* For payment/revenge for burning his face, he tried to kill me.

Past participles. The affix *-i* can be used to form a past participle in a NP as illustrated in (316).

(316) *pāūā   ta-ri-i-ka*
　　　hammock rip-EP-STAT-n
　　　ripped hammock

The suffix *-e?ka* is also used to form participles. Often the role of a verb marked with *-e?ka* is more descriptive than other past tense marked verbs. If the embedded clause in (317) was predicative, it would have the meaning: 'they saw him kill the cayman'. Instead, the verb is more descriptive, modifying the noun phrase 'cayman' like a participle.

(317) *dā-īā-re?ka kahua   ki-hāā-e?ka*
　　　3p-see-PST cayman 3ms-kill-PST
　　　They saw the cayman he killed.

Participles can also be derived from nouns by using *-i* as illustrated in (318).

(318) *i?ka yābāka yōāka yīka-i-ka*
　　　this deer   long leg-STAT-n
　　　This deer is long legged.

Verb Phrase

The same derivation with the general past suffix *-e?ka* is also possible. In (319), the noun *iyebaka* 'fat, lard' drops the suffix *-ka* (neuter) for *-e?ka* to create a participle.

(319) *iyeba-e?ka   sa-ībā-ko?o*
 fat-PST   3ns-be-PST
 It was greased.

(320) Past participles

| *-i* | | *-e?ka* | |
accidental/natural nonagentive		deliberate implied agent	
yapu	*būturi-i-ka*	*saya*	*hūhē-e?ka*
log	rot-STAT-n	dress	wash-PST
'rotten log'		'washed dress'	
yaiwēkoa	*hī-rī-i-ka*	*yapua*	*ta?te-e?ka*
dog	die-EP-STAT-n	log	cut-PST
'dead dog'		'cut log'	
tūparăperia	*yora-i-ka*	*ba?arika*	*koa-e?ka*
candle	melt-STAT-n	food	cure-PST
'melted candle'		'cured food'	
kara-ria	*si-rī-i-ka*	*wārō-e?ka*	
hen-egg	break-EP-STAT-n	teach-PST	
'broken egg'		'teachings, lessons'	
aiya-herāka	*bitabā-rī-i-ka*	*aiya-herāka*	*hie-e?ka*
sun-measure	damage-EP-STAT-n	sun-measure	fix-PST
'damaged watch'		'fixed watch'	

Participles marked with *-e?ka* involve tense and imply an event. They differ from those marked by *-i* in that they seem to imply deliberate action by an implied agent. Thus, they often appear on transitive verbs. Participles marked with *-i* have no tense marking, with the result that they describe rather than express an event. Generally they express accidental or natural, nonagentive processes and generally appear on intransitive verbs.

More study is needed to substantiate this hypothesis,[39] but a consideration of (320) illustrates the possible distinction.

Although the past tense suffix -e?ka seems to roughly parallel constructions with -i regarding the environments in which they both occur, it is more action- or event-oriented and has a broader usage in that it can occur on the event line of a discourse. The contrast in the environments in which -e?ka occurs and the other past tenses is not as great as that between -yu (present) and -i (stativizer).

5.22. Directionals. There are three directional affixes that suffix directly to the verb root. They modify the verb by indicating a direction of the action. The suffixes are: -ra?a 'toward', -wa? 'away', and -ta 'vertical'. The following examples illustrate their usage and effect on the meaning of the verb e?e 'get'.

(321) *arturu-ka   īpa-rā   yapu-hā?ā   yiha-e?e-ta-rape*
Arturo-COM two-p tree-stump 1p-get-VERT-PST
With Arturo, the two (of us) pulled up stumps.

(322) *okoa   bī-e?e-ra?a-be*
water 2s-get-TWRD-IMP
Bring water!

(323) *wi?ia-rā   yiha-re   ki-e?e-wa?-rape*
house-LOC 1p-TERM 3ms-get-AWAY-PST
He took us (by some vehicle) to the house.

Usually the point of reference for -ra?a 'toward' is the speaker. The action is directed toward the one who speaks. The point of reference with -wa? 'away' can be any point of origin in the speaker's mind. The action thus moves away from that point. For example in (323), the point of reference was probably the location from which they started in their journey to the house. The vertical direction of -ta 'vertical' can be either up or down. The point of reference is the original position before the movement.

Most commonly directionals occur on action or motion verbs. They can, however, imply motion on nonmotion verbs. In (324), wa? 'away' occurs with the verb rā?ī 'to be late'.

---

[39]To date one exception to this hypothesis has been found in which 'striped fish' is marked with the 'agentive' participle affix -e?ka.

Verb Phrase

(324) *bāē ki-rāʔĩ-waʔ-ri-reʔka*
 now 3ms-late-AWAY-EP-PST
 Now he went late.

5.23. Intensifiers. There are two types of intensifiers which are suffixed to the verb root. The first type intensifies the verb by extending the range of the verb's effect, while the second type simply intensifies the strength of the action.

The verbal affix *-pata* 'all' extends the range of the of the verb to include everyone as a participant or subject in the action. It serves to give emphasis to the completion of the action as in (325) and (326). *-pata* can also be used to extend the effect of a transitive verb to all of the object as in (327).

(325) *dā-wea-pata-i-ka potohĩ*
 3p-finish-all-STAT-n when
 When they all finish...

(326) *bikitoho dā-peʔ-ri-pata-yu*
 early 3p-return-EP-all-PRES
 They all return (home) early.

(327) *baʔarika bī-baʔa-pata-be*
 food 2s-eat-all-IMP
 Eat all the food!

A second affix, *-tapa* 'everywhere', serves to intensify or extend the range of the verb by indicating that the action occurred everywhere, not just in one specific location. Example (328) illustrates its use in conjunction with the continuative aspect suffix *-yūhū*. In (329), *-tapa* intensifies the verb *tu* 'travel' by extending the range of the travel to everywhere.

(328) *sa-bī-hĩʔĩ-tapa-yūhū-i-ka*
 3ns-2s-carry-everywhere-CONT-STAT-n
 You continue to carry it everywhere.

(329) *iʔsupaka-ha yi-tu-ri-tapa-rape*
 like^that-ADVLZR 1s-travel-EP-everywhere-PST
 I traveled all over like that.

A third affix, *-tiya* (intensifier), serves to generally intensify the strength of an action. Its usage is illustrated in (330) where 'like, want' is intensified to 'really like, love'. It can also intensify a negative construction such as in (331).

(330) *anita-re   yi-yapa-tiya-yu*
Anita-TERM 1s-like-INTS-PRES
I really like/love Anita.

(331) *riaka tē-rī-tiya-be-yu-rā*
river cross-EP-INTS-NEG-PRES-p
They cross the river very little.

5.24. Evidentials. Unlike many Tucanoan languages, the evidential system in Retuarã is small and not frequently used. There are three evidential affixes in my corpus. Whereas in other Tucanoan languages, evidentials are a mandatory feature of the independent verb, in Retuarã the evidentials are optional.[40]

The affix *-ko* (auditory) follows the verb stem and indicates that the source of information for the statement is auditory. In (332), the speaker's evidence that 'there are people down river' is that he can hear them talking.

(332) *peta-rā   pōʔībāhā-re   ībā-ko-yu*
downriver people   be-AUD-PRES
There are people downriver.

(333) *dōʔōka   yābī   yapua   yāʔ-rī-ko-rape*
yesterday night tree   fall-EP-AUD-PST
Last night a tree fell. (i.e., I heard it from my house.)

A second evidential *-rihi* (assumed) indicates that the basis for the speaker's statement is assumption. Examples (334) and (335) illustrate its use.

(334) *kūpahī-ki ki-ībē weheherāka ki-eya-waʔ-ri-rihi-yu*
small-ms 3ms-be year   3ms-reach-AWAY-EP-ASSM-PRES
He's small; I think he may be one year old.

(335) *ire   ki-eta-rihi-yu*
today 3ms-arrive-ASSM-PRES
(I believe) he's arriving today.

In tenses other than present, the present tense suffix *-yu* is retained in the construction with the past or future tense suffixed to *-rihi* as in (336).

---

[40]In other Tucanoan languages, the tense, subject agreement (number gender), and evidential system are bound together in one portmanteau suffix. Thus every declarative sentence must indicate evidentiality.

(336) *waeroka dā-eta-rihi-yu-rāyū*
tomorrow 3p-arrive-ASSM-PRES-FUT
Tomorrow (I believe) they will arrive.

A third evidential is *-re* (reportative). Using this evidential, the speaker indicates that the source of the information is not first hand; he or she is just passing on what was reported to him or her. The reportative evidential is suffixed to the tense marker. The following exchange between speaker 1 and 2 was related by speaker 2 (in (338)) to a third person who in turn related it to a fourth person.

(337) *doʔorā bī-aʔ-yu ki-re dā-hērīā-rape-re*
where 2s-go-PRES 3ms-TERM 3p-ask-PST-RPT
"Where are you going," they asked him. (speaker 1)

(338) *limon eʔe-rī yi-aʔ-yu dā-re ki-ā-rape-re*
lemon get-PURP 1s-go-PRES 3p-TERM 3ms-say-PST-RPT
"I'm going to get lemons," he said to them. (speaker 2)

5.25. Compound verbs. Verb roots can be combined to create compound verbs. This often occurs with phasal verbs such as *ūʔbū* 'begin' and *wea* 'finish' to modify the aspect of the main verb. Examples of both these phasal verbs are illustrated in (339) and (340). In (341), a phasal sense is created by the compounding of the verbs 'return' and 'arrive'.

(339) *bāē sa-dā-hoe-ūʔbū-yu*
now 3ns-3p-burn-begin-PRES
Now they begin to burn it.

(340) *dā-uʔya-wea-i-ka dā-re ki-baʔa-rōhe-yu*
3p-bathe-finish-STAT-n 3p-TERM 3ms-eat-CAUS-PRES
When they finish bathing, he makes them eat.

(341) *yābī ki-peʔ-ri-eta-reʔka*
night 3ms-return-EP-arrive-PST
He returned (and) arrived at night.

Many other creative combinations are evident in the language. Some of these combinations have become lexicalized, while others appear to be novel creations to express a new idea. In (342) the compound of 'to dress' and 'to try' means to try on clothing to see if it fits. In (343), the verb 'to recognize' is formed from the compounding of *ĩã* 'to see' and *wãrũ* 'to learn'. The resulting compound has probably been lexicalized as a single verb now.

(342) *sa-dã-habã-kori-yu*
      3ns-3p-dress-try-PRES
      They try it on.

(343) *ki-heyẽ-bãka   ki-re   ko-ĩã-wãrũ-reʔka*
      3ms-greet-COND 3ms-TERM   3fs-see-learn-PST
      When he greeted (her), she recognized him.

Some further illustrations of verb compounding may serve to demonstrate the variety of possibilities that exist in the language.

(344) *parua   yi-baʔa-ri-yapa-yu*
      banana   1s-eat-DVBL-want-PRES
      I want to eat a banana.

(345) *iʔsia   ãʔbĩti-ri-tirã   ko-re   ki-ĩã-ri-peyo-rape*
      that   hear-EP-after   3fs-TERM 3ms-see-DVBL-reject-PST
      After hearing that, he was hostile toward her.

It is also possible to have a compound verb construction made up of three verbs as in (346), but this is not common.

(346) *uʔya-bã-rĩ-eta-tirã   dã-kaRi-baʔa-wai*
      bathe-walk^up-EP-arrive-after   3p-tucupi-eat-HAB
      After going up and arriving from bathing, they eat tucupi.

5.26–5.28 Causatives

The morphological causative is formed by adding a causative suffix immediately after the verb root.[41] The causee is the object or recipient of the verb. There are two causative suffixes: *-rõhe* and *-ta*. In addition there are evidences of a variety of past processes of causative formation that are no longer productive. One of these processes is still productive in some of the Tucanoan languages while two others may have come from Arawakan languages. They will be discussed below.

---

[41]For the discussion of the analytical causative see §11.4.

Verb Phrase

5.26. Volitional causation. The volitional causative morpheme, *-rōhe*,[42] is used when the causee is compliant. The force of the causation is often verbal, (e.g., the causee is told to do something), but the coercion may involve physical threat or societal pressure as well. Also it must involve a situation in which the causee can comply (whether willingly or grudgingly). Constructions with *-rōhe* imply that the caused event did occur. Shibatani (1976:240) states that one characteristic of causative sentences is that they '... commit the speaker to the belief that the caused event has taken place.'

Example (347), is an independent clause that closely corresponds to the causative construction in (348). A comparison of the two examples shows that *ki-* (masculine singular) is marked with *-re* (term) in (348) as it changes from subject in (347) to recipient in (348). (Recall that *-re* (term) marks free subjects (usually full noun phrases) and objects that are proper names or human. Clitic pronouns such as *ki-* that are marked with *-re* (term) are always objects or recipients since subject clitic pronouns, when they occur, are always prefixed to the verb as in (347).)

(347) OBJ   S-VERB

yapua ki-kōke-re?ka
log   3ms-carry-PST
He carried the log.

(348) OBJ   REC   S-VERB-CAUS

yapua ki-re   dā-kōke-rōhe-re?ka
log   3ms-TERM 3p-carry-CAUS-PST
They made him carry the log.

In (348), the subject is *dā-* (third-person plural) while *-yapua* 'log' remains the direct object of the verb 'carry'. Thus the causee (subject of (347)) *ki-* (masculine singular) becomes the indirect object (or recipient). This is consistent with Comrie's observation (1981:169) that, in the formation of a causative, the causee generally fills the highest available position on the hierarchy of grammatical relations illustrated below.[43]

---

[42] A variant form, *rūhe* also occurs in some communities.

[43] The hierarchy's explanation of the properties of morphological causatives is consistent with Frantz (1979:33), in his discussion of clause union from the perspective of relational grammar.

(349) Position 1   Position 2   Position 3   Position 4
     Subject   Direct   Indirect   Oblique
                      object   object   object

In Retuarã, I have not proposed a category of indirect object since there is no firm grammatical distinction between direct and indirect objects. Objects are better distinguished on the basis of their semantic case roles of patient and recipient. Nonetheless, there is a tendency for the recipient to immediately precede the verb. Thus the two objects are often (but not always) distinguished by word order. (See §7.3 for a discussion of word order regarding objects.) Typical of causative constructions, the transitive verb becomes ditransitive, as in (350). The valence of the verb is increased by one. So, intransitive verbs become transitive and the subject of the intransitive verb becomes the object of the causative as in (351).

(350) OBJ(REC)   OBJ(PATIENT)
       dã-re   bī-hãã-rōhe-be   ki-re
       3p-TERM 2s-kill-CAUS-IMP 3ms-TERM
       Order them to kill him!

(351) bãẽ dã-re   ki-bayatãã-rōhe-yu
      now 3p-TERM 3ms-dance-CAUS-PRES
      Now he makes them dance.

The causative suffix *-rōhe* may also indicate 'allow' as illustrated by comparing (352) and (353) which shows the pronoun causee *ko-* (feminine singular) as object marked with *-re* (term) in (353).

(352) *ko-po-ri-be-ri-koʔo   wiʔia-pi*
      3fs-leave-EP-NEG-EP-PST house-INSTR
      She didn't leave the house.

(353) *anita-re   ko-re   po-ri-rōhe-be-ri-koʔo   wiʔia-pi*
      Anita-TERM 3fs-TERM leave-EP-CAUS-NEG-EP-PST   house-INSTR
      Anita didn't allow her to leave the house.

5.27. Nonvolitional causation. A second morphological causative, *-ta* (causative), is used when volition or compliance by the causee is not

Verb Phrase

involved, that is, the causee may be inanimate or without volition concerning the caused effect.[44]

A comparison of (354) and (355) shows that 'candle', the subject of intransitive verb *ya* 'go out, extinguish' in (354), becomes the object of the causative in (355).

(354) *tūparāperia ya-yu-a*
     candle   extinguish-PRES-n
     The candle goes out.

(355) *tūparāperia ki-ya-ta-yu*
     candle   3ms-extinguish-CAUS-PRES
     He puts the candle out.

In (356), the intransitive verb *bita* 'to become damaged, hurt' is made transitive by *-ta*.

(356) *radio ko-bita-ta-yu*
     radio 3fs-damage-CAUS-PRES
     She damages the radio.

The causative suffix *-ta* is also used with animate causees when it appears that compliance by the causee is not involved as illustrated by (357) and (358).

(357) *opirekoa ki-re tara-ta-e?ka*
     spirit   3ms-TERM tremble-CAUS-PST
     The spirit made him tremble/convulse.

(358) *ihia ko-re yūta-ta-ko?o-a*
     heat 3fs-TERM faint-CAUS-PST-n
     The heat caused her to faint.

The proper usage of the two causative affixes is determined by whether compliance by the causee is involved or not. This is illustrated by (359) which is judged to be the correct usage and (360) which is not. The reason is that this specific situation requires a command (or some kind of pressure) and some degree of compliance by the causees.

---

[44]It is likely that the nonvolitional causative suffix *-ta* has come from Arawakan; probably through Yucuna whose speakers intermarry with the Retuarã and Tanimuca. See Schauer and Schauer (1978:46).

(359) tãʔãpika dã-re   ki-tũã-rōhe-yu
      coca   3p-TERM 3ms-pound-CAUS-PRES
      He makes them pound coca.

(360) *tãʔãpika dã-re   ki-tũã-ta-yu
      coca   3p-TERM 3ms-pound-CAUS-PRES
      *He makes them pound coca.

When volitionality is not involved, constructions using -rōhe are considered incorrect as seen in a comparison of (361) and (362).

(361) yi-re   ki-yãʔ-ta-yu
      1s-TERM 3ms-fall-CAUS-PRES
      He made me fall.

(362) *yi-re   ki-yãʔ-rōhe-yu
      1s-TERM 3ms-fall-CAUS-PRES
      *He made me fall.

5.28. Lexicalized causatives. Other causative constructions can be seen in the language which are evidences of past processes that are no longer productive. A change in the final vowel in some verb stems distinguishes transitive and intransitive verbs. The vowel change occurred according to causative forming processes that may have been borrowed from other languages. I have considered the process causative rather than transitivizing according to Shibatani (1976: 240) who says

> In traditional grammar, verbs like *melt* and *kick* are classified as transitive verbs, but the terms CAUSATIVE VERBS and TRANSITIVE VERBS do not coincide. The verb *kick*, for example, is not a causative verb by itself, since a sentence such as *John kicked the ice* does not necessarily convey that there was any caused event following John's kicking the ice. One can, thus say the sentence *John kicked the ice, but nothing happened to the ice* without involving any contradiction. However, the causative verb *melt* creates contradiction, as shown in the sentence *John melted the ice, but nothing happened to the ice.*

The examples below all imply that the object was affected in the manner indicated by the verb. It may be that several processes were at work; one from Tucanoan languages, and perhaps two from Arawakan. Payne's (1990:78) list of common features of South American languages indicate that causatives are often formed by a vowel prefix to the verb. Although

Verb Phrase

his list is largely composed of the back vowels *a-* and *o-*, it also cites *e-* from two Maipuran Arawakan languages. Wise (1990:107) lists three other Maipuran Arawakan languages that have a *a-/e-* variation for their causative prefix. It is possible that the causative suffix *-a* and the *-e/-o* vowel changes, both discussed below, may have their origin from neighboring Arawakan languages. In Retuarã, it is not a prefix, but rather a change in the final vowel in some verb stems that distinguishes transitive and intransitive verbs.[45] The following examples compare the intransitive verb 'cool off' in (363) with its transitive counterpart in (364). The final vowel *-i* of the intransitive verb root has been replaced by *-e* in the transitive form.

(363) *kape   hihi-ko?o-a*
coffee cool^off-PST-n
The coffee cooled off.

(364) *kape   yi-hihe-ko?o*
coffee 1s-cool^off-PST
I cooled off the coffee.

The replacement of final verb root vowels with *-e* is now nonproductive in Retuarã. In fact, there are several examples where the lexicalized transitive form of this process undergoes the causative process with the suffix *-ta*. In (366) the verb root *yābē* 'sink' is the causative (lexicalized) form of the intransitive verb root *yābī* 'sink' in (365). Example (367) with the causative suffix *-ta* on the verb root *yābē* gives the sense of indirect causation. The causation by the agent in (366) is more direct than that of (367).

(365) *riaka-rā   dā-yābī-rape*
river-LOC 3p-sink-PST
They sank in the river.

(366) *pota   yi-yābē-rape*
hook 1s-sink-PST
I sank the hook into the water.

---

[45]In Payne's data there are many affixes in his first two categories (negative and causative) with the same form across the various language families, but they vary between being suffixes and prefixes. Therefore, it seems likely that the forms and functions of the prefixes were borrowed without retaining their prefixing natures. This is especially so because the Tucanoan languages are overwhelmingly suffixing languages.

(367) *pekapakiaka dā-yābē-ta-rape*
   shot^gun   3p-sink-CAUS-PST
   They sank the shot gun (when their canoe overturned).

In the Tucanoan languages there is a causative suffix *-o*. In Barasana, Tucano, and Carapana, for example, it is still productive with some verbs, but has become lexicalized with others. From the following Retuarã example one could argue that the same causative suffix *-o* has come to replace the final vowel *-ū* (without a loss of nasalization) in the lexicalized form. Apparently vowel harmony has caused the other verb root vowel to change to *-õ* also. In Retuarã, this process has become nonproductive with only several lexicalized examples remaining.

(368) *la cinco   rõʔõhirã yi-tūrū-koʔo*
   five^o'clock at   1s-wake-PST
   I woke up at 5 o'clock.

(369) *bikitoho ki-re   dā-tōrō-koʔo*
   early   3ms-TERM   3p-wake-PST
   They woke him up early.

A third, nonproductive morphological causative suffix exists. The suffix *-a* 'cause' occurs with several verb roots to create a nonvolitional causative verb. The resulting verbs seem to have become lexicalized with some slight shift in the semantics or usages away from the intransitive form. Constructions with causative suffix *-a* are illustrated below. In (370), the verb root *poihi* means 'to be born'. When the verb root is made causative by the suffix *-a* in (371), it has the meaning 'to create' which is not far from the expected meaning 'to cause to be born'.

(370) *yi-maki poihi-yu-ka*
   1s-son be^born-PRES-ms
   My son is born.

(371) *tūparã-te wehea poihia-eʔka*
   God-TERM land create-PST
   God created the land (world).

In (372) the verb root *yekari* means 'to forget'. When *-a* is suffixed to the root it has the meaning to cause one to forget or cease doing something (such as a bad habit).

(372) ba?ia-ha   yi-baa-i-ka   ki-yekaria-e?ka   yi-re
     bad-ADVLZR 1s-do-STAT-n 3ms-forget^cease-PST 1s-TERM
     He caused me to forget/cease doing badly.

5.29. Reciprocals. As with reflexives, some verbs are inherently reciprocal. Givón (1984) labels these 'verbs with a reciprocal/associative object'. They are verbs like fight, meet, join, etc. in which the object is equally the agent and patient. In Retuarã one of the co-agents is marked with the comitative case marker *-ka* as in (373). These verbs do not take an object.

(373) yi-bāyēki-ka   yi-hī-rī-rāyū
     1s-father^in^law-COM 1s-fight-EP-FUT
     I will fight with my father in law.

(374) bāki-ka   ki-wa?ībā-yū
     son-COM 3ms-play-PRES
     He plays with his son.

Grammatically the above two examples are intransitive since there is no overtly marked object. Some verbs which one might assume to be inherently reciprocal are not, for example, *pitayīā* 'to marry' and *tue* 'to accompany'. In (375), the noun phrase (*ko-* (feminine singular)) is marked as a term (and thus an object) rather than a coparticipant. Reciprocality may be overtly marked by *-bua* (reciprocal) following the verb root as in (376) and (377).

(375) OBJ

     ko-re   ki-pitayīā-rape
     3fs-TERM 3ms-marry-PST
     He married her.

(376) dā-yapa-bua-yu
     3p-like-RECPR-PRES
     They like each other.

(377) ee-ri-ka   hai-tirā   dā-ee-bua-yu
     laugh-DVBL-n talk-after 3p-laugh-RECPR-PRES
     After joking, they laugh at each other.

Often the clause containing the reciprocal construction will also have the adverb *tiyiaha* (emphatic) with the same subject prefix as the verb. It serves to clarify that the action occurs between members of the group referred to by the subject. In (378) and (379), *tiyiaha* is translated 'themselves' but it is not indicative of reflexive, only emphasis. Verbs made reciprocal by *-bua* never have an overt object; thus, *-bua* appears to intransitivize the verb.

(378) dã-tiyiaha dã-hãã-*bua*-koʔo
　　　3p-EMPH　3p-kill-RECPR-PST
　　　They themselves killed each other.

(379) dã-tiyiaha dã-kareʔe-*bua*-yu
　　　3p-EMPH　3p-steal-RECPR-PRES
　　　They themselves are robbing each other.

5.30. Incorporation. Sometimes objects and instruments are incorporated into the verb. The incorporated constituent directly precedes the verb root. In (380), *peka* 'fire, fire wood' is the object of *sĩã* 'feed'. (381) and (382) illustrate the incorporated objects *ĩkoa* 'medicine' and *tãʔãpika* 'coca'.

(380) bãẽ　sa-bĩ-*peka*-sĩã-be　　　bui
　　　now 3ns-2s-firewood-feed-IMP brother-in-law
　　　Now stoke the fire, brother-in-law.

(381) kabĩã　hũhẽ-riha-ri-tirã　　sa-bã-*ĩko*-roa-hĩ-yũ
　　　wound wash-CONT-EP-AFTER 3ns-12-medicine-put^on-PSBL-PRES
　　　After one has continuously washed the wound, one should put medicine on it.

(382) kopakaha dã-*tãʔãpi*-hãã-ti-koʔo
　　　now　　　3p-coca-put^in-PERF-PST
　　　Now they have chewed coca.

In (382), the incorporation of the object reduces the valence of the verb to make it grammatically intransitive. In other cases of incorporation, the compounded verb becomes lexicalized as transitive and takes a new object. The verb in (383) is a compound of the object *terĩ* 'seat' and *hãã* 'put in' meaning 'to put in seats' (in a canoe). The new object is a canoe referred to by the prefix *sa-* (neuter singular). Example (384) is an illustration of an incorporated instrument (or perhaps object). Table (385) illustrates some other examples of verbs with incorporated objects and instruments.

(383) bikitoho sa-ki-*terĩ*-hãã-rãyũ
　　　　morning 3ns-3ms-seat-put-FUT
　　　　In the morning he will put seats in it (canoe) (lit., he will seat put it).

Verb Phrase

(384) *dã-re   ki-bĩʔrõ-pupu-yu*
3p-TERM 3ms-tobacco-blow-PRES
He tobacco-blows them (or blows with tobacco).

(385) Object   Instrument

    tãʔãpi-tũã   *tebũ-hãã*
    coca-pound   bow-kill
    'to pulverize coca'   'to shoot with a bow'

    karõ-baa   *bũã-koa*
    string-do   salt-cure
    'to string a trap'   'to cure with salt'

6
Adverbs

The category of adverbs includes those words that indicate manner, time, location, speaker comment, mood, and aspect. Their classification as an adverb or an adjective depends on their function in the clause.

6.1. Manner. Most manner adverbs in Retuarã are usually derived from noun or verb phrases (see §6.6.). Manner adverbs have only the verb in their scope (rather than the whole sentence). They typically occur on the periphery, that is, sentence-initially or finally. In (386), the underived adverb *hãhĩã* 'hard, fast' occurs in sentence-initial position. The adverb may occur in final position when another constituent (such as a time adverb) already occurs sentence-initially as in (387). The adverb *yēbētahi* in (388) clarifies the extent of the action of pouring (i.e., pour until the cup is half full.)

(386) *hãhĩã yiha-iʔta-reʔka*
 fast 1p-come-PST
 We came fast.

(387) *bãẽ yiha-iʔta-reʔka hãhĩã*
 now 1p-come-PST fast
 Now we came fast.

(388) *yēbētahi yi-re bī-paa-be*
 half 1s-TERM 2s-pour-IMP
 Pour me half.

6.2. Time. Time adverbs are sentential in scope, that is, they modify or characterize the entire event or state.

(389) *bikitoho ki-aʔ-ri-koʔo*
 early 3ms-go-EP-PST
 He left early.

(390) *yābāhi yi-peʔ-yu*
 later 1s-return-PRES
 I will return later.

(391) *rōbīha-te o-ri-reʔka piyia*
 women-TERM cry-EP-PST last
 The women cried for the last time.

The adverb *piyia* 'last' in (391) can also function as an adjective (modifying the classifier *-bi*) as in (392). Its classification as an adjective or adverb depends on its function in a sentence.

(392) *piyi-bi ki-eʔe-ri-koʔo*
 last-1DIMEN 3ms-take-EP-PST
 He took the last one.

6.3. Location. Location adverbs have the entire sentence in their scope. They are bound forms that are marked with a case marker such as *-kaka* (ablative), *-pi* (instrument, source), or *-rā* (location). The adverb *poʔi-rā* 'to, toward' in (393) may have been derived from *poʔia* 'body' plus *-rā* (location) meaning 'a person's location'.

(393) *policia poʔi-rā ki-re dā-eʔe-waʔ-ri-reʔka*
 police to-LOC 3ms-TERM 3p-get-AWAY-EP-PST
 They took him to the police.

(394) *rōbī-ha-te kaʔia taa-reʔka yoe-rā*
 women-p-TERM dirt throw-PST far-LOC
 The women threw the dirt far away.

(395) *yoe-pi yi-iʔta-koʔo*
 far-INSTR 1s-come-PST
 I came from far away.

Adverbs

6.4. Speaker attitude adverbs. Some adverbs express the speaker's evaluation of the probability of a statement. These adverbs seem to carry some of the load that evidential suffixes do in many other Tucanoan languages. The adverbs are usually clause-final following the verb, but they can occasionally follow other constituents.

The adverb *he?e* (suppositon) can be translated 'surely' or 'I think' and is used to indicate that the speaker feels something lacks solid evidence for belief. Thus, there is some doubt implied.

(396) *yi-re   ō-rī-be-yu-a   he?e ki-ārī-re?ka*
       1s-TERM know-EP-NEG-PRES-n SUP   3ms-say-PST
       "Surely he's forgotten me," he said.

Quite often sentences with *he?e* (supposition) also contain sentential scope adverbs that highlight the speaker's comment. In (397) *apeyari* 'perhaps' occurs sentence-finally like an uncertain afterthought. The interactional *ahī?ī* 'I don't know' is also often used with *he?e* (supposition) as in (398).

(397) *wiyawaia i?ta-rā-ka   he?e apeyari*
       airplane come-FUT-n   SUP   perhaps
       I think the airplane will come, perhaps.

(398) *ahī?ī   i?ta-be-sa-rā-ki   he?e*
       1s^don't^know come-NEG-EP-FUT-ms   SUP
       I don't know, I think he may not come.

The adverb *ruku* (assertion) is used to express the opinion of the speaker. Often it invites a response to the asserted opinion. Example (399) illustrates one usage of *ruku* where a character asserts his belief to a turtle that he (the turtle) has transformed himself and is actually the man they are looking for. In (400), *ruku* occurs twice. The first occurence follows a time word, 'now', rather than a verb, demonstrating that *ruku* can have a fairly free distribution in the sentence.

(399) *i?ka-ro?si yi-ha-ri-ye?e   bī-ā-rī-ko?o   ruku*
       this-BEN   1s-become-EP-CNTGN   2s-say-EP-PST   ASRT
       So, you must have said, "I could change into this."

(400) *bāē ruku ki-re   dā-ria-yu   ruku*
       now ASRT 3ms-TERM   3p-kill-PRES ASRT
       Now surely they are killing him (do you suppose?).

A typical greeting in (401) illustrates that the use of *ruku* creates an expectation of a response much as a question does. However, unlike a true question, the speaker is asserting something obvious (since he knows who the person is that he is greeting) but is inviting a response or interaction.

(401) *bĩʔĩ ruku*
 2s   ASRT
 (Is it) you?

(402) *āʔā yiʔi*
 yes 1s
 Yes (it is) me.

The opinion marker *ruku* can also be used in questions. It does not assert an opinion in this usage but rather expresses the notion of 'I wonder who or what... etc.'. Again it indicates that the speaker is asking for or inviting the hearer's opinion.

(403) *bāki eta-koʔo-ka ruku*
 who arrive-PST-ms ASRT
 I wonder who arrived? *or* Who do you suppose arrived?

(404) *daʔkoa ki-eʔe-raʔa-koʔo ruku*
 what 3ms-get-TWRD-PST ASRT
 I wonder what he brought? *or* What do you suppose he brought?

6.5. Mood/aspect adverbs. An additional group of adverbs, which I have labeled mood/aspect adverbs, are adverbs that frequently support or lend prominence to the mood and aspect suffix system. For example, *kopakaha* means 'now' but with a telic sense of the end or finish of something. It often occurs with the aspect suffix *-ti* (perfect) as in (405) and (406). In both examples, the same meaning is communicated with or without *kopakaha* 'now'. It seems, therefore, to add emphasis rather than to alter the meaning.

(405) *aʔpe-ika kopakaha kā-rī-ti-i-ki*
 other-ms now   sleep-EP-PERF-STAT-ms
 Now another one is already asleep.

(406) *kopakaha bīhā-ka yi-ībā-ti-kope-yu*
 now   2p-COM 1s-be-PERF-CONTRA-PRES
 Now I have been with you (but...). *or* I soon will no longer be with you.

Adverbs

Another adverb of the mood/aspect category is *koiʔtēhe* 'almost' which can occur with the modal *-kope* (contra-expectation) as in (407).

(407) *koiʔtēhe yi-yāʔ-rī-kope-yu*
   almost 1s-fall-EP-CONTRA-PRES
   I almost fell.

Other adverbs such as *aʔte* 'again' and *rupu* 'yet, still' serve an aspectual function but they do so without supporting an aspectual suffix in the verb. For example, in (408) *aʔte* indicates that the action is repeated at a different time. The adverb *rupu* 'yet, still' expresses the aspectual notion of continuance in an imperative construction. The normal continuative suffix is *-yūhū*, but the imperative construction does not allow aspect or mood suffixes. Thus *rupu*, as a free adverb, is used to indicate continuing action as in (409).

(408) *aʔte yiha-tuʔa-reʔka yiha-bāleta eʔe-rī*
   again 1p-go^to^port-PST 1p-suitcase get-PURP
   Again we went down to the port to get our suitcase.

(409) *bī-bōʔā-be rupu*
   2s-search-IMP still
   Keep searching!

In other situations where an element of contra-expectation exists, *rupu* 'yet, still' is also used. In (410), a taboo associated with childbirth is explained using *rupu* to indicate contra-expectation.

(410) *ibīrīhā īā-be-ri-hī-i-rā rupu*
   men see-NEG-EP-PSBL-STAT-3p still
   The men still cannot see (the child).

6.6. Derived adverbs. Adverbs are also derived from other classes, typically nominals and adjectives, by the suffix *-hV* (adverbializer). Adverbial clauses can also be derived from verb phrases. The form that the adverbializer takes is variable since its vowel copies the preceding vowel's features (including nasalization). Examples (411) and (412) illustrate the harmony.

(411) *kūpahī-hī*
   little-ADVLZR
   scarcely, sparingly

(412) *ĩʔrã-to-ho*
    one-2DIMEN-ADVLZR
    just one flat thing

In (413), *-hV* (adverbializer) is suffixed to the nominal *ĩʔrã-ika* 'one person' to give the meaning 'alone' or 'by one self'. The adverbializer is suffixed to a proper name in (414).

(413) *ĩʔrã-ika-ha*   *ki-baʔirabe-yu*
    one-ms-ADVLZR 3ms-work-PRES
    He works alone.

(414) *migelito-ho*   *ĩõ-i-ki*   *ki-ībē*
    Miguelito-ADVLZR appear-STAT-ms 3ms-be
    He resembles Miguelito.

The *-hV* can also be suffixed to locative phrases as in (415). The locative phrase *yoerã-bã-rĩ-ã* 'not far' thus modifies the verb *ruʔ* 'to flee' as a locative adverbial phrase.

(415) *aʔpe-rã rōbī-ha*   *ruʔ-yu-rã*   *yoe-rã-bã-rĩ-ã-hã*
    other-p women-p flee-PRES-p far-LOC-not^be-DVBL-n-ADVLZR
    Other women flee not too far.

In (416), *-hV* is suffixed to a verb phrase to create a time adverbial clause with the sense of 'while'. The verb of the adverbial clause can only be inflected for present tense.

(416) *ki-hai-yu-hu*   *dã-eta-koʔo*
    3ms-talk-PRES-ADVLZR 3p-arrive-PST
    While he was talking, they arrived.

Manner adverbial phrases derived from verbs are negated with *-be* or *-pe* (negative). Notice in (416)–(418) that the verbs of the adverbial phrases have been reduced in the range of verbal morphology that they display. In (416), only the present tense is allowed. In (417) and (418), there is no tense marking nor epenthetic syllable *-ri* following the single syllable roots. This is consistent with Hopper and Thompson's (1984) claim that the less the verb performs the function of a prototypical verb, the fewer morphosyntactic features typical of verbs it will exhibit.

Adverbs

(417) *hī-pe-ka-ha   bīhā-waʔibā-pe*
fight-NEG-n-ADVLZR 2p-play-IND.IMP
(Go and) play without fighting.

(418) *hai-be-ka-ha   ki-baʔirabe-yu*
talk-NEG-n-ADVLZR 3ms-work-PRES
He works without talking.

The variation in the form of the negative (*-be, -pe*) may have been conditioned phonologically at one time, but a plausible environment for that conditioning is no longer apparent. It may also be that there is a slight difference in meaning between the two forms that is not yet understood. (419) further illustrates the environments.

(419)   *-pe*   *-be*
        hī-pe-ka-ha   *hai-be-ka-ha*
        'without fighting'   'without talking'

        ā-pe-ka-ha   *baʔa-be-ka-ha*
        'without saying'   'without eating'

        aʔ-pe-ka-ha   *uʔya-be-ka-ha*
        'without going'   'without bathing'

The morpheme *-hV* (adverbializer) also has a limitative function. In (420) it is suffixed to the demonstrative pronoun *iʔsia* 'that' to indicate the extent of the verb and in (421) it is suffixed to a verb.

(420) *iʔsia-ha   ki-baʔa-yu*
that-ADVLZR 3ms-eat-PRES
He eats only that.

(421) *ki-re   ībā-ha   ki-baʔa-rōhe-yu*
3ms-TERM be-ADVLZR 3ms-eat-CAUS-PRES
He makes him eat whatever there is.

The adverbializer has the form *-hi* in (422). Its meaning seems to be 'same' because it limits the source of the action to the locative to which it is suffixed.

(422) *sa-pirita-waʔ-ri-reʔka   sa-pi-hi*
3ns-sprang-AWAY-EP-PST 3ns-INSTR-ADVLZR
It sprang up and away from the same (spot).

Example (423) illustrates *-hV* suffixed to a time expression, again with the meaning 'same'.

(423) *i-rībī-hī   ki-bayatāā-rāyū*
this-day-ADVLZR 3ms-dance-FUT
This same day he will dance.

A final limitator *ya* 'just' may occur after nouns or pronouns. In answer to 'who is he?', it occurs with the person pronoun *yiʔi* (first-person singular)

(424) *bāki iʔki?*
who 3ms
Who is he?

(425) *yiʔi ya*
1s just
Just me.

7
Sentence Structure

This section discusses the basic sentence types (intransitive, transitive, ditransitive, existential, and copular), locationals (comparing predicate nominal, possessive, locative, and existential constructions), spatial relators, reflexives, and subordinate clauses. In the following discussion, the gloss will indicate the verb as V, subject as SUB, object as OBJ, obliques as OBL, and a recipient as REC. Pronominal subjects that are prefixed to the verb are glossed PRSUB.

The basic or most common sentence structure of Retuarã has the following characteristics.

1. A subject noun phrase will be sentence initial.
2. The verb will usually be sentence final.
3. In a transitive clause, the object often precedes the verb.
4. Obliques will be sentence initial or final, not medial. The sentence-initial position predominates.
5. Word order is somewhat flexible. The most common (and least ambiguous) order is given in a formula in (426).

(426) (OBL)　SUBJ　(OBJ)　(REC)　　V　　　(OBL)
or:
　　　(OBL)　　　　(OBJ)　(REC)　PRSUB+V　(OBL)

6. Subjects, objects, and the copula may be omitted. A clause that is subordinated by a subordinating suffix often demonstrates

suppression of the subject (see §§11.8–11.17). If the identity of the object is clear, it may be omitted. It is common to omit the verb in copular sentences.

7.1. Intransitive. The basic constituents of an intransitive sentence are an intransitive verb preceded by a free subject or a subject prefix (though not both except under highly marked conditions). (427) and (428) give examples of an intransitive sentence with a free subject and a subject prefix, respectively.

(427)   SUBJ   V
       bāē sa-baiʔpo-te   aʔ-yu
       now 3ns-owner-TERM go-PRES
       Now it's owner goes.

(428) PRSUB+V
       ko-kā-yū
       3fs-sleep-PRES
       She sleeps.

The most common peripheral constituents are the obliques of location and time. These often precede the verb, even when both are present in the sentence as illustrated by (429) and (430). When time and location phrases occur together, time precedes location as in (431).

(429) LOC   PRSUB+V
       waye-rā   yiha-aʔ-ri-reʔka
       upriver-LOC 1p-go-EP-PST
       We went upriver.

(430) TIME   PRSUB+V
       bikitoho ki-aʔ-yu
       morning 3ms-go-PRES
       He goes in the morning.

(431) TIME   LOC   PRSUB+V
       īʔrā-rībī bāʔkaka-rā dā-kā-yū
       one-day jungle-LOC 3p-sleep-PRES
       They sleep in the jungle one day.

Sentence Structure

Obliques may follow the verb when there would otherwise be too much material preceding the verb. In (432), the locative *ātabākarākarā* 'La Pedrera' follows the verb.

(432) TIME   PRSUB+V   LOC
bāēkaraka-kuri herītarika yiha-ībā-reʔka ātabākarākarā
three-time week 1p-be-PST La^Pedrera
We were in La Pedrera (a town) for three weeks.

Occasionally locatives follow the verb when it is a verb of motion. There may be a symbolic or iconic reason for this since a locative or goal marks the end point of some motion. In (433), *yu* 'go downriver' is a motion verb and the goal *wiʔia* 'house' is sentence final. Though the subject in the example is pronominal, the order would be the same for a free noun phrase.

(433) TIME   PRSUB+V   LOC
bikitoho yiha-yu-rape   wiʔia-rā
morning 1p-go^downriver-PST house-LOC
In the morning we went downriver to the house.

Other constituents such as manner, generally precede the subject and verb as in (434). A manner phrase can also follow the verb as in (435). Perhaps this order is more frequent when other constituents are present, such as *bāē* 'now', which often occurs sentence initially.

(434) MANNER PRSUB+V

hiaha   ki-baʔirabe-yu
slowly   3ms-work-PRES
He works slowly.

(435) TIME PRSUB+V   MANNER

bāē yiha-iʔta-reʔka hāhīā
now 1p-come-PST   fast
Now we came fast.

To summarize, the basic order of an intransitive sentence is (TIME) (LOC) [PRSUB+V] with the possiblity of the locative following the verb.[46] The

---

[46]Locative constructions are the exception to this as they allow location obliques to occur clause medially (see §7.6).

number of constituents is usually three or four but can range from one to six.

7.2. Transitive. The basic order of a transitive clause is SOV. The obliques occur on the periphery though they generally precede the clause to which they apply. Although obliques do not occur between a main clause and one subordinated by a suffix, clauses subordinated by conjunction do not have these constraints.

A subject noun phrase precedes the object so that in potentially ambiguous sentences where the subject and object can not be distinguished by case marking nor semantic clues, (e.g., when the subject and object are equally animate as in (436) and (437)), they are distinguished by word order. Thus, in (436), the noun phrase, Ernesto, is understood to be the subject since it precedes Alvaro. The object usually precedes the verb as in (436), but can also occur in a postverbal position as in (437).

(436) SUBJ   OBJ   V
ernesto-te alvaro-te heyobaa-rape
Ernest-TERM Alvaro-TERM help-PST
Ernest helped Alvaro.

(437) SUBJ   V   OBJ
ernesto-te heyobaa-rape alvaro-te
Ernest-TERM help-PST Alvaro-TERM
Ernest helped Alvaro.

When the subject and object are both pronouns (and animate), the pronoun marked with *-re* (term) is the object or recipient. Subject pronouns are usually cliticized and prefixed to the verb (and thus are not case-marked) as in (438). When not prefixed, subject pronouns do not receive *-re* (term) case marking[47] and a number/gender suffix on the verb agrees with it in number and gender as illustrated in (439). Note that the subject pronoun *yiʔi* (first-person singular) is not case-marked with *-re*.

(438) OBJ   PRSUB+V
ko-re ki-īā-koʔo
3fs-TERM 3ms-see-PST
He saw her.

---

[47]There is an infrequent and highly marked exception to this (see §1.17).

(439) SUBJ OBJ   V+PRSUB

     yiʔi   sa-kaʔsia baʔa-rā-ki
     1s   3ns-liver   eat-FUT-ms
     I will be the eater of its liver.

Free subject pronouns are always postverbal in negative declarative sentences which results in the order O V+S S as illustrated in (440). In such cases there is no ambiguity between the equally animate pronouns since the subject is expected to occupy the postverbal position in a negated clause. Also, the term casemarking on the clitic personal pronoun *ko-re* (feminine singular) marks it as the object or recipient.

(440) OBJ   V+S   SUBJ

     ko-re   īā-be-ri-koʔo-ki   iʔki
     3fs-TERM see-NEG-EP-PST-ms 3ms
     He didn't see her.

Transitive sentences with subjects low in agentiveness follow the same word order as other transitive sentences. For example, (441) is low in agentiveness while (442) is increasingly agentive. In both of them, the grammatical object is marked with *-re* (term) and the subject is a prefix on the the verb.

(441) OBJ   PRSUB+V

     ki-re   yi-īā-yu
     3ms-TERM 1s-see-PRES
     I see him.

(442) OBJ   PRSUB+V

     ki-re   yi-hoe-reʔka
     3ms-TERM 1s-burn-PST
     I burned him.

In a discourse in which an object is discussed (e.g., procedural discourse), the object is introduced as a full noun phrase. After that it is referred to by the pronoun prefix *sa-* (neuter singular) or there may be no overt reference. The object pronoun cliticizes to the verb, which is already inflected for subject, giving the morphological order OBJ+PRSUB+V as in (443).

(443)   OBJ+PRSUB+V
   waeroka   sa-yi-rēā-rāyū
   tomorrow 3ns-1s-gather-FUT
   Tomorrow I will gather them.

It is also common to have just the object pronoun prefixed to the verb when the subject is a full noun phrase as in (444). Occasionally the object noun phrase follows the verb. It may be that this is more common when objects are presented as a list.

(444) SUBJ   OBJ+V+PRSUB
   yi-bāki īʔrīka-ha   sa-ō-yū-ka
   1s-son alone-ADVLZR 3ns-know-PRES-3ms
   My son alone is the one who knows it.

An object can follow a verb in a right dislocation construction. In this construction the object is referred to by a pronoun and then, as an afterthought, the speaker adds the specific object noun phrase referred to by the pronoun at the end of the sentence. In (445) therefore, there are two references to the same object with the specific reference *pōrāka* (a type of palm tree) following the verb.

(445) *bāē   sa-dā-ko-yu   pōrāka*
   now 3ns-3p-cut^down-PRES pōrāka^palm
   Now they cut it down, pōrāka (palm tree).

As in intransitive clauses, obliques such as location and time usually precede the subject or object of a transitive clause.

(446) TIME   SUBJ   OBJ   V
   bikitoho arturu-te   tāʔāpika baa-rape
   morning Arthur-TERM coca   make-PST
   In the morning Arthur made coca.

(447) LOC   TIME OBJ   PRSUB+V
   to-rā   bāē pesiwiʔia yiha-baa-rape
   there-LOC now shelter 1p-make-PST
   There now we made a shelter.

Sentence Structure

Obliques can be sentence final following the clause to which they apply. The sentence structure does not allow obliques to come between verbs subordinated by subordinating suffixes and matrix verbs. In (448), the matrix clause 'they dry it' follows the dependent adverbial clause 'after they finish gathering it'. Thus the locative and time obliques which apply to the matrix clause, occur sentence finally rather than between the two clauses.

(448) OBJ+VSUBOR   OBJ+PRSUB+VMATRIX LOC   TIME
sa-eʔe-wea-tirā   sa-dā-pōpo-yu   aiya-peka-rā ĩʔrā-rībĩ
3ns-get-finish-after 3ns-3p-dry-PRES sun-fire-LOC one-day
After (they) finish gathering, they dry it in the sun one day.

Manner phrases also generally occur sentence initially as in (449), but may follow a transitive verb, as in (450), when an oblique such as time also occurs in the sentence. This may suggest that there is a preference to reduce the sentence-initial load of obliques or adverbial constituents.

(449) MANNER   OBJ+PRSUB+V
hai-be-ka-ha   sa-dā-baʔa-yu
talk-NEG-n-ADVLZR 3ns-3p-eat-PRES
They eat it without talking.

(450) TIME OBJ+PRSUB+V MANNER
bāẽ sa-dā-taʔa-yu karea-ha
now 3ns-3p-wait-PRES quiet-ADVLZR
Now they wait for it quietly.

When there is an overt subject or object noun phrase, the manner phrase may not be in sentence-initial position as demonstrated in the following examples where (452) is judged ill-formed.

(451) OBJ   MANNER   PRSUB+V
juā-re   baʔia-ha   bĩ-baa-aʔsi
Juan-TERM bad-ADVLZR 2s-do-NEG.IMP
Don't treat Juan badly.

(452) MANNER   OBJ   PRSUB+V

*ba?ia-ha juā-re bī-baa-a?si
bad-ADVLZR Juan-TERM 2s-do-NEG.IMP
*Don't treat Juan badly.

7.3. Ditransitive.
Ditransitive clauses have the following characteristics.

1. Ditransitive verbs take two objects.
2. The roles of the object noun phrases are semantically interpreted, not grammatically marked.
3. There is a fairly strong tendency for the object noun phrase, which is semantically the recipient, to immediately precede the verb.

Even though there is no grammatical distinction between the two kinds of objects in Retuarã, for the sake of clarity, they will be marked as OBJ (object) and REC (recipient).

The most common order of constituents (without a free subject noun phrase) is OBJ REC VERB as in (453). Other orders do occur as illustrated in (454) and (455), but they are not common.

(453) OBJ   REC   PRSUB+V

wa?ia pisarāka ki-hi?a-ko?o
fish cat 3ms-feed-PST
He fed the fish to the cat.

(454) REC   OBJ   PRSUB+V

yi-re wa?ia bī-īhī-be
1s-TERM fish 2s-give-IMP
Give me (some) fish.

(455) REC   PRSUB+V   OBJ

yi-re bī-īhī-be wa?ia
1s-TERM 2s-give-IMP fish
Give me (some) fish.

The preferred order is for the recipient to immediately precede the verb. This is supported by (456) in which the interpretation is ambiguous unless the word order is significant in determining the roles of the noun phrases. The example also illustrates that word order is significant rather than animacy since the objects are equal in their ranking on the animacy hierarchy (see §12.5). It might be argued that the object highest in animacy occupies the position closest to the verb.

(456) OBJ REC PRSUB+V
   ko-re *ki-re* *yi-bea-yu*
   3fs-TERM 3ms-TERM 1s-show-PRES
   I show her to him.
   *I show him to her.

When the subject is a noun phrase rather than a person prefix on the verb, the recipient can occupy any position in the clause that follows the subject noun phrase.

(457) SUBJ (REC) OBJ (REC) V (REC)
     position   position   position
      1   2   3

The position the recipient takes depends on its form. When the recipient is a pronoun, it generally occupies position 2, and less commonly position 1 (both preceding the verb), as in (458) and (459). The word order in these cases is freer because meaning allows the hearer to interpret both sentences.

(458) SUBJ REC OBJ VCOMP VMATRIX
   lui-re *ki-re* *baʔarika ĩhĩ-rĩ* *eta-royi-reʔka*
   Lui-TERM 3ms-TERM food give-PURP arrive-IMPF-PST
   Lui was coming to give him food.

(459) SUBJ   OBJ REC V
   yolanda-te *dōkoa yiha-re sia-reʔka*
   Yolanda-TERM soup 1p-TERM feed-PST
   Yolanda fed us manioc soup.

When the recipient is a proper name, it often follows the verb as in (460). This helps to distinguish the subject from the recipient. However, any position of recipient preceding the verb would probably be understood correctly since the subject noun phrase would precede it in the clause, but the clause-final position of the recipient is more common. It is likely that ordering the recipient clause finally is easier for the hearer to process. Example (460) illustrates the recipient in clause-final position.

(460) SUBJ   OBJ   V   REC
    anita-re   baʔarika īhī-koʔo betania-re
    Anita-TERM food   give-PST Bethanie-TERM
    Anita gave the food to Bethanie.

There are also occasional examples of a repetition of the recipient but with benefactive case marking. In (461), *dā-* (third-person plural) occurs both as the recipient (marked with *-re*), and the benefactive (marked with *-roʔsi*).

(461) *dā-re   ki-piba-yu   waʔia   dā-roʔsi*
    3p-TERM 3ms-share-PRES fish   3p-BEN
    To them he distributes fish for them.

As in sentences with one object, obliques fill positions on the periphery. Time obliques are usually sentence initial as in (462). The free translation suggests that the recipient, *ko-* (feminine singular) is a benefactive but it receives term case marking (perhaps as eventual recipient.) This blurring of the distinction between recipient and benefactive is common in Retuarã.

(462) TIME   OBJ   REC   PRSUB+V
    bābārī   āūā   ko-re   ki-koa-yu
    first   casava   3fs-TERM   3ms-cures-PRES
    First he cures casava for her.

There are few examples of ditransitive sentences with obliques other than time. This may be due to a tendency to avoid overloading the sentence. More information would be spread over two or more sentences.

Finally, an ordering of the object after the verb can also occur. It may be that lists of objects generally follow the verb. In (463), there are two objects in the list followed by an afterthought that specifies the type of meat.

(463) TIME   REC   PRSUB+V   OBJ   OBJ   OBJ
    bikitoho yiha-re   dā-boapā-koʔo   āūā   riʔia waibikirāka
    early   1p-TERM   3p-serve-PST   casava meat   tapir
    Early they served us casava, and meat, tapir meat.

It is not uncommon, however, for a speaker to choose to order a single object after the verb as in (464).

(464) *la tres* *rõʔõhirã dã-wea-reʔka kopea*
three^a.m. at 3p-finish-PST grave
At 3 a.m. they finished (digging) the grave.

A consideration of causative constructions is relevant in the discussion of distinguishing (or not distinguishing) the objects in Retuarã. Frantz (1979:33) in his discussion of clause union from the perspective of relational grammar, states a strong universal tendency that the causee of an intransitive verb becomes the direct object while the causee of a transitive verb becomes the indirect object of the causative construction. In a Retuarã causative construction, the causee immediately precedes the verb. Thus, a causative with a transitive verb would have the order OBJ REC VERB as illustrated in (466).

(465) OBJ   S-VERB
 karia   dã-baʔa-yu
 yucca^soup 3p-eat-PRES
 They eat yucca soup.

(466) OBJ   REC   S-VERB
 karia   dã-re   ki-baʔa-rõhe-yu
 yucca^soup 3p-TERM 3ms-eat-CAUS-PRES
 He makes them eat yucca soup.

This order (OBJ REC VERB) is the same as the generally preferred order in declarative ditransitive clauses. Thus, one could argue that causative constructions support distinguishing a category of indirect object. However, Comrie (1981:170) does not believe the evidence from causative constructions alone to be sufficient to propose a category of indirect object.

> In many languages, it seems that causative constructions would be the only ones where indirect object is a relevant grammatical relation, and, as discussed in section 3.3, the language-internal justification of a grammatical relation really requires a number of logically independent parameters.... Yet, in the cross-linguistic study of causative constructions, indirect object seems to be one of the best justified positions, the use of indirect objects to express the causee in the causative of a transitive verb being extremely widespread across the languages of the world.

Following Comrie, it would seem that the category of indirect object can not be justified on the basis of causatives alone. The preferred order in declarative sentences of OBJ before REC has many exceptions. Therefore, the object has been labeled by its semantic case role, REC because there does not seem to be adequate grammatical grounds for the category indirect object.

When a causative construction has two animate objects, as in (467), it apparently is more difficult to decode if both objects precede the verb. In such cases, it is common for the causee to retain its position preceding the verb while the object of the verb follows. This ordering takes precedence even though it disrupts the more common order of OBJ before REC. Thus it would seem that the most important order is simply that the recipient (when it occurs) immediately precedes the verb.

(467) REC   PRSUB+V   OBJ
      dã-re   bī-hãã-rōhe-be   ki-re
      3p-TERM 2s-kill-CAUS-IMP 3ms-TERM
      Order them to kill him.

If the valence of a ditransitive construction is increased by causativization, the resulting construction has two recipients. Comrie (1981:171) addresses this apparently widespread phenomena:

> The next problem to consider with regard to the formal approach outlined above is that many languages allow doubling on one of the positions in this [causative] hierarchy.... When, however, we turn to indirect objects, [as opposed to accusative objects] then the possibilities for doubling are much more widespread, indeed it seems to be the case that every language that allows the causee to be expressed in the causative of a ditransitive verb construction allows doubling on indirect object in this position, ... In some languages, such examples may be ambiguous ... or stylistically infelicitous for other reasons in certain instances, but there is no doubt that they exist as possible constructions.

Example (469), which is the causative of the ditransitive sentence (468), has two recipients. As mentioned above, the example is ambiguous with both glosses given by speakers.

(468) OBJ   REC   S-VERB
      dīyẽrũ   yi-re   ko-peata-rape
      money 1s-TERM 3fs-return-PST
      She returned the money to me.

Sentence Structure

(469) OBJ   REC   PRSUB+V   REC
dīyẽrũ ko-re ki-peata-rōhe-rape yi-re
money 3fs-TERM 3ms-return-CAUS-PST 1s-TERM
He made me return the money to her. *or* He made her return the money to me.

Causative constructions provide some perspective regarding the question of distinguishing direct and indirect objects. However, word order is the only other distinction in declarative sentences and it is variable. If there were other areas that supported the categorization of the preverbal noun phrase as indirect object, then the causative data would have more significance in that Retuarã would match the crosslinguistic pattern of putting the causee where the language usually puts the indirect object. Lacking other evidence, there is not enough justification to posit the category of indirect object.

7.4. Copular sentences. The copula in Retuarã is the verb *ībā* (sometimes *ībē*) 'to be'. It is irregular in that it has no tense marking for present tense. The copula is clause final in predicate nominals with the formula [NP/ADJ] [NP/PRONOUN] V.

The order is somewhat unusual because the subject noun phrase comes between the predicate complement and the copula. Example (470) illustrates this order in a copular construction with a predicate adjective while (471) illustrates a predicate nominal indicating identity.

(470) *ho?baka yi-wi?ia ībē*
     big   1s-house be
     My house is big.

(471) *būyūā sa-ībē*
     piranha 3ns-be
     It is a piranha.

It is very common to omit the copula (see discussion in §7.7) leaving the noun or adjective as predicate. The predicate nominal or adjective agrees with the noun class of the subject as seen in (472)–(475). See §3.1 for discussion of noun classes.

(472) *ho?ba-ka ki-wi?ia*
     big-n   3ms-house
     His house is big. (class 1)

(473) hoʔba-ki bī-paki
   big-ms   2s-father
   Your father is big. (class 2)

(474) hoʔba-ko iʔko
   big-fs   3fs
   She is big. (class 3)

(475) hoʔba-rā iʔrā
   big-p   3p
   They are big. (class 4)

Sometimes the singular masculine agreement varies between -ka and -ki just as was described with number/gender suffixes on a verb (see §5.2). Thus, both (476) and (477) are acceptable.

(476) hoʔba-ki yiʔi
   big-ms   1s
   I am big.

(477) hoʔba-ka yiʔi
   big-ms   1s
   I am big.

7.5. Existential. Constructions that express experience are often existentials. That is, the experience 'exists to or for someone'. Existentials are analyzed here as copular sentences in which the grammatical and logical subjects are different. The morphosyntactic characteristics of both subjects are listed.

The grammatical subject.

1. The grammatical subject is indefinite.
2. It occupies the normal slot for subjects of declarative sentences (prior to the other major constituents).
3. Negative existentials have number/gender suffixes on the verb which agree with the grammatical subject but positive existentials may or may not be marked.

The logical subject.

1. The logical subject's role as an experiencer is indicated by its grammatical marking as an object (recipient) by -re (term).

2. Its role as the logical subject is reflected by its position in the construction. In positive existentials it occupies the normal preverbal slot for subjects of copular constructions. In negative existentials it occupies the postverbal subject slot of negative declaratives.

In (478) the experiencer (and logical subject) *yi-* (first-person singular) is marked as REC with *-re* (term).[48] The sensation, *ihia* 'hot', is the grammatical subject and occupies the normal position for subjects in declarative sentences.

(478) SUBJ REC V
ihia yi-re baa-yu
hot 1s-TERM do-PRES
I am hot. (lit., there is hot to me)

Example (479) illustrates subject agreement in a negative existential with the grammatical subject 'male children'. The number/gender suffix *-rā* on the verb agrees with the grammatical subject 'offspring'. The grammatical object *yi-* (first-person singular) is the logical subject.

(479) SUBJ V REC
ībīrīhā bāka-rā ībā-be-yu-rā yi-re
male offspring-p be-NEG-PRES-p 1s-TERM
I don't have any male children.

Notice in (479) that the logical subject, *yi-* (first-person singular) is postposed. This parallels the normal and unique position of subject pronouns in negative declarative sentences as illustrated in (480). This postverbal position is also unusual for the recipient since it is not commonly postposed in ditransitive sentences. The position of the logical subject in a positive existential construction parallels the position of the subject in a positive copular construction. The subject follows the complement and precedes the verb as illustrated in (481).

(480) V SUBJ
daʔkoa baa-be-yu-ka yiʔi
what do-NEG-PRES-ms 1s
I'm not doing anything.

---

[48]Pronoun clitics such as *yi-* prefix to the verb as subjects. When they are case marked as terms with *-re* they can only be an object (patient or recipient), never the grammatical subject.

(481) CMP   SUBJ   V
   hoʔbaka yi-wiʔia ībē
   big   1s-house be
   My house is big.

Constructions with a definite subject that, otherwise, are similar to existentials expressing experience, do not have different logical and grammatical subjects. They are not existential and are expressed with a normal copular construction as in (482). For further examples of existentials see §7.6.

(482) *baēkaraka-bāki yi-bāka-rā   ībā-rā*
   three-p   1s-offspring-p be-p
   I have three children. or My children are three.

7.6–7.8 Locationals

Locationals consist of four categories: predicate nominal, possessive, locative, and existential constructions. They are often related by the verbs and structures they share. Lyons (1968) has attributed much of their similarity to their implicitly locative origin. Clark (1978) has further demonstrated that in many languages the four constructions share the same verbs and that the word order of each construction can be determined by the two discourse rules in (483).

(483) Rule 1: +Definite nominals precede –definite nominals
   Rule 2: +Animate nominals precede –animate nominals

The locationals in Retuarā are related to one another by the copula *ībā* 'to be' being used to form all except some possessive constructions which employ the verb *rika* 'to have'. It will be shown, however, that Retuarā is not constrained to the word order pattern that Clark's two discourse rules or tendencies predict. Perhaps, as she suggests, these tendencies are overridden by topic/focus considerations.

7.6. Locative/existential. Locative and existential constructions are formed using the copula *ībā* 'to be'. It has not been possible to syntactically distinguish the two constructions from each other. Lyons (1968:390) says

> Existential sentences typically have an indefinite, rather than definite, subject: this fact raises the possibility that they should be treated, in a syntactic analysis of their deep structure, as indefinite locatives...

Retuarã, however, has no definite or indefinite article so the definiteness of a subject nominal must be subjectively determined by the hearer. Clark (1978) has demonstrated that in many languages without a definite or indefinite article, word order of the locative (LOC) and nominal (NOM) may be the only way to distinguish locative and existential constructions. She states that "Roughly speaking, whenever the Nom is definite, it occurs in initial position. When indefinite, it is normally preceded by some other constituent" (p. 88).

She demonstrates that existential constructions often have the order LOC-NOM (twenty-seven of thirty-five languages). Since the location in an existential construction is usually definite, rule 1 (+definite nominals precede −definite nominals) predicts this order. The locative construction usually has the opposite order, NOM-LOC, (thirty-two of thirty-eight languages). In Retuarã, however, the word order does not distinguish a locative construction from an existential one. For example, (484) can be interpreted as locative or existential by the hearer. If Clark's observations from her language sample held for Retuarã, one would expect (484) to be an existential construction (i.e., 'there is a canoe in the rapids'). *kubũa* 'canoe' can be interpreted as definite or indefinite regardless of the initial position of the locative. Speakers seem to distinguish a locative from an existential simply by context. If the nominal is perceived as indefinite (such as a mass noun), it is existential as in (485) and (486). Note that when the LOC-NOM order of (485) is reversed as in (486), it is still interpreted as existential.

(484) LOC   NOM
       āta-reka   kubũa ībē
       rock-LOC.SPEC canoe be
       There is a canoe in the rapids. *or* The canoe is in the rapids.

(485) LOC   NOM
       waye-rã   hia   puyũa ibã
       upriver-LOC good leaves be
       Upriver there are good (roof) leaves.

(486)   NOM   LOC
       hia   puyũa ibã waye-rã
       good leaves be   upriver-LOC
       There are good (roof) leaves upriver.

When the nominal is +definite, such as the proper name in (487) and (488), the construction is locative even with the opposite word orders. Notice that locative constructions such as these allow the location oblique to occur clause medially rather than just on the periphery. Perhaps the choice of order depends on whether the locative or nominal is in focus.

(487) NOM   LOC
     anita-re   wiʔia-reka   ĩbẽ
     Anita-TERM house-LOC.SPEC be
     Anita is in the house.

(488) LOC   NOM
     wiʔia-reka   anita-re   ĩbẽ
     house-LOC.SPEC Anita-TERM be
     Anita is in the house.

A nominal can be made +definite by the use of a demonstrative such as *iʔka* 'this' or *iʔsia* 'that' as in (489). The +definite nominal allows only a locative interpretation. A nominal can also be made specific or definite by indicating possession with a genitive construction (possessor plus head) as in (490).

(489) NOM   LOC
     iʔsi-bĩʔrõa   wiʔia-reka   ĩbã
     that-tobacco house-LOC.SPEC be
     That tobacco is in the house.

(490) NOM   LOC
     yi-wiʔia pusi-pebā-rā ĩbẽ
     1s-house hill-top-LOC be
     My house is on a/the hill.

Generally, then, locative and existential constructions are distinguished by context rather than by word order. It is also likely that the form of the nominal indicates whether the clause is locative or existential. Because nominals that are indefinite or that indicate new information are more likely to be expressed in their full form, clauses with a fully expressed nominal are more likely to be existential. Definite nominals or nominals that are topical are often left implicit or are referenced by a pronoun and are more likely to be locative.

Although both orders (LOC-NOM and NOM-LOC) are allowed, there is a tendency for locatives to occur on the periphery of the clause. Thus, they tend to occur clause initially or finally, independent of any constraints such as Clark has proposed.

Sentence Structure

7.7. Predicate nominal and possessive 'to be'. Predicate nominals indicate the identity, class membership, or predicate adjective description of the subject and one type of possessive. These functions are indicated in several ways. First, identity, class membership and predicate adjectives can be indicated using the copula *ībã* 'to be' as in (491), (492), and (493), respectively.

(491) *yi-rīʔī   ki-ībē*
     1s-younger^brother 3ms-be
     He is my younger brother.

(492) *haʔuraka sa-ībē*
     macaw   3ns-be
     It is a macaw.

(493) *hoʔba-ki ki-ībē*
     big-ms   3ms-be
     He is big.

Predicate nominals can also be formed using a deictic pronoun 'this, that', or a personal pronoun ('he, her', etc. . .) when the copula is omitted. The previous three examples can be expressed with a small change in meaning produced by the deictic pronoun.

(494) *yi-rīʔī   īʔī*
     1s-younger^brother this
     This (one) is my younger brother.

(495) *haʔuraka iʔsia*
     macaw   that
     That is a macaw.

(496) *hoʔba-ki iʔki*
     big-ms   3ms
     He is big.

Finally, predicate adjectives can be expressed with no copula in present tense as in (497).

(497) *werika   āyāka*
     dangerous snake
     The snake is dangerous.

When identifying something as belonging to someone, the case marker *-rika* (possession) is suffixed to the noun phrase that is the owner or possessor (POSSR). The other nominal is the possessed being or object (POSSD). This type of possessive construction is essentially the same as the identity class predicate nominals in that it identifies the possessed nominal. For example, compare the parallel constructions of predicate adjective (498), class membership (499), and possessive (500).

(498) *hoʔba-ka iʔka wiʔia ībē*
     big-n   this house be
     This house is big.

(499) *iʔsia wiyāka haʔuraka sa-ībē*
     that bird   macaw   3ns-be
     That bird is a macaw.

(500) POSSR   POSSD
     hose-rika iʔka wiʔia ībē
     José-POSS this house be
     This house is José's.

Clark argues that possessive constructions are basically the same type of construction as the locative and existential. She states:

> ... that the possessor in the two possessive constructions is simply an animate **place**. The object possessed is located in space, just as the object designed in existential or locative sentences. In possessive constructions, the place happens to be an animate being, such that a +Animate Loc becomes a Pr [possessor]. (1978:89)

She posits two types of possessive constructions. The first possessive which she labels 'poss 1' mirrors the existential construction in that it contains a −definite possessed nominal, such as 'a book' in 'there is a book on the table' (existential) and 'Tom has a book' (poss 1). The second type of possessive construction, 'poss 2', contains a +definite possessed nominal and mirrors the locative construction, such as 'the book is on the table' and 'the book is Tom's'. She demonstrates that in many languages the possessor and locative are equated in locational constructions, and that the possessed and the nominal are treated the same.

In (500), the possessor 'José' precedes the possessed *wiʔia* 'house'. This order, however, is quite variable. Clark's two discourse rules predict that for the dominant word order in a possessive construction, the possessor nominal will precede the possessed nominal. Thus, in (500), rule 1 does not apply in predicting word order since both nominals are +definite. Rule 2 predicts the possessor to precede the possessed since the possessor is +animate. In Clark's sample, the dominant word order in thirty-three of thirty-eight languages is possessor-possessed. The languages with a different order were mainly those with two different verbs in the two possessive constructions, i.e., 'have' versus 'be'.[49] In Retuarã, however, the word order of 'to be' possessive constructions can be either POSSR-POSSD as in (500) or POSSD-POSSR as in (501). This order holds even though all possessive 'to be' constructions are ones where the owned objects (POSSD) are +definite.

(501)   POSSD   POSSR
  i?ka dīyērū paulina-rika
  this money Pauline-POSS
  This money is Paulina's.

There may be a slight preference for the POSSR-POSSD order in Retuarã but this is not an overwhelmingly dominant order.

As Clark points out, the choice of verb 'be' versus 'have' in a possessive may depend on whether the possessor or possessed is theme of the sentence. Therefore to express the possessed as theme, the verb ībā 'to be' is used with the optional POSSD-POSSR order as in (501) where dīyērū 'money' is theme.

7.8. Possessive 'to have'. The other possessive construction employs the verb rika 'to have'. It denotes possession, but not necessarily ownership, as in (502) which is a poss 2 because the possessed yi-sara 'my machete' is +definite. The dominant word order is POSSR-POSSD just as Clark's discourse rules would predict. Rule 1 does not apply in predicting word order since both nominals are +definite, but rule 2 predicts POSSR-POSSD word order since the possessor is +animate and the possessed is −animate.

(502) huā-re   yi-sara   ki-rika-yu
      Juan-TERM 1s-machete 3ms-have-PRES
      Juan has my machete.

Rule 1 predicts POSSR-POSSD word order in (503) because the possessed 'much money' is −definite but the possessor (Juan and Miguel) are +definite. It is an example of a poss 1 (i.e., −definite POSSD).

---

[49]English is one of the five languages that had the reverse order, 'the book is Tom's', but it also has a possessive construction using 'have'. Retuarã has a second verb, rika 'to have', to express possession, as described in §7.8.

(503) *hūā bīgel-ka dīyērū rīkibāka dā-rika-yu*
　　　Juan Miguel-COM money much 3p-have-PRES
　　　Juan and Miguel have much money.

The two possessive constructions using 'to be' or 'to have' tend to differ in the definiteness of the possessed nominal. The *rika* 'to have' possessive construction may have either a definite possessed object, as in (504), or indefinite as in (505).

(504) *hose-re bī-yaiwēkoa ki-rika-yu*
　　　Jose-TERM 2s-dog 3ms-have-PRES
　　　José has your dog.

(505) *mauricio-re rīkibāka iyaka ki-rika-yu*
　　　Mauricio-TERM much grape 3ms-have-PRES
　　　Mauricio has lots of grapes.

The possessive construction using *ībā* 'to be' places the possessed nominal as subject instead of as object in 'to have' possessives. The possessed nominal is definite because the possessive case marker *-rika* indicates ownership which makes them poss 2 constructions. One would expect the possessed nominal to precede the possessor since it is both definite and the subject or theme of the sentence. Clark points out, however, that in many languages there is a strong tendency for the +animate possessor to be in initial position. In languages without a definite article, the definite nature of the possessed is then indicated by an emphatic or topicalization marker. Retuarā does this with either of the demonstratives *ika* 'this' or *i?sia* 'that' as in (506).

(506) POSSR　　　POSSD
　　　hūā-rika i?ka yaiwēkoa ībē
　　　Juan-POSS this dog be
　　　This dog is Juan's.

The demonstrative is retained even in the alternate word order, when the possessed occurs before the possessor as in (507).

(507)　　　POSSD　　POSSR
　　　i?ka īpa-rā yaiwēkoa lui-rika ībē
　　　this two-p dog Lui-POSS be
　　　These two dogs are Lui's.

Sentence Structure

7.9. Reflexives. Overtly marked reflexives are rare in Retuarã. Instead, when the subject receives the action of a verb that could be transitive, the absence of an object noun phrase makes the reflexive implicit as in (508), which is opposed to (509).

(508) *ki-uʔya-koʔo*
 3ms-bathe-PST
 He bathed (himself).

(509) *bāko-re   ko-uʔya-koʔo*
 daughter-TERM 3fs-bathe-PST
 She bathed her daughter.

In other cases, intransitive verbs are inherently reflexive. In (510), the transitive verb *taʔte* 'to cut, chop' requires something other than the subject to receive the action of the verb. In contrast, the intransitive verb *tote* 'to cut, chop (oneself)' in (511) is inherently reflexive; it can only mean that the subject receives the action of the verb.

(510) *sara-pi   ko-re   ki-taʔte-koʔo*
 machete-INSTR 3fs-TERM 3ms-chop-PST
 He cut her with the machete.

(511) *sara-pi   ki-tote-koʔo*
 machete-INSTR 3ms-chop-PST
 He cut himself with the machete.

The only overt method to express a reflexive is to use *poʔia* 'body' as the object as in (512). There is a coreference requirement in this type of construction where *poʔia* 'body' has to be possessed by the subject.

(512) *ki-poʔia ki-hāā-koʔo*
 3ms-body 3ms-kill-PST
 He killed himself.

Often an overt reflexive construction will contain an adverbial phrase such as *ō-yū upaka-ha* 'knowingly' as in (513). The subject of the adverbial phrase is coreferential with the subject of the main verb. This adverbial phrase only occurs in clauses that have a reflexive intent, so it no longer means 'knowingly', but rather, its usage has changed and become lexicalized as a signal of the reflexive nature of the clause.

(513) bã-õ-yũ   upaka-ha   bã-po?ia bã-paki-yu
      12-know-PRES like-ADVLZR 12-body   12-deceive-PRES
      We deceive ourselves.

The above constructions are rare. They seem to be used in unusual or unexpected situations where a reflexive would not be readily inferred without some overt marking such as *po?ia* 'body'. In such cases, the lexicon does not contain an intransive verb that matches the transitive verb's meaning. Thus, the transitive verb is used with *po?ia* to indicate the reflexive meaning.

7.10. Subordinate clauses. Subordinate clauses have a basic word order of OBJ V just like main clauses. Most subordinate clauses tend to precede the main clause. The verb can be nominalized with a number/gender suffix (see §§5.4–5.9), made stative by the suffix *-i*, or adverbialized by a subordinating suffix (see §§11.8–11.17). Example (514) illustrates subordinate clauses with nominalized verbs. Example (515) illustrates a subordinate clause in which the verb has been made stative by the suffix *-i*. Example (516) illustrates an adverbial clause subordinated with the suffix *-bāka* (condition).

(514) *wei-ko?o-a   yiha-i?ta-ko?o ofisidã-rã*
      finish-PST-n 1p-come-PST   office-LOC
      (When) it was finished, we came to the office.

(515) *sa-õbēã   dã-tea-wea-i-ka   sa-itopea a?te*
      3ns-prow   3p-shape^cut-finish-STAT-n   3ns-stern again

   dã-tea-yu
   3p-shape^cut-PRES
   (When) they finish shaping the prow, then they shape its stern.

(516) *werika   bã-re   sa-ībã-bāka   bã-re   hia*
      dangerous   12-TERM   3ns-be-COND   12-TERM   good

   ki-tue-hī-yũ
   3ms-accompany-PSBL-PRES
   When it is dangerous for you, he can accompany you.

8
Imperatives

Retuarã has second-person imperatives, indirect imperatives, negative imperatives, hortatory forms, and third-person imperatives. In all but one of the imperative forms, the verb is inflected for person by the subject prefixes. Imperative constructions do not allow the verb to take aspect or mood affixes.

8.1. Second-person imperatives. Second-person imperatives are marked by *-be* (imperative) and *-pe* (indirect imperative). In (517) and (518), *-be* is suffixed to the verb root to form an imperative. The imperative can also be suffixed to compound verbs as in (519) and can have a continuative aspect when the adverb *rupu* follows the construction.

(517) *bĩ-ĩã-be*
   2s-see-IMP
   Look!

(518) *bĩhã-uku-be*
   2p-drink-IMP
   Drink!

(519) *bĩ-baʔarika bĩ-baʔa-pua-be*
   2s-food   2s-eat-use^up-IMP
   Eat (up) all your food.

(520) bī-baʔirabe-be   rupu
      2s-work-IMP   still
      Keep on working.

8.2. Indirect imperative. The indirect imperative morpheme *-pe* presupposes an intermediate action (usually 'go') before the action of the verb. In (521), the command 'see' requires that the person first go to the location of the event.

(521) ōterikia   bī-rēā-pe
      fruit   2s-collect-IND.IMP
      (Go and) collect fruit!

The implied, normal direction of an indirect command is away from the speaker, which is translated 'go'. If the speaker wants to indicate 'come', then the directional affix *-ra* 'toward' is suffixed to the verb root.[50]

(522) ki-re   bī-īā-ra-pe
      3ms-TERM   2s-see-TWRD-IND.IMP
      (Come and) see him!

The indirect imperative is also used for courtesy; it seems to soften a command. For example, when a person is about to leave another's house, he says 'I am going now' (523). The proper response from those of the house is 'Go!', but it is the indirect form as in (524).

(523) bāē   yi-aʔ-yu   (speaker 1)
      now   1s-go-PRES
      I am going now.

(524) bī-aʔ-pe   (speaker 2)
      2s-go-IND.IMP
      Go!

Another indirect imperative construction exists using the suffix *-korī* (intention). When the construction has a subject prefix, it is a modal of intention as discussed in §5.16. When a subject prefix is absent, it is understood to be a second-person indirect imperative as illustrated in (525).

---

[50]The normal form of the directional is *-raʔa* but the form is always shortened to *-ra* when used with the indirect imperative suffix *-pe*.

Imperatives

(525) *aʔte   hiapũʔrē-korī*
again blow-INT
Go and blow on the fire again.

8.3. Negative imperative. A negative command is formed by suffixing -*aʔsi* to a verb root, like the other imperative-forming suffixes.

(526) *iʔsia bīhā-baʔa-aʔsi*
that 2p-eat-NEG.IMP
Don't eat that!

(527) *ki-re   baʔia-ha   bī-baa-aʔsi*
3ms-TERM bad-ADVLZR 2s-do-NEG.IMP
Don't treat him badly!

The negative imperative can also be used with first- and third-person subjects, in which case it means 'lest'.

(528) *waruā bī-hoe-be   bī-re   yi-hāā-aʔsi   yi-behoa-pi*
fast   2s-burn-IMP 2s-TERM 1s-kill-NEG.IMP 1s-spear-INSTR
Burn it fast lest I kill you with my spear!

(529) *bī-iʔta-be   õʔõ-rā   bī-re   ki-pahe-aʔsi*
2s-come-IMP here-LOC 2s-TERM 3ms-hit-NEG.IMP
Come here lest he hit you!

8.4. Hortatory. A common hortatory construction is formed with the first-person plural inclusive prefix *bā-* (we inclusive i.e., 12), a verb root, and -*ērā* (purpose) as in (530). Other hortatory constructions are possible and are formed by replacing the purpose suffix -*ērā* with -*yeʔe* (contingency) as in (531), or with *aʔri go*, or with *rāyũ* (future).

(530) *sa-bā-ko-ri-ērā*
3ns-12-try-EP-PURP
Let's try it.

The hortatory can be softened to show courtesy or friendship by using the suffix -*yeʔe* (contingency). The construction is an imperative that has the force of a suggestion. It clearly gives the addressee the option of replying or not.

(531) bā-baʔa-yeʔe
12-eat-CNTGN
Let's eat, (shall we)?

Example (533) occurs in the context of a friend encouraging another who killed two game animals, but was unable to kill more due to a lack of ammunition. The speaker is the same in both (532) and (533). For illustrations of the use of -yeʔe (contingency) in adverbial clauses, see §11.12.

(532) hee kopakaha īpa-rā bī-hāā-ti-koʔo
ok now two-p 2s-kill-PERF-PST
Ok, now you have killed two (animals).

(533) iʔsia-raka-bāki-hi bā-baʔa-yeʔe
that-number-p-ADVLZR 12-eat-CNTGN
Let's eat that many (then).

There is also an indirect hortatory form just as with the second-person imperative. The verb stem is inflected for person bā- (we inclusive), and the verb stem aʔri 'go' is suffixed to the verb. The interactional daho 'let's go' is optional, but is often added.

(534) daho riaka-rā bā-uʔya-aʔri
let's^go river-LOC 12-bathe-go
Let's go to the river and bathe.

Though not a grammatical imperative, a future declarative sentence can also be used as a polite imperative. They are used to give instructions or exhortation in a courteous manner.

(535) waeroka bī-ūʔbū-rāyū
tomorrow 2s-begin-FUT
Tomorrow you will begin.

(536) dā-re bā-wayuīā-riha-ri-rāyū
3p-TERM 12-have^compassion-CONT-EP-FUT
We will continue to show them compassion.

8.5. Third-person imperatives. The affix -rū (optative) indicates a third-person imperative which is used to express a wish or desire as illustrated in (537) and (538).

Imperatives

(537) *tŭparã-te   bī-re   heyoa?-ri-rŭ*
God-TERM 2s-TERM accompany-EP-OPT
May God accompany you.

(538) *hia   sa-ībã-rŭ   bī-ro?si*
good 3ns-be-OPT 2s-BEN
May it be good for you. *or* Good luck.

Sometimes *-rŭ* has the meaning 'let, allow' as illustrated in (539).

(539) *bãkarã-te   ba?a-rŭ   bãbãrĩ*
children-TERM eat-OPT first
Let the children eat first.

Example (540) is a phrase often said to children with the intent of a command.

(540) *sa-ībã-rŭ*
3ns-be-OPT
Let it be! (i.e., Don't touch it!)

8.6. Responses to imperatives. The response to any imperative if positive is *hee* 'ok'. A negative response uses *herõ?õ* 'no' and is usually followed with some type of rebuttal or reason for refusal. A negative response may also simply be silence and noncompliance with the imperative.

9

Questions

Questions are formed by adding a question marker (content and one type of yes/no marker) to an indicative clause. The question marker is usually clause initial. Typically the intonation of a question rises slightly at the end.

9.1. Yes/no questions. There are two yes/no question markers. One, *yahe* is usually clause initial and sentential in its scope. It does not occur in negative questions. The scope of the other yes/no question marker, *bai*, extends only to constituents of the sentence and can occur in positive or negative questions.

In (541), the scope of *yahe* includes both the time *waeroka* 'tomorrow' and locative *ātabākabākarā* 'La Pedrera' (a town).

(541) *yahe waeroka ki-aʔ-ri-rāyū ātabākabāka-rā*
    Y/N tomorrow 3ms-go-EP-FUT Pedrera-LOC
    Will he go to Pedrera tomorrow?

The constituent Y/N question marker *bai* does not occur in clause-initial position. Its scope only extends to the constituent that precedes it. In (542), the verb *wiri* 'to appear' precedes *bai*. The speaker is not questioning the spirit's existence, but rather if it appeared to the addressee. The English gloss has the form of a tag question to give the sense, but it is not a tag question in Retuarā.

(542) *siparā upaka bī-re wi-ri-be-yu-a bai heʔe*
    spirit like 2s-TERM appear-EP-NEG-PRES-n Y/N SUP
    Something like a spirit didn't appear to you? (did it?)

Since *bai* focuses on a constituent, it lends prominence to a specific part of the question. As a result, it is sometimes used to form a rhetorical question that has a scolding intent. In (543), *bai* focuses on the verb and, in particular, the continuative aspect *-yūhū* which is translated 'still'. In (544), the constituent 'also' is questioned.

(543) *bīhā-re oka-be-ri-yūhū-i-ka   bai*
      2p-TERM satisfy-NEG-EP-CONT-STAT-n Y/N
      It is **still** not enough for you?

(544) *i?ki oka bai īpi*
      3ms also Y/N chief
      Is he **also** a chief?

A negative question can also be formed with a negative indicative clause and rising intonation clause finally. There is no overt question marker in the construction apart from the intonation. Example (545) illustrates a negative clause which is intended as a question as seen by the fact that it is answered in (546). The intonation rises on *bī-re* (second-person singular)

(545) *ba?arika ībā-be-yu-a   bī-re*
      food   be-NEG-PRES-n 2s-TERM
      You don't have food?

(546) *herō?ō ībā-be-yu-a   yi-re*
      no   be-NEG-PRES-n 1s-TERM
      No, I don't have (any).

9.2. Content questions. All content questions have interrogative pronouns in clause-initial position. Following is a variety of examples of content questions.

(547) *dō?ō-rā   bī-a?-yu*
      where-LOC 2s-go-PRES
      Where are you going?

(548) *dī?ī   yi-heyobāki*
      which 1s-friend
      Which friend of mine?

(549) *bārākā?ā yahe to-rā   bī-ībē*
      how   Y/N there-LOC 2s-be
      How are you doing there?

Questions

The interrogative pronouns can also be used in negative declarative sentences to indicate nonexistence. For example, *da?koa* 'what' means 'nothing' when the verb is negated as in (550). Similarly, *bāki* 'who' has the sense of 'no one' when used in the negated declarative sentence in (551).

(550) *da?koa a?pea ībā-be-yu-a*
what other be-NEG-PRES-n
There's nothing like it.

(551) *bāki herō?ō ki-re   ā-rī-be-ri-hī-i-ka*
who no   3ms-TERM say-EP-NEG-EP-PSBL-STAT-n
No one can say no to him.

9.3. Alternate questions. Alternate questions are like content questions in form except that the alternative statement follows the question. The two alternatives are differentiated by rising intonation on the first, followed by a pause and falling intonation on the second. In (552), the intonation rises on the word *ire* 'today' and falls on *waeroka* 'tomorrow'. In (553), the intonation rises on 'coca cola' and falls on 'fanta'.

(552) *bārāpate ki-a?-ri-rāyū ire   waeroka*
when   3ms-GO-EP-FUT today tomorrow
When will he go, today or tomorrow?

(553) *dika bī-uku-ri-yapa-wai-a kokakola fanta*
which 2s-drink-EP-like-HAB-n coca^cola fanta
Which do you usually like to drink, coca cola or fanta?

9.4. Indirect questions. Indirect questions occur embedded within indicative sentences, imperatives, and other questions. These constructions are a subset of constructions (with sensory, cognition, or utterance verbs) that take object complements (see §11.5). The embedded questions have the same form as a simple content question. (554) is an indirect question in an indicative sentence, and is marked by brackets. Example (555) illustrates the question *bāki eta-ko?o-ki* 'who arrived?' in an imperative sentence and (556) is a question within a question.

(554) *yi-ō-rī-be-yu   [bāki eta-rāyū]*
1s-know-EP-NEG-PRES who arrive-FUT
I don't know who will arrive.

(555) bī-īā-pe   [bāki eta-koʔo-ki]
      2s-see-IND.IMP who   arrive-PST-ms
      (Go and) see who arrived!

(556) yahe bī-re   ki-ā-rī-koʔo   [dōʔō-hi-rā   dā-eta-koʔo]
      Y/N 2s-TERM   3ms-say-EP-PST where-EXTENT-LOC   3p-arrive-PST
      Did he say to you how many arrived?

9.5. Courtesy in question-asking. Because a question imposes some obligation or pressure on the addressee to answer, speakers will occasionally lessen the obligation of the question with the adverb *heʔe* (supposition). This is translated 'perhaps' and functions much the same way as it would in English to soften the imposition of a question.

(557) yahe ki-re   bī-yapa-yu heʔe bāko   ko-re   ki-ā-yū
      Y/N 3ms-TERM   2s-like-PRES SUP daughter 3fs-TERM   3ms-say-PRES
      "Do you like him perhaps, daughter?" he says to her.

The effect of *heʔe* is to lessen the demand for an answer, thus coaxing or inviting a response. This is similar to the use of *-yeʔe* (contingency) with courteous imperatives, where compliance to the imperative is overtly put into the hands of the addressee (see §8.4).

9.6. Answers to questions. Yes/no questions are often answered with single words. Most commonly they are answered affirmatively with *āʔā* 'yes' or negatively with *herōʔō* 'no'. Content questions will also often have abbreviated answers as in (559). The section marked by brackets is necessary for grammatical accuracy but is often omitted in actual speech.

(558) dōʔō-rā   bī-aʔ-yu
      where-LOC   2s-go-PRES
      Where are you going?

(559) waʔi-baa-rī   [yi-aʔ-yu]
      fish-catch-PURP   1s-go-PRES
      [I'm going] to fish.

Responding in the negative to a question or request can cause embarrassment or shame. Thus, such questions or requests often go unanswered to avoid the problem for both parties.

10
Negation

This section will discuss negation at both the sentence level and the constituent level. There are two other areas of negation in Retuarã including manner adverbial constructions (see §11.3) and the negative imperative (see §8.3).

10.1. Sentential negation. Sentence negation is expressed by the verbal suffix *-be* (negative), which immediately follows the verb root. Negated declarative sentences with pronominal subjects most commonly have (O) V+S S word order. Affirmative declaratives are typically (O) S+V. A comparison of (560) and (561) illustrates the more common word order for the affirmative and negative respectively.

(560) OBJ   PRSUB+V

wiyawaia yi-ĩã-yu
airplane 1s-see-PRES
I see the airplane.

(561) OBJ   V+S   SUBJ

wiyawaia ĩã-be-yu-ka   yiʔi
airplane see-NEG-PRES-ms 1s
I don't see the airplane.

These examples have the same form as copular sentences with predicate nominals. It seems that (562) could be translated literally as, 'I am a not-knower'.

(562) õ-rī-be-yu-ka   yi?i
      know-EP-NEG-PRES-ms 1s
      I don't know.

Negative declaratives with noun phrase subjects, however, often exhibit a preverbal order for the subject noun phrase. In (563), the number/gender suffix -a agrees with the subject āūā 'cassava'.

(563) āūā   ībā-be-ri-ko?o-a
      cassava be-NEG-EP-PST-n
      There wasn't any cassava.

The negated declarative can also have S+V word order like the affirmative although postposing the subject pronoun is not as common as the (O) V+S S order. (564) illustrates the S+V order. Examples (565) and (566) illustrate both word orders for negative sentences in the past tense.[51]

(564) OBJ   PRSUB+V
      ki-re   dā-īā-wārū-be-ri-re?ka
      3ms-TERM 3p-see-able-NEG-EP-PST
      They didn't recognize him.

(565) bikitoho a?ri-be-ri-ko?o-ko i?ko
      early   go-NEG-EP-PST-fs   3fs
      She didn't go early.

(566) bikitoho ko-a?ri-be-ri-ko?o
      early   3fs-go-NEG-EP-PST
      She didn't go early.

Although the negated declarative sentence can exhibit either ordering of the pronominal subject and verb, the affirmative declarative can only have the free subject pronoun preceding the verb. Thus, (567) is judged grammatical, but (568) is not.

---

[51]In the immediate and remote past tenses, the suffix -be (negative) is followed by the epenthetic syllable -ri. The affix -ri has a function related to stress, independent of the negator. For further discussion see §1.17.

(567) SUBJ OBJ   V+S

  yiʔi wiʔia baa-rapa-ki
  1s   house make-PST-ms
  I built the house.

(568) OBJ   V+S   SUBJ

  *wiʔia baa-rapa-ki yiʔi
  house make-PST-ms 1s
  *I built the house.

The negation of a verb extends to just the clause that contains the negative morpheme; it does not extend, for example, to an object complement. Thus in (569), the negation of the matrix verb does not imply whether the event of the complement occurred or not.

(569) *yi-aʔ-ri-ri-ka   ki-wiʔia-rã   ko-yapa-be-ri-koʔo*
  1s-go-EP-DVBL-n 3ms-house-LOC 3fs-want-NEG-EP-PST
  She didn't want me to go to his house.
  *She wanted me to not go to his house.

With causative constructions, negation applies to the lexical verb. Example (570) implies that they did not, in fact, eat rather than a negation of the causative with the meaning 'he did not make them eat'.

(570) *dã-re   ki-baʔa-rõhe-be-ri-koʔo rupu*
  3p-TERM 3ms-eat-CAUS-NEG-EP-PST yet
  He didn't let them eat yet. *or* He caused them to not eat.

10.2. Negative verb. The negative verb *bã* 'to not be' is used to negate constituents of the clause by expressing the lack or absence of the constituent.[52] It most often occurs with the deverbalizer *-ri* (which becomes nasalized *-rĩ*) and a nominalizer. In this nominal form it takes modifiers such as nouns, verbs, adjectives, or adverbs which express the object or quality that is absent. Its scope extends to just that constituent. In (571),

---

[52]In the majority of other languages in the Tucanoan family, the negative verb 'to not be' occurs with a form such as *bãdĩ* (Barasana and Tuyuca), *bã* (Guanano), and *bãrĩ* (Tucano). All of these (including Retuarã *-bã*) are realized phonetically as [ma], [mani], or [mañi]. Payne (1990) notes that there is "a widespread form of a negative morpheme, usually similar to the shape *ma* [which] extends outside the bounds of the usual South American context...to include Mayan." In his data the morpheme *ma* occurs crosslinguistically as a free form, a suffix, and a prefix.

the noun *parua* 'plantain' is negated by *bā* 'not be'. In its role as a modifier, final *-a* drops off the noun *parua*.

(571) *herōʔō paru-bā-rī-a   iʔsia*
      no   plantain-not^be-DVBL-n that
      No, that's not a plantain.

In other usages an animate number/gender suffix may follow the negator as illustrated by *-rā* (plural) in (572). A literal translation such as 'we saw no hands people' might illustrate the modifier role of the noun.

(572) *pita-bā-rī-rā-te   yiha-īā-rape*
      hand-not^be-DVBL-p-TERM   1p-see-PST
      We saw people without hands.

In (573) and (574), the negated constituents are verb roots. In (575) the verb *bā* negates an adverb of location. The nominalization *-bā-rī-a* is subsequently adverbialized by *-hV*.

(573) *ki-heyo-bā-rī-ka   yiʔi*
      3ms-help-not^be-DVBL-ms 1s
      I'm not his friend.

(574) *īā-bā-rī-ki   iʔki*
      see-not^be-DVBL-ms 3ms
      He is blind.

(575) *ruʔ-yu-rā yoe-rā-bā-rī-a-ha*
      flee-PRES-p far-LOC-not^be-DVBL-n-ADVLZR
      They don't flee far.

(576) illustrates negation of predicate adjectives and (577) illustrates negation of quantifiers.

(576) *hāhī-bā-rī-a   ki-haa-ri-koʔo*
      strong-not^be-DVBL-n 3ms-become-EP-PST
      He became weak.

(577) *kūpahī-bā-rī-a   sa-ībē*
      little-not^be-DVBL-n 3ns-be
      There's a lot (not a little).

Negation

The negative verb *bā* may also occur with the interrogative pronoun *daʔkoa* 'what' to mean 'nothing' or 'empty'. Locations or areas that are negated can be expressed with *bā* plus the locative *-to* 'there'.

(578) *āūā   bā-baʔa-rā-ka daʔko-bā-rī-a*
cassava 12-eat-FUT-n   what-not^be-DVBL-n
If one eats cassava, nothing (happens to you).

(579) *rata-koʔa   daʔko-bā-rī-a   sa-ībā-koʔo*
can-CLAS^(bowl) what-not^be-DVBL-n 3ns-be-PST
The can was empty.

(580) *yapu-bā-to-rā   ki-tu-rape*
tree-not^be-there-LOC 3ms-travel-PST
He traveled in an area without trees.

(581) *īʔrā-ri-kōrī-bā-to   yi-ō-rī-be-yu*
one-INDEF-place-not^be-there 1s-know-EP-NEG-PRES
I don't understand some (story) parts. *or* More than one place I don't understand.

11
Subordination

Clauses may be subordinated as internally headed relative clauses, object complements, or adverbial clauses.

11.1–11.2 Relative clauses

11.1. Internally headed classification. Relative clauses in Retuarã are not common. They are of the internal-head type which Comrie (1981:138) defines as follows:

> In the clearest examples of the internal-head type of relative clause, the head noun remains expressed within the relative clause, in the usual form for a noun of that grammatical relation within a clause, and there is no overt expression of the head in the main clause.

The restricting clause in Retuarã is nominalized by a number/gender suffix which agrees with the head rather than the subject. This agreement is another area of the grammar that rests on the noun class system. The embedded clause takes a case marker where applicable following the number/gender suffix to show the clause's case role in the matrix clause. This type of construction is consistent with Keenan's (1985:161) data on internal relative clauses in which he states:

> First let us establish that internal RCs are indeed NPs, a point which in some cases at least is not immediately obvious since the domain noun occurs in a normal NP position in Srel [restrictive clause] and

consequently Srel may appear to be simply some sort of subordinate clause rather than an NP ... it seems best to treat Srel as a clause which has been sufficiently nominalized to take determiners, case markings, and adpositions, all properties which are characteristic of NPs.

Example (582) illustrates this type of internally headed construction. The head of the relative clause, *bē?rō* 'girl', is contained within the restrictive clause. The restrictive clause is nominalized by the number/gender suffix *-ko* (feminine singular) which agrees with the head, and the entire clause is related to the main clause by the case marker *-te* (term) which follows *-ko*.[53]

(582) *[bē?rō-te āyāka rīka-ko?o]-ko-te   yi-īā-ko?o*
girl-TERM snake step^on-PST-fs-TERM 1s-see-PST
I saw the girl who stepped on the snake.

As mentioned previously (see §5.2), the number/gender suffixes, *-ko* (feminine singular) *-ki* (masculine singular), *-ka* (neuter, masculine singular), *-rā* (plural) and *-a* (neuter) can be optionally used in independent clauses to mark agreement with the subject. In a relative clause, however, these suffixes do not agree with the subject, but rather with the head as in (583). The subject person marker prefix *ko-* (feminine singular) is feminine but the number/gender suffix *-ki* (masculine singular) is masculine and agrees with the head *bē?rī* 'boy'. Thus the verb of the restricting clause may often have both prefix and suffix person markers (with different referents).

(583) *[bē?rī-te ki-ro?si īkoa   ko-wapahī-rapa]-ki-te o-yu*
boy-TERM 3ms-BEN medicine 3fs-buy-PST-ms-TERM   cry-PRES
The boy she bought medicine for is crying.

The form of the term case marker may be either *-re* or *-te* within the restricting clause, but when the head is a term (human subject, object, or recipient) in the main clause, the case marker suffixed to the restricting clause is always *-te,* never *-re*. When the head is animate but not human or a proper name as in (584), the number/gender suffix *-a* (neuter) is used and agrees with the head of the restricting clause. The case marker *-te* (term) is not present since the subject of the main clause 'snake' is nonhuman. The reader will remember that term case marking occurs only

---

[53]In all the examples, the head will be bold and the restrictive clause will be bracketed.

on human or proper name subjects, objects, or recipients. Thus there is no case marking on restrictive clauses when a nonhuman head has the role of subject (584), object, or recipient in the main clause. In (585) the restricting clause is case-marked since it is the benefactive in the matrix clause.

(584) *[āyāka bē?rī-te   kuku-ko?o]-a werika   sa-ībā-ko?o*
      snake boy-TERM bite-PST-n   dangerous 3ns-be-PST
      The snake that bit the boy was dangerous.

(585) *[yaiwēkoa bī-īā-ko?o]-a-ro?si i?ka ba?a-ri-ka ībē*
      dog   2s-see-PST-n-BEN   this eat-DVBL-n be
      This food is for the dog you saw.

If the head is inanimate as in (586) and (587), the number/gender suffix may be *-a* or *-ka* depending on the tense.

(586) *waibikirāka yi-hāā-ko?o [dā?ōka   peka*
      tapir   1s-kill-PST yesterday shot^gun

   yi-wapahī-rapa[54]*]-ka-pi*
   1s-buy-PST-n-INSTR
   I killed the tapir with the shot gun I bought yesterday.

(587) *[sara-pi   karaka ki-hāā-ko?o]-a-pi āyāka yi-hāā-ko?o*
      machete-INSTR chicken 3ms-kill-PST-n-INSTR snake 1s-kill-PST
      With the same machete he killed the chicken, I killed the snake.

Case markers occurring at the end of the restricting clause following the number/gender suffix, indicate the role of the relative clause in the matrix clause. For example, in (587) the case marker *-pi* (instrument) indicates that the nominalized clause referring to *sara* 'machete' is the instrument in the main clause. In (585), *-ro?si* (benefactive) indicates that the nominalized clause has the benefactive case role in the matrix clause. Diegueño (a language from S. California–N. Mexico) operates the same way. Comrie says it is clear that "... a clause is functioning as a noun phrase referring to the head ... where the clause in question can take the appropriate suffix to indicate its syntactic role in the main clause ... " (p. 138).

---

[54]The recent past tense suffix *-rape* has the form *-rapa* when it takes number/gender suffixes. The suffix *-ka* is always used with *-rapa* (recent past) for agreement with neuter subjects, or for nominalizing the verb phrase.

When relativizing into the subject, object, or recipient and the head of the relative clause is pronominal (referring to a human) rather than a full noun phrase, the pronoun is omitted and the head is referred to only by the number/gender suffix. This is a gapping strategy and is illustrated by comparing the independent clause of (588) with the relative clause of (589) which relativizes into the object. The clitic pronoun *ki-* (masculine singular) and its case marker *-re* (term) are omitted in (589). The location where one would expect to find the pronoun is marked with 'Ø'.

(588) *kūāparāka ki-re   tute-koʔo*
      scorpion   3ms-TERM   sting-PST
      The scorpion stung him.

(589) *[kūāparāka Ø tute-koʔo]-ki-te   hī-yū*
      scorpion   sting-PST-ms-TERM sick-PRES
      The one that the scorpion stung is sick.

When the full noun phrase *bēʔrī* 'boy' is substituted for the pronoun, it is expressed in the relative clause as in (590).

(590) *[kūāparāka bēʔrī-te   tute-koʔo]-ki-te   hī-yū*
      scorpion   boy-TERM   sting-PST-ms-TERM sick-PRES
      The boy that the scorpion stung is sick.

Pronominal subject prefixes are also omitted when relativizing into the subject. In (591), the pronominal subject prefix *ki-* (masculine singular) is omitted, yet is understood because of the number/gender suffix *-ki* (masculine singular).

(591) *yi-ō-yū   [yi-re   Ø-kareʔe-koʔo]-ki-te*
      1s-know-PRES   1s-TERM   Ø-rob-PST-ms-TERM
      I know the one who robbed me.

Thus pronominal heads that are terms are omitted while pronouns with other case roles are retained. In (592), the pronominal head *ki-* (masculine singular) is retained with the comitative case marker *-ka*.

(592) *[peta-rā   ki-ka   yi-tu-ri-koʔo]-ki-te   hī-rī-koʔo*
      downriver-LOC 3ms-COM 1s-travel-EP-PST-ms-TERM sick-EP-PST
      The one (masc) I traveled downriver with was sick.

Examples (593) and (594) contain slots for two pronominal clitics, both *ki-* (masculine singular) with term and benefactive case roles. The head of the

Subordination

relative clause can be determined by the omission of the pronominal in the term case role. Thus, in (593), the omission of the the subject prefix *ki-* (masculine singular) (marked by ∅) indicates that the missing subject of the restricting clause is the head of the relative clause. In (594), the inclusion of the subject prefix indicates that the subject of the restricting clause is not the head of the relative clause and thus the clitic pronoun in the benefactive case role, *ki-roʔsi* 'for him', is the head of the relative clause.

(593) *[īkoa   ki-roʔsi   ∅-wapahī-rapa]-ki-te po-ri-rāyū   waeroka*
      medicine 3ms-BEN   ∅-buy-PST-ms-TERM   leave-EP-FUT tomorrow
      The one who bought the medicine for him will leave tomorrow.

(594) *[īkoa   ki-roʔsi   ki-wapahī-rapa]-ki-te po-ri-rāyū   waeroka*
      medicine 3ms-BEN   3ms-buy-PST-ms-TERM leave-EP-FUT tomorrow
      The one for whom he bought medicine will leave tomorrow.

When both pronouns are terms as in (595) and (596), the omitted pronoun is the head. Example (595) illustrates relativization into the object, while (596) illustrates relativization into the subject.

(595) *[∅ ki-īā-koʔo]-ko-te   boebaa-yu*
      3ms-see-PST-fs-TERM be^angry-PRES
      The one (fem) he saw is angry.

(596) *[ko-re   ∅-īā-koʔo]-ki-te   boebaa-yu*
      3fs-TERM ∅-see-PST-ms-TERM be^angry-PRES
      The one (masc) who saw her is angry.

In the present tense, relative clause constructions with pronominal heads also omit tense marking. A comparison of (597) and (598) illustrates the omission of any tense marker in (598), indicated by ∅.

(597) *[ki-īā-rapa]-ko-te   ki-yapa-yu*
      3ms-see-PST-fs-TERM 3ms-like-PRES
      He likes the one (fem) he saw.

(598) *[ki-īā-∅]-ko-te   ki-yapa-yu*
      3ms-see-∅-fs-TERM 3ms-like-PRES
      He likes the one (fem) he sees.

In summary then, a gap strategy can be used for pronominal heads when the head is a subject or object in the restricting clause. Pronominal heads that are not subjects or objects are not gapped but rather are expressed (i.e., a nonreduction strategy of relativization). Similarly, all full noun phrase heads are expressed in the restricting clause regardless of their case role. These observations are consistent with Keenan and Comrie's (1977) Accessibility Hierarchy in (599) which summarizes the ease of relativization into various positions in the restricting clause.[55]

(599) Accessibility hierarchy of Keenan and Comrie

Subject > Direct object > Indirect object >
Object of pre- or postposition > Possessor

Keenan (1985) states:

... if a given language can relativize a position low on the Hierarchy by gapping then it can generally relativize all higher positions by gapping. Thus NPrel [position relativized into] is most likely to be gapped if it is the subject of Srel [restricting clause], next most likely if it is the direct object, etc. And at the bottom of the Hierarchy we find that possessors are very rarely relativized by gapping... (p. 154)

He further suggests the generalization that "more positions can be relativized if personal pronouns are presented in the NPrel position than if they are not" (p. 155).

11.2. Relativization into different syntactic positions. It is possible to relativize into the following syntactic positions: subject, object, recipient, instrument, comitative, locative,[56] and possessive.

Relativization into subject.

(600) *[yaiwēkoa yi-re   wape-ko?o]-a yapa-be-yu-ka   yi?i*
      dog   1s-TERM bark-PST-n   like-NEG-PRES-ms 1s
      I don't like the dog that barked at me.

---

[55]The Accessibility Hierarchy cited in Keenan and Comrie (1977) is slightly different from what appears here. The table in (599) is taken from Keenan (1985) since the following quote by Keenan refers to the modified version.

[56]Relativization into the locative position deviates from the normal pattern of using number/gender suffixes to agree with the head. All relativizations into locative use *-rō?õ* 'place' to mark agreement with the locative head.

Subordination

(601) *[bē?rī-te sara riata-ko?o]-ki-te yi-bō?ã-yu*
 boy-TERM machete lose-PST-ms-TERM 1s-search-PRES
 I am searching for the boy that lost the machete.

Relativization into object.

(602) *[bē?rō-te ko-wape-ko?o]-ko-te o-yu*
 girl-TERM 3fs-scold-PST-fs-TERM cry-PRES
 The girl she scolded is crying.

(603) *[bē?rī-te sara riata-ko?o]-a yi-bō?ã-yu*
 boy-TERM machete lose-PST-n 1s-search-PRES
 I am searching for the machete that the boy lost.

Relativization into recipient.

(604) *[ba?a-ri-ka bākarā-te yi-īhī-ko?o]-rā-te o-ri-tiyi-ko?o*
 eat-DVBL-n children-TERM 1s-give-PST-p-TERM cry-EP-stop-PST
 The children I gave the food to stopped crying.

Relativization into instrument.

(605) *[sara-pi yapua yi-ta?te-ko?o]-a rīkia sa-ībē*
 machete-INSTR tree 1s-cut-PST-n heavy 3ns-be
 The machete I cut the tree with is heavy.

Relativization into benefactive.

(606) *[yaiwēkoa-ro?si ba?a-ri-ka yi-pātā-ko?o]-a yi-re wape-ko?o*
 dog-BEN eat-DVBL-n 1s-leave-PST-n 1s-TERM bark-PST
 The dog that I left the food for barked at me.

Relativization into comitative.

(607) *[bē?rī-ka ko-tu-rapa]-ki-te hī-yū*
 boy-COM 3fs-travel-PST-ms-TERM sick-PRES
 The boy she traveled with is sick.

Relativization into locative.

(608) *[wiʔia-rā aʔpe-rā-te   ībā-rapa]-rōʔō-rā dā-kāka-rape*
       house-LOC other-p-TERM be-PST-place-LOC 3p-enter-PST
       They entered the house where the others were.

Relativization into possessive

(609) *[ki-rika iʔka yaiwēkoa ībā]-ki-te   yi-ō-yũ*
       3ms-POSS this dog   be-ms-TERM 1s-know-PRES
       I know the one whose dog this is.

11.3–11.7 Complementation

Retuarã allows a variety of object complements, that is, clauses embedded as the object of the verb, but I have found no examples of subject complements.

There are various categories of verbs that take object complements, including modality, manipulative, cognition, utterance, sensory, and motion verbs. Transitive constructions with complements that express frustrated intent will also be discussed.

The table in (610) summarizes some of the distinctive features of the verb categories that take object complements. Included in the the table is a column describing the 'boundedness' of the complement verb. Hopper and Thompson (1984:743) discuss matrix verbs that are high on the binding scale and the corresponding reduction of prototypical verbal characteristics in their complement verbs. The table briefly illustrates the various categories of verbs that take object complements and describes some of the main indicators of the reduction of the complement verb.

> Givón (1980a) shows a strong correlation between the degree to which the event described by a V is 'bound' by another V and the degree to which it is formally 'reduced'. A V is high in the 'binding scale' to the extent that its agent or experiencer exerts a strong influence over that of the complement clause (as in Eng. *force*), or is strongly purposive in accomplishing the event in the complement (as in Eng. *succeed*), or has a strong emotional commitment to the possibility of the realization of the complement event (cf. Eng. *want*).
>
> Givón presents evidence from a range of languages to demonstrate that, in general, the higher a V is on the binding scale, the more

its complement V (a) will tend to not be independent, but will be structurally integrated into the main clause; and (b) will fail to express independent tense/aspect/modality. That is, the HIGHER a V is on the binding scale, the LOWER the degree of categoriality of the complement V.

(610) Verb categories that take object complements

Verb Category	Switch Reference	Examples of Verb Types	Complement Clause Bound or Free
Modality	either s.s. or d.s.	plan want remember	bound—comp. clause has infinitival form plus equi-subj. deletion
Manipulative	different subject	do help	bound—subject of comp. clause raised to obj. of manipulative verb comp. verb subordinated
Sensory Cognition Utterance	different subject	see think say	free—comp. clause has form of an independent clause (no raising to obj.)
Motion verbs with purpose complements	same subject	go come run	bound—no overt subject marking. Subordinating suffix on comp. verb
Preventative	different subject	all transitive verbs	bound—subject of comp. clause raised to obj. of preventative verb comp. verb subordinated

11.3. Modality verbs. Givón (1984:117) defines modality verbs as those that take a complement whose subject is coreferential with its own. Accordingly the equi-subject is deleted in the complement leaving simply an infinitival verb. In Retuarã, however, some modality verbs such as *yapa* 'want' can also take a complement whose subject is not coreferential with its own. In such cases, the subject of the complement is not deleted. Example (611) illustrates a modality verb and complement with the same subject. The complement 'she gets fish' drops subject marking since it has the same subject as the matrix verb (and all other inflection) and is nominalized. In (612), the subject prefix *yi-* (first-person singular) is retained in the complement since it is different from the the subject of the modality verb *yapa* 'want'.

(611) *waʔia eʔe-ri-ka   ko-yapa-yu*
      fish   get-DVBL-n 3fs-want-PRES
      She wants to get fish.

(612) *waʔia yi-eʔe-ri-ka   ko-yapa-yu*
      fish   1s-get-DVBL-n 3fs-want-PRES
      She wants me to get fish.

Additionally, when the subject of the complement is the same as a modality verb like *yapa* 'want' or *peyo* 'reject', the complement verb can occur in a compound verb construction such as (613). Like (611) and (612), the modality verbs require a complement with nominal characteristics, so the complements in (613) and (614) are deverbalized by the affix *-ri*.

(613) *yi-kā-rī-rī-yapa-yu*
      1s-sleep-EP-DVBL-want-PRES
      I want to sleep.

(614) *ko-re   ki-īā-rī-peyo-rape*
      3fs-TERM 3ms-see-DVBL-reject-PST
      He rejected seeing her. *or* He was hostile toward her.

Givón semantically subdivides modality verbs according the property of implicativity (positive, negative, or neutral). When an implicative verb is itself true, it implies the truth of its complement clause or verb. Neg-implicative verbs are those that imply the falsity of their complements when the neg-implicative verb is true. Verbs that are neutral in regards to implicativity he calls non-implicative. That is, if the verb is true, it does not imply the truth or falsity of its complement.

The verb 'remember' in (615) is implicative. Since it is true, it implies that the complement clause is also true, i.e., that the speaker did bring water.

(615) *okoa eʔe-raʔa-ri-ka   yi-ō-rī-koʔo*
      water get-TWRD-DVBL-n 1s-remember-EP-PST
      I remembered to bring water.

Subordination

Example (616) with *yekari-* 'forget' is neg-implicative, i.e., its truth implies that the complement is false (or did not occur). Thus, the speaker did not bring water.

(616) *okoa eʔe-raʔa-ri-ka   yi-yekari-ri-koʔo*
water get-TWRD-DVBL-n 1s-forget-EP-PST
I forgot to bring water.

The main verb *yapa* 'want' in (613) is true, but does not imply whether or not the subject did indeed sleep, thus it is non-implicative. The verb *pupahoa* 'think, plan' in (617) is also non-implicative. It does not imply that the subject actually went, or will go. The actuality (or non-actuality) of the event of the clause cannot be determined.

(617) *aʔ-ri-ri-ka   yi-pupahoa-yu*
go-EP-DVBL-n 1s-plan-PRES
I plan to go.

A non-implicative verb becomes neg-implicative if followed by *-kope* (contra-expectation). In (618), it is implied that the event referred to by the complement did not or will not occur. The parenthesis in the gloss supplies the implicit context of the utterance.

(618) *baya-rã   aʔ-ri-ri-ka   yi-pupahoa-kope-yu*
dance-LOC go-EP-DVBL-n 1s-plan-CONTRA-PRES
I plan to go to the dance (but I probably won't).

11.4. Manipulative verbs. Complements to manipulative verbs often require a subordinating suffix on their verb. The subjects of the complement and the main clauses are always different because the subject of the subordinate clause is raised to the role of grammatical object of the main clause. This category includes implicative verbs like *heyobaa* 'help' and an analytical causative construction using *baa* 'do, make'.

If the implicative manipulative verb is true, it implies the truth of its complement. Non-implicative verbs like *hãʔbẽ* 'order' and *hẽyẽ* 'ask, request' do not imply the truth or falsity of their complements. In Retuarã, I have not encountered neg-implicative verbs such as 'prohibit' or 'prevent' that would imply the falsity of the complement when the neg-implicative verb is true. The sense of 'not allow' is expressed using a negated causative construction rather than a verbal complement.

An analytic causative construction is formed with the verb *baa* 'to make' and a subordinate clause. In (619), the intransitive verb, *kã* 'sleep', has *ko-* (feminine singular) as the subject, its single argument. In (620), the same argument (now the causee) is the object marked with *-re* (term).[57] Note that in (620) the verb *kã* 'sleep' is subordinated by *ẽrã* (purpose), and is uninflected for person, number, and tense as would generally be the case for a main verb. The construction in (620) is implicative since the complement is considered true.

(619) *ko-kã-yũ*
3fs-sleep-PRES
She sleeps.

(620) *ko-re   kã-ẽrã   yi-baa-yu*
3fs-TERM sleep-PURP 1s-make-PRES
I make her sleep.

The construction in (621) using 'help' is not a causative, but also has a complement to a manipulative verb that is implicative. Example (622) is non-implicative. One can not infer that the subjects of the complement, 'they', did in fact leave.

(621) *wiʔia baa-ri-ka   yi-re   ki-heyobaa-rape*
house make-DVBL-n 1s-TERM 3ms-help-PST
He helped me make the house.

(622) *wiʔi-baĩpi   dã-re   hãʔbẽ-eʔka-ki dã-po-ri-ẽrã*
house-owner 3p-TERM order-PST-ms 3p-leave-EP-PURP
The house owner ordered them to leave.

11.5. Cognition/utterance/sensory verbs. Cognition, utterance, and sensory verbs all take object complements with subjects that are usually not coreferential with their own subject. The complement and main clauses are not tightly bound, unlike manipulative verbs, since the subject of the complement is not raised to the role of grammatical object of the main clause. The complement clause is identical to an independent clause and shows no subordinating suffixes. Cognition verbs include *õrĩ* 'know' and *pupahoa* 'think'. Examples of utterance verbs are *ãrĩ* 'say' and *boha* 'tell'. Examples of sensory verbs include *ĩã* 'see' and *ãʔbũtiri* 'hear'. These verbs can be divided by the property of 'factivity'. Givón states:

---

[57]The person prefix marker *ko-* can only be an object since it is case-marked with *-re*. Person prefixes in the role of subject only occur prefixed to the verb, never case marked (see §4.1). The noun phrase has been raised to the grammatical object of the matrix verb.

Subordination

A verb is said to be factive if its complement sentence is true either when the main clause/verb is true or false... A verb may be considered neg-factive if either its affirmative or negative implies the falsity of the complement. (p. 119)

Factive. The complement in (623) and (624) 'José loved her' is true whether the cognition verb 'know' is affirmative as in (623), or negative as in (624).

(623) *dā-ō-rī-reʔka   jose-re   ko-re   ki-yapa-reʔka*
3p-know-EP-PST José-TERM 3fs-TERM 3ms-love-PST
They knew José loved her.

(624) *dā-ō-rī-be-ri-reʔka   jose-re   ko-re   ki-yapa-reʔka*
3p-know-EP-NEG-EP-PST José-TERM 3fs-TERM 3ms-love-PST
They did not know José loved her.

Example (625) illustrates a factive utterance verb *boha* 'tell'. The complement 'he saw her' is true whether the utterance verb is affirmed or negated. It is *boha* 'tell' that is negated in the example.

(625) *dā-re   ki-boha-be-ri-koʔo   ko-re   ki-īā-rape*
3p-TERM 3ms-tell-NEG-EP-PST 3fs-TERM 3ms-see-PST
He did not tell them he saw her.

Sensory verbs by their nature always imply the truth of their complements, thus they are factive and never non-factive or neg-factive. Examples (626) and (627) illustrate factive sensory verbs.

(626) *ki-īā-reʔka   pōʔībāhī-te   sa-pekahāā-reʔka*
3ms-see-PST man-TERM 3ns-shoot-PST
He saw a man shoot it.

(627) *ki-ee-ko-ri-koʔo   yi-āʔbīti-ri-koʔo*
3ms-laugh-AUD-EP-PST 1s-hear-EP-PST
I heard him laugh.

Neg-factive. A neg-factive cognition verb can be derived by suffixing *-kope* (contra-expectation) to a cognition or utterance verb. Thus in (628), the cognition verb, *ōrī* 'know', becomes neg-factive with the addition of *-kope*, and the complement is interpreted as false.

(628) ki-re   yi-īā-rāyū, yi-ō-rī-kope-rape
3ms-TERM 1s-see-FUT 1s-know-EP-CONTRA-PST
I would see him, I knew/thought (but I didn't see him).

Example (629) illustrates *hāʔbē* 'order' as a neg-factive verb after the suffixing of *-kope*. Compare this with the earlier example (622) with the same gloss.

(629) *wiʔi-baīpi   dā-re   hāʔbē-kope-eʔka-ki   dā-po-ri-ērā*
house-owner 3p-TERM order-CONTRA-PST-3ms 3p-leave-EP-PURP
The house owner ordered them to leave, (but they didn't).

Non-factive. Some cognition and utterance verbs are non-factive, i.e., they do not imply that the complement is either true or false. An example of a cognitive non-factive verb is *pupahoa* 'think'. An example of an utterance non-factive verb is *ārī* 'say' or its negation 'don't say'. The following examples with the verb 'say' are non-factive although (631) is stated negatively, and (632) is stated positively.

(630) *ko-tibī-te   boebaa-yu   ko-pupahoa-yu*
3fs-husband-TERM be^angry-PRES 3fs-think-PRES
She thinks her husband is angry.

(631) *bī-bāyēki-te   kīki-be-yu-ka   yiʔi'   bī-ārī-aʔsi*
2s-father^in^law-TERM fear-NEG-PRES-ms 1s   2s-say-NEG.IMP
Don't say to your father-in-law, "I'm not afraid (of you)."

(632) *yi-re   bī-hīʔī-rāyū   ki-re   ko-ārī-royi*
1s-TERM 2s-carry-FUT 3ms-TERM 3fs-say-IMPF
"You will carry me!", she always says to him.

11.6. Motion verbs with purpose complements. Motion verbs such as *iʔta* 'come', *aʔri* 'go', and *eta* 'arrive' can take purpose complements made up of a verb root and its arguments made subordinate by the suffix *-rī* (purpose). The subordinated verb always has the same subject as the motion verb although there is no overt marking. The motion verb is non-implicative since the accomplishment of the complement's purpose can not be verified.

(633) *uʔya-rī   yi-aʔ-yu*
bathe-PURP 1s-go-PRES
I go to bathe.

(634) bĩ-re   tue-rĩ   yi-iʔta-koʔo riobĩka
     2s-TERM accompany-PURP 1s-come-PST orphan
     I came to accompany you, orphan.

The suffix -rĩ can also be used on the interrogative pronoun *daʔko* 'what'. In (635), the slot filled by *daʔko* 'what' matches the slot of the subordinated verb *baʔa* 'eat' that answers the question in (636).

(635) daʔko-rĩ   bĩ-iʔta-koʔo
     what-PURP 2s-come-PST
     For what did you come?

(636) baʔa-rĩ   yi-iʔta-koʔo
     eat-PURP 1s-come-PST
     I came to eat.

When *-kope* (contra-expectation) is suffixed to the motion verb, it becomes neg-implicative. In example (637), it is implied that the event referred to by the complement did not or will not occur. The parenthesis in the gloss supplies the implicit context of the utterance.

(637) yapua ki-rupu   ko-ri-wea-rĩ
     tree 3ms-before cut^down-EP-finish-PURP

     yi-aʔ-ri-ri-yapa-kope-koʔo
     1s-go-EP-DVBL-want-CONTRA-PST
     I wanted to go in order to finish cutting down (my) tree before him, (but he won).

(638) baʔa-rĩ   yi-eta-kope-koʔo
     eat-PURP 1s-arrive-CONTRA-PST
     I came to eat (but there isn't any food.)

11.7. Preventative constructions. The clause subordinated with *-yaka* (intention frustrated) only occurs in negated verb constructions and indicates the frustrated intention of the subject of the subordinated clause which is the grammatical object of the matrix clause. It is the inability of the animate object referent to accomplish his or her intent due to someone or something's interference or prevention. The suffix *-yaka* always indicates switch reference in that the subjects of the subordinate and matrix clause are different. All transitive verbs may be used in the matrix clause.

In (640), the understood subject of *e?e* 'get' is (first-person singular). The context of the example is that an orphan is unable to bring home any fish because a talking deer in the forest keeps taking his catch. Example (639) is the independent form of (640) in the subordinate clause.

(639) *wa?ia e?e-be-yu-ka   yi?i*
       fish   get-NEG-PRES-ms 1s
       I'm not getting/catching (any) fish.

(640) *wa?ia e?e-be-yaka   yi-re   ki-baa-royi*
       fish   get-NEG-INT.FRUS 1s-TERM 3ms-make-IMPF
       He makes me never get/catch fish.

The subordinator *-yaka* cannot be used to express a positive result. Its use in a non-negated clause, as in (641), is judged ungrammatical. Therefore *-yaka* may indicate frustrated intent, but it cannot express this without the negative suffix *-be*.

(641) **e?e-yaka   ki-re   sa-baa-royi-re?ka*
       get-INT.FRUS 3ms-TERM 3ns-do-IMPF-PST
       He got (fish) because it was always doing (this) for him.

The subject of the matrix clause can be inanimate. Thus the cause of the prevention can be a thing or event. For example, the subject of (642), *sa-* (neuter singular), refers to 'coughing' which prevents someone from eating.

(642) *ba?a-be-yaka   ki-re   sa-ībā-royi*
       eat-NEG-INT.FRUS 3ms-TERM 3ns-be-IMPF
       It (coughing) was preventing him from eating.

(643) *kā-rī-be-yaka   ki-re   sa-yi?a-rape*
       sleep-EP-NEG-INT.FRUS 3ms-TERM 3ns-hurt-PST
       He could not sleep because it hurt him.

Although the subject of the matrix clause can be inanimate, the object must be animate or volitional since frustrated intention is involved. A construction containing an inanimate object, as in (644), is judged ungrammatical.

(644) **be-ri-be-yaka   sa-ko-hie-ko?o*
       rip-EP-NEG-INT.FRUS 3ns-3fs-fix-PST
       *She fixed it (hammock) so that it would not rip.

11.8–11.17 Adverbial clauses formed by suffixes

Adverbial clauses are formed in two ways in Retuarã. First, a clause may be subordinated with a subordinating suffix. The subordinated clause may be no more than a verb root and the suffix, with or without other inflection and arguments of the subordinate verb. A second way to form an adverbial clause is with a subordinating conjunction and a clause.

The construction that uses a subordinating suffix is less explicit and more tightly bound to the matrix verb than are clauses subordinated by conjunctions. That is, much information such as tense, aspect, mood, and frequently person and number marking are absent on the subordinate verb and must be inferred from the matrix clause. Several of the suffixes, however, indicate switch reference, i.e., that the subjects of the subordinate and matrix clauses are same or different. Adverbial clauses formed with subordinating suffixes are used with familiar topics in which a lot of information can be left implicit.

Clauses subordinated by conjunctions are more explicit and display more inflection. Where there exists a choice between a suffix or a conjunction (such as that between -*tirã* 'after' and *be?erõ?õ* 'prior'), the conjunctions tend to be used more often when the material discussed is unfamiliar and requires more detailed explanation. They also are more likely to be used when, due to insufficient shared knowledge between speaker and hearer, the speaker must be more explicit. Subordination by suffix may be governed to some degree by discourse constraints since suffixes are often used in clause chaining which can lend cohesion to a text.

A sentence can be constructed of several subordinate clauses followed by a matrix clause. The subordinate clauses indicate the logical, or temporal succession of events. Example (645) illustrates this clause chaining in which the subordinating suffix -*tirã* 'after' subordinates two clauses. In (646), the clauses are subordinated by -*pakã?ã* (reason) and -*tirã* 'after'.

(645) *ibī bõ?ã-tirã   sa-ba?a-i-ka   ĩã-tirã   sa-dã-tuyu-yu*
 day search-after 3ns-eat-STAT-n see-after 3ns-3p-track-PRES
 After searching in daylight, upon seeing (what) it ate, they track it.

(646) *a?pe-ri-kuri   īki-rã   sa-hī-pakã?ã   sa-hea-tirã*
 other-INDEF-time deep-LOC 3ns-die-REAS.DS 3ns-dig-after

 sa-dã-e?e-yu
 3ns-3p-get-PRES
 Sometimes because it dies deep (in a hole), after digging it up, they get it.

The order of the dependent and matrix clauses in the sentence is not rigid. It is more common for the dependent clause to precede the matrix clause, but the order may vary. Clauses subordinated by some suffixes and conjunctions vary their position more than others. In general, they seem to follow an iconic principle that clauses are in temporal/logical order. Thus, purpose clauses (see §11.10 and 11.13) follow main clauses while others, which encode prior and/or simultaneous events, usually precede them.

The word order in adverbial clauses is overwhelmingly SOV. When a verb is subordinated by a suffix, the verb must be clause final in the subordinate clause to bear the subordinator, which always occurs as the final element. In (647), a clause is subordinated by *-tirā* 'after'. The subject of the subordinate clause is coreferential with the subject of the matrix clause. In (648), 'the women said to them' is subordinated by the conjunction *upaka* 'like' and has the order SOV followed by the subordinating conjunction.

(647) [OBJ   V] SUBOR   OBJ   PRSUB + VMATRIX
      bīhia eʔe-tirā   ki-re   ki-piʔpe-reʔka
      vine get-after   3ms-TERM   3ms-tie-PST
      After getting vine, he tied him.

(648) [SUBJ   OBJ   V]   SUBOR   PRSUB + VMATRIX
      rōbītika dā-re   ā-rī-reʔka   upaka-ha   sa-ībā-reʔka
      women   3p-TERM   say-EP-PST   like-ADVLZR 3ns-be-PST
      It was like the women said to them.

11.8. Time: after. The suffix *-tirā* 'after'[58] indicates that the event of the subordinate clause immediately precedes the event of the matrix clause. Some subordinating suffixes, such as *-tirā*, require that the subject of the subordinated clause be the same as that of the matrix clause. In such cases, the subject of the subordinate clause is omitted. Example (649) has no overt subject in the subordinate clause but it is understood to be the same as the subject of the matrix clause.

(649) *iʔsi-roka   hai-tirā   ki-pupa-ri-reʔka*
      that-word   speak-after   3ms-spirit-lose-PST
      After speaking that message, he died.

---

[58]This suffix may derive from the aspect suffix, *-ti* (perfect) and the case marker *-rā* (locative). It is analyzed as a single suffix here because of its particular function to form adverbial clauses and because it is probably now a single, morphologically frozen form.

(650) ī?rā-ika aiya	ībā-tirā	a?te	ki-bīa-re?ka
one-ms moon be-after again 3ms-go^upriver-PST
After (he) being (home) a month, he again went upriver.

11.9. Time: simultaneous. The suffix *-baraka* indicates that the event of the subordinate clause is simultaneous with the event of the matrix clause. In (651), 'laughing' and 'talking' are simultaneous with 'working'.

(651) ee-baraka hai-baraka dā-ba?irabe-yu
laugh-SIM talk-SIM   3p-work-PRES
Laughing, talking, they work.

The construction always has the same subject as the matrix verb. When the subjects of the the subordinate and matrix clauses are different, the derivational affix *-hV* (adverbializer) is used to subordinate the verb phrase instead of *-baraka*. The verb phrase subordinated by *-hV* always has the present tense form. In (652), the adverbializer has the form [-hu] since its vowel harmonizes with the preceding vowel.

(652) ki-ba?irabe-yu-hu	dā-wa?ibā-rape
3ms-work-PRES-ADVLZR 3p-play-PST
While he worked, they played.

11.10. Purpose. The suffix *-ērā* (purpose) is used to create a subordinated clause of purpose. It differs from the complement subordinator *-rī* (purpose) (see §11.6) in that it occurs with nonmotion verbs. Clauses subordinated by *-ērā* often follow the main clause. In addition, the main and adverbial clause may have different subjects.

(653) yapu-kotoa yi-pope-re?ka kope-wi?ia tāte-ērā
wood-box 1s-break-PST hole-house cover-PURP
I broke the box in order to cover the grave (with the boards).

Again, the action of the matrix verb is seen as serving to accomplish the event indicated by the subordinate clause. When the subordinated verb is not marked for person, it is understood to have the same subject as the matrix clause as in (653) and (654).

(654) ko-re	bā-hai-hī-yū	ko-yapa-ri-ka	īā-ērā
3fs-TERM 12-talk-PSBL-PRES 3fs-want-DVBL-n see-PURP
One can talk to her in order to see if she wants (to marry).

When the subordinate clause has a different subject than the matrix clause, the subordinated verb has person marking indicating the subject. In (655), the subject of the subordinated verb *taʔa* 'guard' is indicated by the pronominal prefix *ki-* (masculine singular). The subject of the matrix clause is *dā-* (third-person plural).

(655) ki-re   dā-wapahī-reʔka kopereka ki-taʔa-ērā
     3ms-TERM 3p-pay-PST   door   3ms-guard-PURP
     They paid him to guard the door.

11.11. Intention. The modal suffix *-korī* (intention) is also used as a subordinator as illustrated in (656).

(656) *rioa hoe-korī yi-oo-yu*
     field burn-INT 1s-burn-PRES
     Intending to burn the field, I burned myself.

The subject of the clause subordinated by *-korī* is the same as the matrix clause. In example (657), it is understood that the subject of the two clauses is (masculine singular) even though it is unmarked on the verb 'spring' in the adverbial clause. For further discussion of *-korī* see §5.16.

(657) *aʔte pirīta-ērā   baa-korī sa-rā-ha   ki-tūrū-rupa-reʔka*
     again spring-PURP do-INT 3ns-LOC-ADVLZR 3ms-roll-sit-PST
     Again as he was going to spring from there, he somersaulted.

11.12. Contingency. The suffix *-yeʔe* indicates a condition or exhortation relation. That is, contingent upon the existence of some condition, the addressee is exhorted to take a particular action. Often the exhortation has only the force of a suggestion. The clause expressing the condition is subordinated by *-yeʔe* and the main clause is an imperative.

In (659), speaker 2 answers the question in (658) using *-yeʔe* (contingency). It indicates that the command or request (implicit in this case) is contingent on the availability of fish.

(658) *yahe waʔia bī-re   yi-wapaīhī-hī-yū*
     Y/N   fish 2s-TERM 1s-buy-PSBL-PRES
     Should I buy you fish (in town)? (speaker 1)

(659) *āʔā waʔia sa-ībā-yeʔe*
     yes fish 3ns-be-CNTGN
     Yes, if there's fish (buy some). (speaker 2)

Subordination

(660) *bī-rū-rī-ye?e   bī-herīta-be rupu*
     2s-tire-EP-CNTGN 2s-rest-IMP   yet
     If you are tired, keep on resting.

(661) *bāē   waeroka   bī-a?-ri-ye?e   hiyia pi?pe-tirā supatirā*
     now   tomorrow 2s-go-EP-CNTGN   tight tie-after   then

     sa-bī-hī?ī-be
     3ns-2s-carry-IMP
     Now if you go tomorrow, after tying (it) tight, then carry it.

The subordinating conjunction *reka* 'if' (see §11.21) is also used to create a condition clause, but the associated matrix clause indicates a consequence rather than an exhortation. In addition, the difference in usage between constructions containing *-ye?e* and those containing *reka* involves the speaker's perception of the condition as hypothetical or potential. Beekman, Callow, and Kopesec (1981:104) consider the condition-consequence relation to consist of two basic types:

1. The condition is known or assumed not to be the case, or not to have happened, and the speaker gives a hypothetical Consequence.
2. The condition is uncertain, so far as the speaker is concerned, as to whether it took place, is taking place, or will do so.
So, in this relation there is always a hypothetical component present, or else one of uncertainty.
The first type is commonly known as a *contrary-to-fact* (or *contrafactual*) condition. The condition is known not to have taken place, or it is assumed that it did not. The assumption may, of course, be wrong, but that does not affect the relation.
The second type is known as a *potential-fact condition,* and it is subcategorized into *general* conditions, which can refer to any number of *particular* cases, and particular conditions, which refer to only one situation.

It seems that the usage of *-ye?e* is limited to potential-facts with particular conditions. The speaker considers the condition possible and to involve specific people. I have no examples of *-ye?e* expressing exhortations contingent on hypothetical conditions. In contrast, *-reka* has a broad usage involving both hypothetical and potential-fact conditions. Also the usage of *-ye?e* with this type of exhortation may have a connotation of courtesy. This is supported by its usage in polite commands (see §8.4).

11.13. Negative purpose. The suffix *-koreka* (negative purpose) subordinates a clause that indicates the negative purpose of the matrix clause. It has the meaning 'so that something does not occur'. Typically the negative purpose clause follows the matrix clause. Its use is illustrated in (662) and (663) where the subjects of the matrix and subordinate clauses are different. But *koreka* (negative purpose) can also have the same subject (unexpressed but understood) as the matrix clause as in (664).

(662) *hotoa tāte-rūki   arowaka   kāka-koreka*
   pot   close-IMPRS cockroach enter-NEG.PUR
   One covers the pot so that cockroaches don't get in.

(663) *dā-baʔirīhia dā-yaye-rape aʔpe-rā-te   tōpo-koreka*
   3p-things   3p-bury-PST other-p-TERM find-NEG.PUR
   They buried their things so that the others would not find them.

(664) *iʔsi-peʔrōto-rā kia   ko-haʔata-rape waruoka   haʔata-koreka*
   that-side-LOC manioc 3fs-leave-PST   merchandise leave-NEG.PUR
   She left the manioc on that side (of the river) so that she would not have to leave the merchandise.

Example (665) further illustrates a negative purpose clause with the same subject as the matrix clause and the prior adverbial clause. Notice also that in this example the purpose clause precedes the matrix clause, but the logical or temporal order is not disrupted. In this case, the negative purpose is associated with the previous adverbial clause 'upon taking off his blanket'.

(665) *ki-bupu-rūki-a   eʔe-ta-tirā   sa-rīkapā-koreka*
   3ms-cover-IMPRS-n get-VERT-after 3ns-trip-NEG.PUR

   ki-bībīrīka-eʔka
   3ms-stood^up-PST
   Upon taking off his blanket, so that he would not trip, he stood.

11.14. Condition/grounds. The suffix *-bāka* (condition) can have various meanings such as 'since', 'because', and 'when'. It can indicate a temporal condition/consequence (when) or a grounds/conclusion (since/because) relation between the subordinate and matrix clause. The condition/grounds subordinate clause has the meaning 'when' in (666) and (667).

(666) *iʔsupaka sa-ībā-bāka yaia bā-re taʔa-yu dā-ā-yā-wai*
like^that 3ns-be-COND tiger 12-TERM wait-PRES 3p-say-EP-HAB
When it's like that, a tiger awaits one, they say. *or* When that happens, it's said that a tiger waits for you.

(667) *bī-aka-bāka dā-iʔta-be-sa-rāyū*
2s-call-COND 3p-come-NEG-EP-FUT
When you call (them), they will not come.

The event of the matrix clause is the consequence or conclusion of the condition of the clause subordinated by *bāka* (condition). In (668), the consequent 'she can bathe' follows the accomplishment of the condition 'when he has cured'. In (669) and (670) *-bāka* is the grounds for a conclusion with the meaning 'because'.

(668) *ki-koa-ti-bāka ko-uʔya-hī-yū*
3ms-cure-PERF-COND 3fs-bathe-PSBL-PRES
When he has cured (her), she can bathe.

(669) *ki-re yi-īārī-ri-reʔka yi-paki ki-ībā-bāka*
3ms-TERM 1s-care^for-EP-PST 1s-father 3ms-be-COND
I took care of him because he was my father.

(670) *kūbūā yiha-re koyi-be-ri-hī-ka rīkibā-iʔtaka yiha-ībā-bāka*
canoe 1p-TERM suffice-NEG-EP-PSBL-n many-INTS 1p-be-COND
The canoe is not sufficient for us because we are many.

The suffix *-bāka* indicates switch reference in that the subjects of the main and subordinate clauses are not coreferential. Interestingly, the object of one clause and the subject of the other are often coreferential. In (668), the understood object (feminine singular) of the subordinate clause 'when he has cured her' is the subject of the main clause. The reverse situation is illustrated in (671) in which the subject of the subordinate clause (first-person singular) is the object of the main clause 'it cursed me'.

(671) *sa-pebā yi-hoe-bāka yi-re sa-kubūpu-rape*
3ns-face 1s-burn-COND 1s-TERM 3ns-curse-PST
When I burned its face, it cursed me.

11.15. Reason (different subject). The subordinating suffix *-pakāʔā* (reason) marks a reason or result relation between the subordinate and matrix clause. The subordinated clause is the reason and the matrix clause is the result. It indicates that the subjects of the two clauses are different. Like *-bāka*, *-pakāʔā* can also have the meaning 'when', but usually it has the meaning 'because', marking the subordinate clause as the reason or explanation of the result expressed by the matrix clause. Unlike *-bāka*, *-pakāʔā* can occur on a negated verb as in (672). Example (673) illustrates *-pakāʔā* marking the subordinate clause as the reason for the result expressed by the matrix clause.

(672) *peka   ībā-be-pakāʔā   yaiwēkoa sa-dā-hāā-yu*
shotgun be-NEG-REAS.DS dog   3ns-3p-hunt-PRES
(When) there isn't a shotgun, dogs hunt it.

(673) *hia āūā   ko-ria-be-pakāʔā   baʔa-tirā*
well cassava 3fs-cook^cassava-NEG-REAS.DS eat-after

   yi-hī-yū
   1s-be^sick-PRES
   Because she didn't make the cassava well, I'm sick after eating it.

Like the other subordinating suffixes, tense is not indicated by *-pakāʔā* (reason). The subordinated clause takes its tense from the matrix clause. Examples (674) and (675) are further illustrations of reason indicated by *-pakāʔā*.

(674) *okoa ha-pakāʔā waʔia yi-baa-tiyi-koʔo*
rain be-REAS.DS fish   1s-do-stop-PST
Because it rained, I stopped fishing.

(675) *bāria-re   boebaa-rape ki-aʔ-pakāʔā*
María-TERM anger-PST 3ms-go-REAS.DS
María was mad because he went.

11.16. Reason (same subject). The subordinating suffix *-waʔri* (reason) generally marks a reason or result relation between the subordinate and matrix clause. It often functions to further clarify or explain the action or the motivation of the subject. It differs from *-pakāʔa* (reason) in that it indicates same subject.

(676) *kīki-tiya-waʔri   dā-akasere-reʔka*
fear-INTS-REAS.SS 3p-scream-PST
For terror, they screamed.

Subordination

(677) *yōā-payāka taʔa-ri-ka   yapa-be-ri-waʔri   ki-re*
long-DIM   wait-DVBL-n   want-NEG-EP-REAS.SS   3ms-TERM

    yi-puāta-rape
    1s-send-PST
    Not wanting to wait a little while, I sent him.

Often *-waʔri* is used with *ā* 'say'. The compound *ārīwaʔri* can be translated 'meaning' or 'for this reason'. It has perhaps become a frozen form as an adverb indicating 'explanation' or answering the question 'why'.

(678) *yahe bī-ībā-kope-yu   ā-rī-waʔri   yi-iʔta-koʔo*
Y/N   2s-be-CONTRA-PRES   say-EP-REAS.SS   1s-come-PST
I came (to see if) you might be home.

(679) *hia   bīhā-pupahoa-be   bīhā-ō-yū   upaka-ha   bīhā-poʔi-rā*
good   2p-think-IMP   2p-know-PRES   like-ADVLZR   2p-body-p

    bīha-paki-aʔsi   ā-rī-waʔri
    2p-deceive-NEG.IMP   say-EP-REAS.SS
Consider well lest you deceive yourselves.

11.17. Contra-expectation. The subordinator *-kobāʔkaha* (contra-expectation) indicates that the event referred to in the matrix clause does not conform to an expectation established in the subordinate clause. In (680), the expectation following from 'not liking him' would be to avoid living with (i.e., marrying) him. The matrix clause 'you will live with him' is contrary to this expectation.

(680) *bī-yapa-be-ri-kobāʔkaha bī-ībā-rāyū*
2s-like-NEG-EP-CONTRA   2s-live-FUT
Even though you don't like (him), you will live with (him).

(681) *bī-aka-kobāʔkaha ko-iʔta-be-yu*
2s-call-CONTRA   3fs-come-NEG-PRES
Although you called, she's not coming.

(682) *peka boʔi-rā sa-ropa-kobāʔkaha ki-baʔa-reʔka*
fire   on-LOC   3ns-mount-CONTRA   3ns-eat-PST
Even though it (food) was still over the fire, he ate it.

11.18–11.22 Adverbial clauses formed by conjunctions

Adverbial clauses formed by conjunctions can be inflected for person, number, tense, and in some cases, aspect and mood. It usually precedes the matrix clause, and the subordinating conjunction follows the subordinated clause. Often the verb of the clause subordinated by the conjunction will have a nominalized form.

11.18. Time: when. The conjunction *potohī* indicates time. The event of the subordinate clause is simultaneous with or immediately prior to the event of the matrix clause.

(683) *wiʔia-rā   ki-ībā-reʔka potohī pēte-rā   ko-tui-reʔka*
house-LOC 3ms-be-PST when outside-LOC 3fs-stay-PST
While he was in the house, she stayed outside.

(684) *ki-hiye-wea-royi-reʔka   potohī ki-re   ko-heriā-reʔka*
3ms-bail-finish-IMPFV-PST when 3ms-TERM 3fs-ask-PST
When he was finishing bailing (water) she asked him.

(685) *bī-rika pu-ri-rā-ka   potohī yi-rika bā-baʔa-rāyū*
2s-POSS run^out-EP-FUT-n when 1s-POSS 12-eat-FUT
When your (food) runs out, we will eat mine.

In (683)–(685), the subordinated clauses indicate the time of the event referred to by the matrix verbs 'stay', 'ask', and 'eat'.

11.19. Time: prior. The conjunction *beʔerōʔō* 'prior' indicates sequential time. The event or state referred to by the subordinate clause is completed or exists prior to that referred to by the matrix clause. It could be translated 'after' or 'before' depending on the context. For example, in the formula [clause 1] *beʔerōʔō* [clause 2], one could say that the event/state of clause 2 occurs 'after' that of clause 1 or that the event/state of clause 1 occurs 'before' that of clause 2. In (686), it is translated 'after', although the sentence could also be translated 'he returned home before the tiger arrived'.

(686) *ki-peʔ-ri-reʔka   beʔerōʔō yai-re   eta-reʔka*
3ms-return-EP-PST prior   tiger-TERM arrive-PST
After he returned (home), the tiger arrived.

Example (687) illustrates the variable order of the clauses with the subordinate clause following the matrix clause, and in (688) *be?erō?ō* is translated 'before.'

(687) *pō?ībāhā-re sa-ba?a-yu dā-kā-yū be?erō?ō*
people-TERM 3ns-eat-PRES 3p-sleep-PRES prior
It eats people after they are asleep.

(688) *werika i?sia be?erō?ō sa-dā-hāā-yu*
dangerous that prior 3ns-3p-kill-PRES
That (animal) is dangerous before they kill it.

The conjunction *be?erō?ō* 'prior' may follow a noun phrase instead of a clause, but a clause may be implied. In (689), the conjunction follows the noun phrase 'three days'. The verb phrase 'had passed' is implicit.

(689) *bāēkaraka-rībī be?erō?ō ki-ba?a-rape*
three-day prior 3ms-eat-PST
After three days (had passed), he ate.

11.20. Comparison: like. A clause subordinated by *upaka* 'like' indicates by comparison the manner in which the event of the matrix clause occurred. The conjunction *upaka* requires the adverbializing suffix *-hV* when the subordinated material is a clause. When nominals take *upaka*, the adverbializing suffix is absent. In (690) and (691), manner is expressed by the clauses 'just like they said' and 'the way you say', respectively. In (692), the conjunction *upaka* relates the noun phrase *yābāhīka* 'small deer' to the verb.

(690) *rōbītika dā-re ā-rī-re?ka upaka-ha sa-ībā-re?ka*
women 3p-TERM say-EP-PST like-ADVLZR 3ns-be-PST
It was just like the women told them.

(691) *bī-ā-yū upaka-ha yi-baa-rāyū*
2s-say-PRES like-ADVLZR 1s-do-FUT
I will do (it) the way you say.

(692) *to-rā ki-re sa-pebākotowi-ri-re?ka yābā-hīka upaka*
there-LOC 3ms-TERM 3ns-appear-EP-PST deer-small like
There it appeared to him, like a small deer.

11.21. Condition: if. A clause subordinated by the conjunction *reka* 'if' indicates either the contrafactual or potential-fact condition in a condition or consequence relation. The consequence of either type of condition is the event referred to by the matrix clause. In (693) and (694), the conditions are assumed by the speaker to be contrafactual. Example (695) illustrates a general potential-fact condition. See §11.12 for examples of particular potential-fact conditions.

(693) dīyērū yi-re   ībā-hī-i-ka   reka bōtoro yi-wapahī-hī-yū
      money 1s-TERM be-PSBL-STAT-n if   motor 1s-buy-PSBL-PRES
      If I had money, I could buy a motor.

(694) karebārīā ipabāki bī-ībā-rā-ka reka hoʔbaka wiʔia bī-baa-rāyū
      suppose   chief   2s-be-FUT-n if   big   house 2s-do-FUT
      If (supposing) you were a chief, you would build a big house.

(695) baʔia-ha   bā-huā-hī-i-ka   reka ki-re
      bad-ADVLZR 12-suffer-PSBL-STAT-n if   3ms-TERM

      bā-hai-hī-yū
      12-talk-PSBL-PRES
      If one should suffer badly, one can talk to him.

11.22. Continue: still/yet. The conjunction *rupu* 'still' subordinates primarily a clause in a time relation to the matrix clause. The event of the matrix clause occurs while the prior event or condition of the subordinate clause still persists as illustrated by (696).

(696) dāī-rā   ki-hī-rī-ērā   baa-reʔka rupu okoa ha-reʔka
      afternoon-LOC 3ms-die-EP-PURP do-PST   still rain be-PST
      In the afternoon while he was still dying, it rained.

Contra-expectation is a natural inference of *rupu*. In (697), the subject José persists in his disbelief despite the efforts to persuade him otherwise.

(697) jose-re   yiʔ-ri-be-ri-reʔka   rupu ki-re
      José-TERM believe-EP-NEG-EP-PST   still 3ms-TERM

      dā-ā-rī-royi-reʔka
      3p-say-EP-IMPFV-PST
      José still didn't believe (what) they were saying to him.

The conjunction *rupu* also functions as an adverb to indicate continuing action (see §6.5).

12
Elements of Discourse

Various topics concerning discourse features of Retuarã are discussed in this section. The section is not intended to be an extensive treatment of the topic, but rather is simply a collection of observations about some of the discourse structures of the language.

12.1–12.5 Participant reference

Participant reference in Retuarã narrative largely conforms to Givón's Iconicity Principle (1983:18) that states "The more disruptive, surprising, discontinuous or hard to process a topic is, the more coding material must be assigned to it."

Applying this principle to participant reference in Retuarã narratives means that the form of the reference (noun phrase, pronoun... etc.) will be dependent upon the speaker's assessment of the audience's expectations or what he or she considers shared information. Reference to participants in a Retuarã narrative can be made in four ways.

1. noun phrase (NP)
2. pronominal prefix (PX—subject on the verb or bound pronoun)
3. number/gender suffix (on the verb)
4. free pronoun

Of the above choices, the first two are the most common, whereas 3 and 4 occur infrequently. While the usages of number/gender suffixes and free pronouns are still under study, it is obvious that rules other than those of participant reference intrude to determine their usage. For example, most negations display number/gender suffixes rather than the more common pronominal prefix. A free pronoun often occurs with the number/gender suffix in negations (see §10.1). Number/gender suffixes are also used in dependent clauses and on a higher level to indicate that the predication is background information (see §12.7).

How the speaker or author chooses to refer to a participant depends both on the role of the participant in the discourse and the form of any previous reference to the participant. Most studies in discourse distinguish the first three participant roles of the following list. A fourth role, that of VILLAIN, needs to be added for Retuarã since it is referenced differently from the other roles in Retuarã narratives.

1. Central character—the participant most involved with the author's purpose in telling the story. The central character may be active and agentive (initiator), or an experiencer or patient. In Retuarã, the story's title usually indicates the central character.
2. Major participant—any other participant that significantly interacts with the central character. A major participant may be the experiencer of the actions of the central character, or the initiator of actions that impinge on the central character in the development of the story.
3. Minor participant—any participant that briefly interacts with a major or central character. Usually a minor participant is a prop or an experiencer of the actions of the central character.
4. Villain—a participant whose name has a negative connotation due to his or her reputation. Noun phrase reference to the villain occurs more frequently than would be expected for a major participant in order to achieve the effect of the negative connotation (see §12.3).

Often it is useful to determine which role a participant has since the participant reference rules will vary with the role of a participant. In Retuarã all the roles are somewhat distinctive in the manner in which they are referenced except for the major and minor participants which appear to be treated the same.

Elements of Discourse 181

12.1. Participant reference rules.

1. All participants are introduced with a NP. In cases where a participant(s) is either not specific or his existence is taken for granted, the reference is by a PX.
2. Once a participant has been introduced, and for as long as the participant remains involved in the action of the narrative:
   a. further reference to him or her is by a full NP, in contexts involving a change of subject and two or more third-person referents of the same gender and number; otherwise,
   b. further reference to him or her is by a PX.
3. Reintroduction of central character(s) is by a PX whereas other participants are reintroduced with a NP.

These participant reference rules are illustrated in §§12.2–12.4, together with a discussion of exceptions. §12.5 describes how a mismatch between the global role of the central character and his or her animacy relative to other major participants leads to a greater use of noun phrases than that predicted by the above rules.

12.2. Introduction of participants. In general, all participants are introduced with a NP, regardless of their status. Often, but not always, the first participant mentioned in the introductory material of the story is the central character. For example, the 'Alligator story' not surprisingly has the alligator (*kahu*) as the central character and is referred to by a NP in the title. In (699), the first line of the story, the reference is a pronominal prefix on the verb and a right dislocated NP.

(698) *kahu   bāharoka (title)*
alligator story
The alligator story

(699) *ĩʔrĩka-ha   ki-ĩbā-reʔka kahu*
alone-ADVLZR 3ms-live-PST alligator
He lived alone, the alligator.

A central character may also be referenced with a PX if the title contains a NP reference, as in (700) which begins with a Spanish title. The 'ancestors' are the central characters.

(700) como tumbaron la chagra los antepasados (title)
How the ancestors cleared land for their gardens.

(701) *pitaka-pi   dā-wae-royi-re?ka   sara-bā-rī-a*
hand-INSTR 3p-weed-IMPFV-PST machete-not^be-DVBL-n
By hand, they weeded without a machete.

Major participants are also introduced with a NP. In a different story with the central character already on stage, the major participants, monkeys, are introduced with a NP as illustrated in (702).

(702) (CENTRAL PX)   (MAJOR NP)
  ki-rio-weya-rā   seraka   eta-re?ka
  3ms-garden-border-LOC monkey(s) arrive-PST
  Monkeys arrived at the borders of his garden.

Likewise, minor participants, such as the caretaker in (703) from another story, are generally introduced with noun phrases. The central characters are referred to by the bound pronominal *dā-* (third-person plural)

(703) *kura   wi?ia   īārī-rī-bāhī-te   dā-ruata-rape*
  priest house   care^for-DVBL-person-TERM 3p-scare^off-PST
  They scared off the caretaker of the priest's house.

Thus, the use of a NP to introduce participants is the expected pattern whatever their status. However, there are some exceptions to this. If the participant is considered part of a larger group that has already been introduced and he or she does not need to be identified as a specific individual, then the reference is a PX because it is considered a further reference (see §12.3). In (704), the central characters, the ancestors, have already been introduced with a NP in the title: 'How the ancestors cleared land for their gardens'. When the story shifts to recount an incident with one ancestor, the reference is a PX (*ki-re* (masculine singular)). He is an individual member of the group of ancestors that plays a major role but is unspecified. The other major participant, the yam chief, is a supernatural character rather than one of the ancestors and is introduced with a NP in the expected way as illustrated in (704).

(704)   (MAJOR NP) (CENTRAL PX)
  supa   baa-riha-ri   bākayābū īparāka   ki-re
  like^3ns do-CONT-DVBL   yam   chief   3ms-TERM

  ki-wi-ri-re?ka
  3ms-appear-EP-PST
  Doing like that, the yam chief appeared to him.

If the author had chosen to use a NP here such as 'man' instead of 'him', then it would probably be understood that this participant was not one of the ancestors. A NP would serve to distinguish the man from the group of ancestors.

Another exception to the use of a NP to introduce a participant is when the author considers the existence of the participant a given in the mind of his audience. For example, it is common in Retuarã narrative for a participant to enter the communal house and speak. The participant(s) that respond are often referenced with a pronominal prefix since the author expects the audience shares his perspective that there are always relatives in the communal house. They are unspecified people in the narrative. Thus they need no formal introduction.

12.3. Further participant reference. After any participant (central, major, or minor) has been introduced, the norm for all further reference to him or her is by a PX, for as long as the participant remains involved in the action of the narrative. (Reintroduction of participants will be discussed in §12.4.) The reference is by a PX regardless of whether the subject is the same as the previous sentence or different. These patterns are illustrated in the following three consecutive sentences of a story in which (705) and (706) have the same subject, but (707) has a change of subject.

(705) ito-rã   sa-ībẽ dã-re   yi-ã-rape
      there-LOC 3ns-be 3p-TERM 1s-say-PST
      "There it is," I said to them.

(706) dã-re   yi-hoata-rape
      3p-TERM 1s-point-PST
      I pointed for them.

(707) dahoa   bã-ī-aʔri yiha-re bī-ruputa-waʔ-pe   yi-re
      let's^go 12-see-go 1p-TERM 2s-lead-AWAY-IND.IMP 1s-TERM

      dã-ã-rape
      3p-say-PST
      "Let's go and see. You lead us," they said to me.

One exception to continuing reference with a PX can be observed in the reporting of conversations where the speech margins are omitted. It does not occur frequently, and when it does it is only in situations involving information familiar to the audience. Such situations would include common repartee such as greetings or recounting of a previous event in the story of which the audience is aware. In the following passage, the central character returns home from the jungle and recounts to a brother what just happened to him. The previous material makes the speech margins superfluous for distinguishing the speaker. In such cases, as seen below, there is no reference to the participant as speaker after the first line.

(708) *daʔkoa payāka to-rā   yi-re   eta-koʔo-a ki-ā-rī-reʔka*
what   like   there-LOC 1s-TERM arrive-PST-n 3ms-say-EP-PST
I wonder what it was that came to me there? he said. (central character)

(709) *bārāpaka īō-i-ka   sa-ībā-koʔo*
how   appear-STAT-n 3ns-be-PST
How was its appearance? (brother)

(710) *pōʔībāhā īō-eʔka   sa-ībā-koʔo*
people   appear-PST 3ns-be-PST
It was/appeared like people look. (central character)

(711) *bārākāʔā bī-re   sa-ā-rī-koʔo*
how   2s-TERM 3ns-say-EP-PST
What did it say to you? (brother)

That there are no references to the participant as speaker accord with Givón's Iconicity Principle. In the above contexts, the topics are not disruptive or surprising. The audience's experience or clues from the story line provide sufficient information to identify the participants with no coding material assigned to them. In this particular case, the events of the story are known to the audience from the previous context. When such conditions are met, the speaker begins the conversation indicating the speaker in the first line and then has the option of omitting subsequent speech margins if he judges them unnecessary for identifying the participants.

Another exception to the exclusive use of a PX for further participant reference occurs in contexts with third-person, same-gender referents. In such contexts, a bound pronominal reference will be understood to be coreferential with the previous referent in the same grammatical role (i.e., subject, object... etc). If the subject or object is different, it requires that the reference be made with a NP. This exception is identical to the participant reference rule that Fox (1987:171) observes in English:

> If a character has been mentioned as participating in an event/ action, then that person can subsequently be referred to with a

pronoun, until another character of the same gender is mentioned participating in another event/action. If two referents of the same gender are involved in the same action, then the grammatical subject of the clauses describing that action can be referred to in the next event-line mention with a pronoun. The other non-subject NP will have its referent indexed on the next event-line mention with a full NP... in the sequence

X actionverb, Y actionverb, PRO

where X and Y are same-gender referents, the pronoun refers to Y, not to X. A full NP must be used to perform a second reference to X.

The above observation is illustrated in (712)–(715). All the characters are singular and masculine. The switch of subjects from (712) to (713) requires the subject (Moses) to be a NP. In (714) the subject is referenced with a PX so it is understood that it was Moses who returned rather than Ernesto. The further bound pronominal reference (masculine singular) in (715) indicates the same subject again as (713) and (714).

(712) yābī yēbātahi ki-pupa-ri-ri-reʔka
night middle 3ms-spirit-lose-EP-PST
At midnight he [Alfonso] died.

(713) muice-te ernesto-te boha-rī tu-ri-reʔka
Moses-TERM Ernesto-TERM tell-PURP travel-EP-PST
Moses went to tell Ernesto.

(714) yābī ki-peʔ-ri-eta-reʔka
night 3ms-return-EP-arrive-PST
In the night he [Moses] returned.

(715) aturu pōʔīrā aʔte ki-tu-ri-reʔka
Aturu to again 3ms-travel-EP-PST
To Aturu's he again traveled.

Participant reference is also affected by the role of VILLAIN which was proposed as a fourth role earlier. The villain role is referenced with a NP more often than the participant reference rules would predict for other roles. There may be two motivations for this type of participant referencing: first, it is used when the speaker wishes to exploit the effect of the negative connotation of the villain's name (NP). Second, he may wish to distance himself or others from the villain by excluding the villain from the same type of PX referencing of the other participants.

This type of villain role is demonstrated in a story in which people unfriendly to Americans repeatedly make reference to one as the 'gringo', rather than by a PX as would be expected of any of the other participant roles. The speaker associates the name 'gringo' with economic greed and communicates his opinion by the more frequent use of the NP rather than the neutral PX.

12.4. Reintroduction of participants. In general, central participants are reintroduced with a PX while major and minor participant reintroductions are done with a NP. The reason that a central character is referenced differently seems to be that they are assumed to be 'in the wings'. It is assumed, that in the minds of the audience, the central character is not completely absent from the stage. Thus, in conformity to the Iconicity Principle, less coding material is needed to reintroduce them than a major or minor participant. In (716), the central character (alligator) is offstage while his adversaries discuss a plot against him. Upon agreeing on a plan, the next sentence reintroduces the alligator with a PX *(ki-re)*.

(716) *bāē aʔte ki-re   dā-ā-rī-reʔka bā-bāeru-uku-ērā*
now again 3ms-TERM 3p-say-EP-PST 12-pineapple-drink-PURP
Now again they said to him, "Let's drink pineapple drink."

In the cases in which major participants are reintroduced, a NP is generally used. In the following examples of three consecutive sentences in a narrative, the author refers to himself pronominally (717), but reintroduces two major characters (Lui and Aturu) in turn with noun phrases.

(717) *bikitoho tāʔāpika taa-rī   yi-tu-rika īpa-rībī*
morning coca^bush throw^out-PURP 1s-travel-PST 2-CLAS^day

   beʔerōʔō
prior
Two days later, in the morning, I went to throw out (his) coca bushes.

(718) *lui-re   peria baya-reʔka opirekoa bīrāka ruata-ērā*
Lui-TERM copai cure-PST spirit former scare^off-PURP
Lui cured (shining with) copai wood in order to scare off (his) former spirit.

(719) yābī   aturu-te   yae-re?ka
     night Aturu-TERM shine-PST
     In the night, Aturu shined (with copai).

In the infrequent examples in which a minor participant is reintroduced, it is likewise with a NP.

A NP is also used to reintroduce a participant into the action of the narrative. In the following six sentences of a text, two major participants, Ernesto and Aturu, arrive at the house of the brother that has just died. The eldest brother Lui talks to each of them separately, so that although Aturu is on stage in (720)–(723), he is not reintroduced into the action until (724). At this point a NP is used. Following that, the minor characters (women) are also reintroduced into the action with a NP.

(720) yābī aka dā-eta-re?ka rō?ōrā lui-re   dā-re   boha-re?ka
     night also 3p-arrive-PST place Lui-TERM 3p-TERM tell-PST
     At the time of their arrival in the night also, Lui told them (Ernesto and Aturu).

(721) hī-yū-ka   bā-bā?bī   dā-re   ki-ā-rī-re?ka
     die-PRES-ms 12-brother 3p-TERM 3ms-say-EP-PST
     "Our brother is dead", he said to them.

(722) ernesto-te   ki-re   yi?-ri-re?ka
     Ernesto-TERM 3ms-TERM answer-EP-PST
     Ernesto answered him.

(723) dā-hai-tiyi-re?ka
     3p-talk-end-PST
     They stopped talking.

(724) aturu-te   a?te ki-hai-re?ka
     Aturu-TERM again 3ms-talk-PST
     To Aturu now (again) he spoke.

(725) rōbīha-te   o-ri-re?ka
     women-TERM cry-EP-PST
     The women cried.

The exception to the use of a NP for reintroducing a major and minor participants is when the context makes a pronominal reference clear. This can occur when the story line leads the audience to anticipate the reintroduction of a major participant. In (726)–(728) taken from a fable, a man has met a supernatural character in the woods. The next day the man returns to the woods and the action of the story slows down, which signals that something important is about to happen. The audience expects the supernatural character to appear again, so when he does in (728), the PX reference for him is appropriate.

(726) *bāē sa-ki-hea-reʔka*
now 3ns-3ms-dig-PST
Now he (man) dug it (yam).

(727) *ki-hea-rupe*
3ms-dig-sitting
He was sitting digging.

(728) *ki-pōʔīrā   ki-eya-reʔka*
3ms-toward   3ms-reach-PST
He (supernatural character) reached him.

When minor participants are reintroduced with a PX, it is for the same reason mentioned earlier, viz. that they are assumed or implicit for the audience. Examples of such PX referencing would include family in the communal house or the soldiers at the frontier town several days travel away.

12.5. Exceptions to rules. Occasionally a story may exhibit more noun phrases in participant reference than would normally be expected. The more frequent use of NP references has the effect of breaking the story up into units or episodes. A particular story that exhibits this type of referencing concerns an old man who undergoes a series of misfortunes. Each of these misfortunes is a short episode. There is no turn of events in which the old man finally wins in the end, only a series of disasters (death of his son, famine, missed hunting opportunity, ridicule by monkeys, and his own death). The overall effect of these short episodes is to give a sense of helplessness in the face of calamity. The frequent use of a NP reference is consistent with Fox's (1987:168) observation that full noun phrases are used to demarcate new narrative units.

The participant reference pattern in the story means that the following modifications to the rules proposed in §12.1 are necessary.[59]

---

[59] The numbering corresponds to that of the original rules.

Addition of 2c: Any major participant that is subject at the beginning of a new narrative unit is referenced with a NP.[60]

Addition to 3: Reintroduction of a major participant as non-subject is usually with a NP. The following sentence will continue to reference the reintroduced participant with a NP as the subject.

These modifications account for the episodic nature of the story since they correlate with episode breaks. Normal reference by a PX implies continuity of situation, action, and participants. The reference by a NP has the effect of signalling a disruption in the continuity and contributes to the episodic atmosphere. In such cases, the NP reference dominates the story line. Stories like these talk about the experiences of a character without emphasis on the development and resolution of the action of the story. In contrast, the majority of stories emphasize the development of the events and most participants are referred to by a PX. The story line is primary and participants are secondary.

The unusual pattern of participant reference in this particular story may be explained by proposing that reference is sensitive to the participants' ranks on an animacy hierarchy similar to that proposed by Comrie (1981). The animacy hierarchy shown in (729) reflects the probability of certain types of referents being the agent or subject of a clause. Givón, in discussing the animacy hierarchy and its relation to agreement, states that ... 'the agent has the strongest claim to subjecthood and the agent is overwhelmingly human or animate' (1984:371). Based on this strong correlation of agents with high animacy, one can expect the best candidates for agents to be found on the left side of the hierarchy while the best patients or experiencers are on the right.

(729) Animacy hierarchy

1,2 PX > 3 PX > proper name > human NP > animate > inanimate

Levinsohn (1978) (following Barnard and Longacre (1968)) distinguishes three global roles in narrative: the initiator, the objective, and props. He defines the initiator as

> the participant who controls the direction of the actions of the discourse; typically the actor or causer of actions in which he participates...

---

[60]A shift to background information also shifts the reference to a NP from a PX.

The objective is

> the participant towards whom the actions of the dicourse are directed: typically the goal or experiencer of actions in which he is (caused to be) a participant. (p.70)

In this scheme, a central character could be either the global initiator or the global objective or experiencer of a narrative. If a central character (CC) is high on the animacy hierarchy, he or she will be a likely candidate for the role of initiator. If the CC is low in animacy then he or she will be a likely candidate for the role of the experiencer. Following the animacy hierarchy, one would expect, however, that the initiator would be higher in animacy than the experiencer.

In Retuarã narrative, if the overall initiator is higher in animacy than the overall experiencer, then the normal participant reference rules apply. Conformity to this expectation is signalled by the introduction of a participant with a NP, and then continuing reference with PX. Any reintroduction would be a NP for major and minor participants, and a PX for the central character.

If the reverse is true, that the overall initiator is lower in animacy than the overall experiencer, then the experiencer will be referenced with a NP much more frequently than would otherwise be expected.

This is illustrated in the story of the old man's calamities. In the story, the old man is a central character that is higher in animacy than the monkeys, but throughout the story he is low in agentiveness. In fact, he is in the role of experiencer while the monkeys are the initiators. The relatively frequent use of a NP, which is further to the right on the animacy hierarchy, to reference the old man, rather than a PX, signals that, for this participant, there is a mismatch of high animacy and low agentiveness for his global role in the story. The frequent referencing with a NP shows the need for a constant restatement that the participant is low in agentiveness or initiative. A normal use of PXs would signal continuity of the story and that the participant high in animacy is agentive.

In another story, an alligator is the central character, while a group of ancestors are the major participants. On the animacy scale, the alligator ranks lower than the men. Thus the expectation is that, since the alligator is lower in animacy, he will be the overall experiencer and the men will be the initiators. This is, in fact, the case, so the participants are referenced according to the normal rules.

Table (730) illustrates the participants' roles in these two stories. The men in both stories are higher in animacy than the other participants.[61] The central characters (CC) in both stories are in the role of experiencer.

---

[61] High animacy is indicated in the table by capital letters.

Story 1 has frequent use of NPs for continuing participant reference of the CC (old man). Story 2, following normal participant reference rules uses PXs for continuing reference.

(730) The effect of animacy on participant reference

	Overall Initiator	Overall Experiencer	Continuing Participant Reference of CC
story 1	monkey	OLD MAN (CC)	(exception) frequent NP
story 2	MEN	alligator (CC)	(normal) PX

12.6. Stative versus active. The speakers of Retuarã have a number of resources available to them to distinguish foreground versus background material in discourse. Among these resources are the use of *-i* (stative) in place of the present tense marker *-yu,* and the use of the prefix verses suffix agreement markers.

In the present tense, most verbs can occur as active/tensed or stative/nontensed. Foreground events in discourse usually have the tense markers while background events are marked by *-i*. In the other tenses, background events are tensed and take the suffix agreement markers *-a/-ka*. For illustrations of these usages, see the Appendix Text 2 and Text 3.

The active/stative selection in relatively isolated sentences also reflects the speaker's choice of focussing on an actual event versus the general situation. For example, both (731) and (732) are acceptable but their usage depends of the speaker's choice.

(731) *daʔkoa bī-baa-yu*
 what 2s-do-PRES
 What are you doing?

(732) *daʔkoa bī-baa-i-ka*
 what 2s-do-STAT-n
 What are you doing? *or* What is your activity?

Speakers may choose prefix versus suffix subject agreement markers (see §5.2) to foreground or background events respectively. Prefix subject agreement marking is the prototypical verbal agreement pattern, whereas the agreement suffixes are typical of nominals. Thus, verbs which do not report main discourse events lose the normal verbal agreement and instead take the agreement marking typical of nouns. Hopper and Thompson (1984:709-10) state the following concerning prototypical nouns and verbs in relation to their discourse function.

> Prototypical N's [nouns], as we have seen, introduce a participant of the discourse... Prototypical V's [verbs], report an actual event of the discourse. We should therefore find that, in discourse environments where participants are introduced or events reported, N and V will display the widest degree of morpho-syntactic contrast, i.e. the largest number of oppositions... In non-prototypical environments, then the CONTRAST between N and V tends to be neutralized... We will demonstrate in this paper a very clear tendency across languages to correlate overt morpho-syntactic markings, characteristic of the categories N and V, with the degree to which the forms in question are performing their respective prototypical discourse functions.

That verbs can take noun-like marking is illustrated in (733)–(735). In (733), the suffixes -*ki* and -*ka* distinguish the singular masculine and neuter noun classes, respectively, for nominals. In (734), they derive nominals from adjectives. In addition, the same forms are used as suffix subject agreement markers as illustrated in (735). This is more fully discussed in §§2.26 and 5.2.

(733) *iʔki iʔka*
     3ms this
     he, this

(734) *hoʔba-ki hoʔba-ka*
     big-ms   big-n
     big one (male), big thing

(735) *iʔki yu-rapa-ki*
     3ms go^downriver-PST-ms
     He traveled downriver. *or* He was the one who traveled downriver.

The following excerpt from a narrative contains a clause backgrounded by the suffix -*ka* in (737) probably because the act of going is of transitional, secondary importance, in comparison with the events performed before and after it. The marking is more typical of nouns than prototypical verbs, which occur in the foregrounded events in (736) and (738).

(736) *yiha-re bī-ruputa-wa?-pe   yi-re   dā-ā-rape*
 1p-TERM 2s-lead-AWAY-IND.IMP 1s-TERM 3p-say-PST
 "You lead us", they said to me.

(737) *yiha-a?-rapa-ka*
 1p-go-PST-n
 We went.

(738) *yiha-eya-rape wi?ia-rā*
 1p-arrive-PST house-LOC
 We arrived at the house.

Although -*i* (stative) and the use of suffix agreement markers both mark background events, they are independent of one another. Verbs marked by -*i* describe a general situation, and focus to a greater degree on the actor, if the subject agreement suffix is animate, or focus on the situation, if the subject agreement suffix is neuter rather than on reporting an event. It may be that verbs marked by -*i* plus a suffix subject agreement marker are more highly backgrounded than those that are marked only by subject agreement suffixes. Hopper and Thompson have demonstrated that there is a correlation between the degree to which a V performs its prototypical discourse function (i.e., "to assert the occurence of an event of the discourse" (p.708)) and the overt morphosyntactic markings characteristic of Vs. Verbs marked with -*i* show very little marking that is typical of Vs. Like Ns, they have suffixes typical of noun classes, and can even take classifiers. The only morphology typical of Vs that occurs on stative constructions is prefix subject marking, but even this may be analyzed as a genitive construction, which is again typical of Ns rather than Vs.

(739) and (741) are examples of stative constructions containing -*i*. Examples (740) and (742), in contrast, report events, even though they are nonprototypical Vs. That they are less like Ns than constructions containing -*i* is reflected in their use of a slightly wider range of verbal morphology, i.e., the addition of tense marking.

(739) *parua   ba?a-i-ki*
  banana eat-STAT-ms
  He is a banana eater.

(740) *parua   ba?a-yu-ki*
  banana eat-PRES-ms
  He is the one eating bananas.

(741) daʔkoa ki-baʔa-i-ka
      what   3ms-eat-STAT-n
      What is his food/meal?

(742) daʔkoa ki-baʔa-yu-a
      what   3ms-eat-PRES-n
      What is it that he is eating?

The stative -i does not occur in constructions that denote past or future.[62] In such cases, backgrounded forms contain the tense marker plus an agreement suffix (usually -a or -ka).

As mentioned previously, the stative -i and the suffix subject agreement markers most frequently occur in dependent clauses which typically contain background material. Hopper and Thompson (1984:736) discuss dependent versus independent verbs in regards to foreground and background.

> In connected discourse, speakers typically distinguish foregrounded reported events from other material which they intend to be taken as background. This background may include descriptive and evaluative material; but it may also include realis or irrealis events which are being presented as DISCOURSE-PRESUPPOSED, in the sense that they are not open to challenge (Givón 1981), and are subsidiary to the foregrounded reported events. Because these events are referred to only in the context of the foregrounded events to which they are viewed as ancillary, the clauses in which they occur are often marked as dependent.

Crosslinguistically, dependent clauses tend to present background events and, not surprisingly, stative -i and suffix subject agreement markers figure in the formation of dependent clauses in Retuarã. (See §5.21 and §§5.4–5.9 for illustrations.) This use of -i and suffix agreement markers in dependent clauses provides additional evidence that the devices contribute to backgrounding.

Nominalization of a verb is the ultimate in backgrounding of an event; presenting the event as a person or prop rather than an event in the discourse. Again -i in (743), and suffix agreement markers, in (744), are the two derivational elements used to nominalize verbs.

(743) ihia baa-i-rõʔõ-rã   ko-po-ri-be-ri-hĩ-yũ
      hot do-STAT-place-LOC 3fs-leave-EP-NEG-EP-PSBL-PRES
      She should not leave a warm place.

---

[62]The stative -i does, however, occur in past participles (see §5.21).

(744) *yiʔi sa-rupukoʔa baʔa-rā-ki*
 1s 3ns-head eat-FUT-ms
I am the one who will eat its head.

In summary, the preceding data suggests that events in the foreground of the discourse will exhibit a wide possible range of verbal morphology (e.g., prefix subject agreement marking, tense markers, etc.). Background material will be marked by suffix subject agreement marking and/or the stative suffix *-i*. In isolated sentences, a speaker may choose either strategy to focus on the event or on a general discription of a situation.[63]

12.7. Backgrounding. The imperfective aspect suffix *-royi* functions on the discourse level to background material. In its normal unmarked usage, the imperfective denotes an incomplete verbal event on the clause level as discussed in §5.11. It is apparent, however, that it also has a marked usage on the discourse level since it can occur with events that are complete and not in process.[64] These usages typically occur in backgrounded introductory material. Less frequently they also occur in the conclusion of a narrative.[65] This marked usage serves to distinguish or separate the backgrounded material from foreground material such as the main body.

In the following examples, the imperfective suffix *-royi* appears in the introductory sentences. Its absence in (747) signals the beginning of the main body of the text which is in the foreground.

---

[63]Derbyshire (1986) has cited evidence that languages from Amazonia tend to share a variety of areal features regardless of language family. He does not mention affix distinctions between foreground and background as one of the common areal features, yet something similar does occur in several Arawakan languages from Brazil. In an earlier work, Derbyshire (1982) reports thematic/perspective distinctions in Jamamadí and Paumarí: "In both languages they consist of a small set of suffixes, which always occur verb-final and which indicate the type of information being conveyed by the sentence in relation to the discourse as a whole: primary/foreground v. secondary/ backgrounded; dialogue v. nondialogue; establishment of topics and settings; descriptive. Most of the forms are marked for gender agreement with some noun phrase in the sentence, and in the case of Paumarí there is a tense component in two of the forms" (p. 49). Thus it may be that Retuarã also marks similar distinctions (i.e., stative/background versus active/foreground) by the suffix *-i* (stative) and the choice of prefix or suffix subject agreement marking.

[64]Although some of the events in the examples could be seen as habitual, or a routine series of complete actions, a true habitual is not marked for tense (see §5.10).

[65]A similar distinction between past tenses in French newspaper accounts has been noted by Waugh and Monville-Burston (1986).

(745) supa   ībá-rī   baʔarika wayuaka dā-baa-royi-reʔka aʔpe-rā
      like^3ns be-DVBL food   poor   3p-do-IMPFV-PST other-p

   baʔarika ībā-be-pakāʔā
   food   be-NEG-REAS.DS
   Therefore they were poor because there was no food from other people.

(746) bākayābūā dā-baʔa-royi-reʔka bākaka-rā sa-bōʔā-tirā
      yam   3p-eat-IMPFV-PST   jungle-LOC 3ns-search-after
      They ate yams after searching for them in the jungle.

(747) supa   baa-riha-ri   bākayābū-īparāka ki-re
      like^3ns do-CONT-DVBL   yam-spirit^chief 3ms-TERM

   ki-wi-ri-reʔka
   3ms-appear-EP-PST
   Doing like that, the yam chief appeared to him.

Interestingly, there are several instances in a long introduction of a narrative in which a sentence is not marked with the imperfective. They seem to occur when a comment is being made. Thus, the absence of the imperfective distinguishes the comment from the context in which it occurs. In this case, the comments appear to be backgrounded even further from the rest of the introduction. Examples (748)–(751) are excerpted from an introduction. In (748), (749) and (751), the material is marked with the imperfective. The absence of the imperfective in (750) distinguishes it from the sequence of thought of the introduction. It must be regarded simply as a comment.[66]

(748) ātakōbēā   dā-kōbēā ībā-royi-reʔka
      stone^axe 3p-axe   be-IMPFV-PST
      Their axes were stone axes.

(749) yapua-rā dā-hiʔahia-royi-reʔka
      pole-LOC 3p-secure-IMPFV-PST
      They secured them onto poles.

---

[66]This particular narrative is unusual in that the introduction has seventeen sentences. The introduction of the story is an explanation of how the ancestors used to clear land for their gardens. There are several instances besides the example cited in which the absence of the imperfective marks the sentence as a comment.

Elements of Discourse

(750) *dā-rupubīhīā kīke-eʔka-pi   sa-dā-piʔpe-eʔka*
　　　3p-long^hair weave-PST-INSTR 3ns-3p-tie-PST
　　　With their long woven hair they tied them on.

(751) *supatirā sa-pi   rioa   dā-ko-ri-royi-reʔka*
　　　then   3ns-INSTR garden 3p-cut^down-EP-IMPFV-PST
　　　Then they cut down (the trees) of their garden with it.

Thus, it may be that the imperfective does not mark backgrounded material but rather contrasts the material it marks from the other material in the context. This would be somewhat similar to the conclusions drawn about the simple past (SP) in French by Waugh and Monville-Burston (1986:872).

> First, SP is eminently contrastive: it differentiates itself from its morphological (grammatical) context. When it occurs in the vicinity of IP's [imperfect] for description, it takes on a punctual interpretation; used after CP [compound past] for setting the scene, it narrates the events which took place; in a narrative predominantly in HP [historical past] or CP, it may open the text, close it, supply interesting detail, or make a parenthetical remark... through this contrast, it establishes differences within the text itself. The contrastive information given by SP is relative in nature: it is necessary to know what tense was used before, or will be used after—and where one is in the text—in order to determine the basis on which the contrast is being made.

The type of contrast presented here in Retuarā is much simpler than that which occurs between the simple past and the other tenses in French. The imperfective distinguishes material of one level from material of a different level in regards to background or foreground. On the discourse level it has this function and often occurs in the introduction and the conclusion. The reverse situation, that of marking the main body with the imperfective to disinguish it from introduction and conclusion, does not occur. In addition, as mentioned above, the imperfective also can occur in the conclusion. In (752)–(754), the imperfective is used to distinguish the body of the story from the conclusion. Example (752) is the last sentence of the main body.

(752) *daʔko-iʔtaka dā-baʔa-reʔka heʔe*
　　　what-INTS   3p-eat-PST   SUP
　　　They had nothing to eat I suppose.

(753) isupaka   wayuaka ba?arika pakia-rā-te   ībā-royi-re?ka
      like^that poor   food   elder-p-TERM live-IMPFV-PST
      Like that, with a scarcity of food the ancestors lived.

(754) wayuaka ba?arika pakia-rā-te   baa-royi-re?ka
      poor   food   elder-p-TERM   do-IMPFV-PST
      The ancestors did with a scarcity of food.

12.8. Agentiveness reduction strategy. Under certain conditions the number/gender suffixes -a/-ka (neuter) occur on the verb phrase.[67] The environments in which -a/-ka are generally found are those that are typical of number/gender suffixes, i.e., clauses with inanimate or nonhuman subjects. In addition -a/-ka are also used to nominalize a clause, and in discourses where the responsibility or involvement of the subject is reduced. The suffixes -a/-ka have been glossed as (neuter) with the various functions mentioned above.

Nominalization. The suffix -a can nominalize a verb as in (755) and (756).

(755) wi-ya-wai-a
      fly-EP-HAB-n
      airplane

(756) turū-rūki-a
      roll-IMPRS-n
      car (a roll thing)

Examples (757) and (758) are illustrations of the nominalization of a verb phrase.

(757) bīhā-ā?bīti-yu-a   hia   bīhā-pupahoa-be
      2p-hear-PRES-n   good   2p-think-IMP
      Think well/hard about what you hear.

---

[67]This produces the variant tense suffix forms -yu-a (present) (realized phonetically as -yua) and -ko?o-a (immediate past) (realized phonetically as -ko?a). The recent past morpheme does not take -a marking. Instead it occurs with the variant form -rapa and takes -ka marking. Thus, it always has the form -rapa-ka in the same environments that produce -a marking on -yu (present) and ko?o (immediate past). It has not been possible to determine if the remote past (-re?ka) is marked with -a since it already ends with -a.

(758) ki-wărō-rapa-ka yi-ā?bīti-rape
 3ms-teach-PST-n 1s-hear-PST
 I heard what he taught.

This nominalizing function of -a/-ka leads to the conclusion that it is the same -a/-ka that occurs on many nouns to distinguish heads from modifiers in a NP. For example, in (759), a?pe 'other' is first a modifier to -rībī 'day' and then nominalized by -a to be head of a NP marked with -ro?si (benefactive). For further discussion see §2.1.

(759) a?pe-rībī a?pe-a-ro?si e?e-rī   ki-a?-yu
 other-day other-n-BEN get-PURP 3ms-go-PRES
 Another day he goes to get others.

Reduced responsibility of subject. The nominalizing function of -a/-ka may serve to reduce the focus on the subject. The reasoning is that, the less verbal a construction is, the less agentive the subject. Thus, it may be that -a/-ka is used to create a shade of meaning somewhat like a passive in English. In (760) and (761), the speaker may want to reduce the attention he has as the subject.

(760) yi-wărū-be-ri-ko?o-a
 1s-learn-NEG-EP-PST-n
 I didn't learn how. *or* I couldn't do it. (shuffle cards)

(761) yi-ō-rī-be-ri-ko?o-a
 1s-know-EP-NEG-EP-PST-n
 I didn't know. *or* I made a mistake. (writing a word)

As a further illustration, (762)–(764) show three ways to say 'I don't know'. It may be that (763) and (764) represent subject defocus strategies by nominalization of the verb constructions. As mentioned previously, the suffixes -a/-ki/-ko/-ka/-rā when used for subject agreement also have a nominalizing effect as opposed to the subject prefixes. Thus (764) is a further example of a reduction of the subject's responsibility according to this hypothesis.

(762) yi-ō-rī-be-yu
 1s-know-EP-NEG-PRES
 I don't know.

(763) *yi-ō-rī-be-yu-a*
    1s-know-EP-NEG-PRES-n
    I don't know. *or* It is not known to me.

(764) *ō-rī-be-yu-ka   yiʔi*
    know-EP-NEG-PRES-ms 1s
    I don't know. *or* I'm one who does not know.

A further example of a reduction of the subject's involvement in the action is illustrated in (765) where the speaker seeks to distance himself from the (repulsive) thought of eating bats.

(765) *oyoa yiha-baʔa-be-yu-a*
    bats 1p-eat-NEG-PRES-n
    We don't eat bats. *or* Bats are not eaten by us.

An interesting exchange in a myth between a deer and a man may illustrate this possibility further. In the myth, the deer has eaten the entrails of a game animal and is apparently hiding this fact from the man, his companion, by telling him that he threw them away. Notice the variation in the past tense between *-koʔo* (man speaker), and *-koʔo-a* (deer speaker) in (767) and (769). It may be that the deer is trying to deflect attention from himself. (Note: the *-a* is not used by the deer in other speeches even though he is a nonhuman subject.)

(766) *yahe bī-itahia-koʔo*
    Y/N 2s-gut-PST
    Did you gut it? (man speaker)

(767) *āʔā bui   yi-itahia-koʔo-a*
    yes brother^in^law 1s-gut-PST-n
    Yes brother-in-law, I gutted it. (deer speaker)

(768) *dōʔō sa-ita bī-baa-koʔo*
    where 3ns-gut 2s-do-PST
    Where did you put its guts? (man speaker)

(769) *ahīʔi   bui   yi-waʔūsa-koʔo-a   heʔe*
    1s^don't^know brother^in^law 1s-throw^away-PST-n SUP
    I don't know brother-in-law, I threw (it) away perhaps. (deer speaker)

(770) dõʔõ-rã   sa-bī-waʔūsa-koʔo
where-LOC 3ns-2s-throw^away-PST
Where did you throw it away? (man speaker)

Tentative conclusions. In addition to their function at the lower grammatical level as number/gender suffixes, it is likely that -a/-ka also express a shade of meaning or shift of emphasis in regards to agentiveness at a higher level that varies according to the speaker's perspective which may explain the wide variation and lack of a fixed pattern in their usage. It is evident that -a/-ka is used to express low agentivity and/or control on the part of the subject. This low agentiveness may be factual in such cases where it marks agreement with inanimate subjects (e.g., 'the hammock ripped.'). Also on nominalizations of intransitive verbs such as 'fly' from which the noun 'airplane' is derived, the agent is entirely absent. Nominalizations of transitive verbs focus on the object rather than the subject so that a nominalization of 'you teach' becomes 'what you teach'. Thus, it may be that -a/-ka has a secondary, nonfactual function on a higher discourse level that is related to the lower level grammatical function. For example, the connotation of low agentiveness may be employed at the discourse level to reduce responsibility or degree of involvement of the subject in the action of the clause. The choice of using this device varies with each speaker and situation. Situations that are potentially embarassing or cause for shame will demonstrate more frequent use of -a/-ka to reduce the speakers' responsibility for the situation.

12.9. Thematic development. The thematic continuity of a narrative discourse is maintained when every proposition demonstrates cohesion to at least one other proposition in the text. The text has logical, temporal, or referential connectedness.

Continuity of the situation is assumed by default. It seems likely that this must be true crosslinguistically. One assumes that the speaker will continue to talk about the same topic or activity without indiscriminantly jumping to others.[68] In the development of any narrative, however, new or distinctive material is necessarily introduced which interrupts the continuity in some

---

[68]Levinsohn (1980:507) in discussing continuity of situation in Koiné Greek concludes "that the absence of a forefronted basis for relating a sentence to its context implies that there is continuity of situation (cast and spatio-temporal setting) with the last events described. Only if a sentence begins with a (thematic, temporal or spatial) basis is continuity of situation with the last event not indicated (and must be determined from the context)."

area such as a change in the type of activity or cast of active participants. These discontinuities of situation are marked in the discourse.

In Retuarã, thematic development is most often marked by the adverb *bãe* 'now'. Typically it occurs sentence initially and marks discontinuities of the situations listed below.[69] These introductions of distinctive information or new developments are judged to be discontinuities (and thus marked by *bãe*) according to the perception of the author or speaker. Typical discontinuities involve:

1. a change in setting (time or location),
2. a change in the cast of participants,
3. a change in the type of activity,
4. a switch back to the main events of the narrative from background information, or
5. a change in the circumstances, state, or attitude of a participant if not anticipated in the context.

The development marker *bãe* is illustrated in (771) and (772) in which it marks the change in the circumstances of the central character from 'together' to 'alone'.

(771) *ĩpa-rã-hã ki-bãki-bĩrãki-ka dã-ĩbã-kope-eʔka*
two-p-ADVLVR 3ms-son-former-COM 3p-be-CONTRA-PST
Together, (he) with his son, they would no longer be.

(772) *bãe ĩʔrã-ika-ha ki-ha-ri-waʔ-rika*
now one-ms-ADVLZR 3ms-become-EP-AWAY-PST
Now he was/became all alone.

In (773) and (774) the change in setting (location) is marked by *bãe*.

(773) *ãburua ĩrẽã dã-wapaĩhĩ-rape*
fariña palm^fruit 3p-buy-PST
They bought fariña and palm fruit.

(774) *bãe dã-yu-ri-waʔ-rape*
now 3p-go^downriver-EP-AWAY-PST
Now they went downriver.

---

[69] Apart from some small adaptations, the thinking behind this list comes from the work of Levinsohn (1978:86–96).

Elements of Discourse

The following text further illustrates the usage of the development marker *bāe* 'now'. In each instance of its use, the type of development is indicated below the gloss line.

(775) *kahu   bāharoka (title)*
   alligator story
   The alligator story

(776) *ĩʔrā-ika-ha   ki-ĩbā-reʔka kahu*
   one-ms-ADVLZR 3ms-live-PST alligator
   He lived alone, the alligator.

(777) *ki-yata-reka   peka ĩbā-reʔka*
   3ms-belly-LOC.SPEC fire be-PST
   There was fire in his belly.

(778) *iʔsia ki-reka   eʔe-ērā   dā-pakata-rika*
   that 3ms-LOC.SPEC get-PURP 3p-strive-PST
   They strove to get that (fire that was) in him.

(779) *bāe ki-re   dā-ōʔyiboha-rika ki-bāeru-uku-ērā*
   now 3ms-TERM 3p-invite-PST   3ms-pineapple-drink-PURP
   Now they invited him to drink (fermented) pineapple juice.

   (Change from background to main events)

(780) *daʔko okoa bĩhā-uku-yu*
   what juice 2p-drink-PRES
   What juice are you drinking?

(781) *bāeruokoa yiha-uku-rāyũ ki-re   dā-ā-rīka*
   pineapple 1p-drink-FUT 3ms-TERM 3p-say-PST
   "We will drink pineapple juice", they said to him.

(782) *hee bĩhā-uku-be dā-re   ki-ā-rīka*
   oh 2p-drink-IMP 3p-TERM 3ms-say-PST
   "Oh, you drink it", he said to them.

(783) *aʔte ki-re   dā-oyiboha-eʔka*
   again 3ms-TERM 3p-invite-PST
   Again they invited him.

(784) dā-re   ki-ā-rīka   daʔko okoa bīhā-uku-rāyū
     3p-TERM 3ms-say-PST what juice 2p-drink-FUT
     He said to them, "What juice will you drink?"

(785) bāeruokoa   yiha-uku-rāyū ki-re   dā-ā-rīka
     pineapple^juice   1p-drink-FUT 3ms-TERM 3p-say-PST
     "We will drink pineapple juice", they said to him.

(786) hee bīhā-uku-be dā-re   ki-ā-rīka
     oh 2p-drink-IMP 3p-TERM 3ms-say-PST
     "Oh, you drink it", he said to them.

(787) bāe dā-pupahoa-eʔka daʔkoa-pi ki-re   bā-paki-hī-yū
     now 3p-think-PST   what-INSTR 3ms-TERM 12-deceive-PSBL-PRES
     Now they thought, "With what can we fool him?"

   (Change in activity, and cast. Exit alligator)

(788) supaka aʔpe-ika ā-rī-reʔka-ki yiʔi ō-yū-ka   ki-ā-rīka
     then   other-ms say-EP-PST-ms 1s   know-PRES-ms 3ms-say-PST
     Then another spoke, "I know," he said.

(789) bārākāʔā ki-re   bā-baa-hī-yū
     what   3ms-TERM 12-do-PSBL-PRES
     What can we do to him?

(790) bāe dā-re   ki-ā-rīka   bāeruka   bīhā-oye-be
     now 3p-TERM 3ms-say-PST pineapple 2p-grate-IMP
     Now he said to them, "You grate pineapple".

   (Change of activity from talking to planning.)

(791) supatirā sa-okoa bīhā-eʔe-ta-be
     then   3ns-juice 2p-get-VERT-IMP
     Then get its juice out.

(792) supatirā āta kayabaka bīhā-haʔyeā-pe
     then   rock pebble   2p-collect-IND.IMP
     Then go and collect gravel.

Elements of Discourse

(793) *i?sia hihibāka ki-uku-hī-i-ka   he?e bīhā-īā-ērā dā-re*
that happy   3ms-drink-PSBL-STAT-n   SUP   2p-see-PURP 3p-TERM

ki-ā-rīka
3ms-say-PST
"If he drinks that happily, you will see," he said to them.

(794) *bāe a?te ki-re   dā-ā-rī-re?ka bā-bāeru-uku-ērā*
now again 3ms-TERM 3p-say-EP-PST 12-pineapple-drink-PURP
Now they said to him again, "Let's drink pineapple juice".

(Change of activity and cast. Reintroduction of alligator.)

(795) *da?koa bīhā-uku-rā-ka*
what   2p-drink-FUT-n
"What will you drink?"

(796) *ki-re   dā-ā-rī-re?ka ātakayaba-ka?būa yiha-uku-rā-ka*
3ms-TERM 3p-say-EP-PST gravel-drink   1p-drink-FUT-n

ki-re   dā-ā-rī-re?ka
3ms-TERM 3p-say-EP-PST
They said to him, "We will drink gravel drink", they said to him.

(797) *supaka ki-yi?-ri-re?ka hēē   hēē   hēē*
like^that 3ms-agree-EP-PST (sound) (sound) (sound)

ki-ā-rī-re?ka
3ms-say-EP-PST
He agreed to that and said, "Hēē, hēē, hēē."

(798) *ki-yi?-ri-re?ka*
3ms-agree-EP-PST
He agreed (to come.)

(799) *bāe dā-pō?īrā ki-a?-ri-re?ka bāeru-uku-rī*
now 3p-toward 3ms-go-EP-PST pineapple-drink-PURP
Now he went to them to drink pineapple juice.

(Change of location/setting)

(800) *ki-eya-re?ka*
3ms-arrive-PST
He arrived.

(801) *ki-re   dā-heyē-re?ka*
3ms-TERM 3p-greet-PST
They greeted him.

(802) *ā?ā ki-ā-rī-re?ka*
yes 3ms-say-EP-PST
"Yes", he said (responding to the greeting).

(803) *āta   kayaba-ka?būa uku-rī   yi-i?ta-yu   ki-ā-rīka*
rock gravel-drink   drink-PURP 1s-come-PRES 3ms-say-PST
"I come to drink gravel drink", he said.

(804) *bāe ki-re   dā-sīā-re?ka   ko?a   pururika*
now 3ms-TERM 3p-feed^pour-PST gourd full
Now they poured a full gourd for him.

(*Change in activity from arrival to drinking*)

(805) *āta   peroa   sa-rā   ha?ata-tirā ki-uku-pata-re?ka*
rock pebbles 3ns-LOC put-AFTER 3ms-drink-all-PST
After putting pebbles in it, he drank it all.

(806) *a?te ki-uku-re?ka a?te ki-uku-re?ka a?te ki-uku-re?ka*
again 3ms-drink-PST again 3ms-drink-PST again 3ms-drink-PST
Again he drank, and again he drank, and again he drank.

(807) *bāe ki-payā-re?ka   be?erō?ō ki-re   dā-wa?a-re?ka*
now 3ms-lay^down-PST prior   3ms-TERM 3p-cut^open-PST

   ki-yata
   3ms-belly
Now after he laid down, they cut open his belly.

(*Change of activity from drinking to next step in plan*)

(808) *bāe ki-peka dā-e?e-re?ka dā-ē?bā-re?ka*
now 3ms-fire 3p-get-PST   3p-take^away-PST
Now they got his fire, they took it (from him).

(*Change of activity to next step in plan*)

(809) *supatirã ki-yata wiʔia dã-tua-reʔka kabãwĕka-pi*
then 3ms-belly rib^cage 3p-put^cover-PST type^of^plant-INSTR
Then they covered (the hole) with kabãwĕka (a plant).

(810) *supa ībã-rī koyua kahu-yata wiʔia ībã-wai*
like^3ns be-DVBL soft alligator-belly rib^cage be-HAB

sa-baʔa-ri-ka reka
3ns-eat-DVBL-n if
Therefore the alligator's belly is always soft when one eats it.

(811) *ikupaka kahu-bãharoka*
like^this alligator-story
This is the alligator story.

Appendix

The following texts are useful for illustrating some of the features of Retuarã, particularly at the discourse level. The texts are divided into sentences which are numbered to aid in reference.

Text 1 Canoe story

The text illustrates the different environments of the present tense suffix *-yu* and the stativizer *-i*.

(812) *bãbãrī sa-dã-bõʔa-yu   bãkaka-rã*
    first   3ns-3p-search-PRES jungle-LOC
    First they search for it in the jungle.

(813) *hia-aka kubū-yapua dã-bõʔa-yu*
    good-? canoe-tree 3p-search-PRES
    Among the good canoe trees they search.

(814) *aʔpe-ri-kuri   dã-tõpo-be-yu*
    other-INDEF-time 3p-find-NEG-PRES
    Sometimes they don't find (one).

(815) *aʔpe-rībī aʔte bõʔa-rī   dã-aʔ-yu*
    other-day again search-PURP 3p-go-PRES
    Another day they go to search again.

(816) *yoe-rã   sa-dã-tõpo-i-ka   sa-dã-ko-yu*
 far-LOC 3ns-3p-find-STAT-n 3ns-3p-cut^down-PRES
 (When) they find it far away, they cut it down.

(817) *bãẽ   sa-dã-ruʔa-yu   herã-baa-tirã*
 now 3ns-3p-cut^out-PRES measure-do-after
 Now they cut out (a section) after measuring (it).

(818) *supatirã   sa-dã-ĩã-yu   hia   sa-ĩbã-ri-ka*
 then   3ns-3p-see-PRES good 3ns-be-DVBL-n
 Then they look at the good part.

(819) *hia   sa-ĩbã-rõʔõ-pi   sa-õbẽã   dã-tea-yu*
 good 3ns-be-place-INSTR 3ns-nose 3p-shape-PRES
 From the good part they shape its prow.

(820) *sa-õbẽã   dã-tea-wea-i-ka   sa-itopea aʔte   dã-tea-yu*
 3ns-nose 3p-shape-finish-STAT-n 3ns-stern again 3p-shape-PRES
 (When) they finish shaping its prow, its stern they again shape.

(821) *to-hi-rã   dã-rãĩ-yu*
 there-EXTENT-LOC 3p-be^late-PRES
 At that point it is late afternoon for them.

(822) *dã-peʔ-yu   wiʔia-rã*
 3p-return-PRES house-LOC
 They return to the house.

(823) *dã-eta-yu*
 3p-arrive-PRES
 They arrive.

(824) *dã-uʔya-yu*
 3p-bathe-PRES
 They bathe.

Text continues...

Appendix

Text 2 Dance story

The text illustrates the contrast in usage between the present tense *-yu* and the stativizer *-i* in a discourse about preparing for a dance. This text is a section from the middle of a larger text.

(825) *bāē sa-dā-ko-yu pōrāka*
now 3ns-3p-cut^down-PRES palm (a type of)
Now they cut it down, pōrāka.

(826) *sa-dā-kaʔre-yu*
3ns-3p-peel-PRES
They peel it.

(827) *bāē sa-dā-paa-yu dā-ībāupatihi*
now 3ns-3p-pound-PRES 3p-all
Now they all pound it.

(828) *sa-dā-wea-i-ka*
3ns-3p-finish-STAT-n
They finish it.

(829) *sa-dā-kīke-yu*
3ns-3p-weave-PRES
They weave it.

(830) *kīke-wea-tirā sa-dā-ruʔa-yu īrātihi*
weave-finish-after 3ns-3p-cut-PRES evenly
After finishing weaving, they cut it evenly.

(831) *sa-dā-turē-yu hāhīā hiyia*
3ns-3p-roll^up-PRES very hard/tight
They roll it up very tight.

(832) *wea-i-ka*
finish-STAT-n
Finish.

(833) *tātā-rā sa-dā-rēā-yu*
mud-LOC 3ns-3p-blacken-PRES
They blacken it in mud.

(834) *hia dēīā*
     good black
     Very black (they make it).

(835) *sa-dā-wea-i-ka*
     3ns-3p-finish-STAT-n
     They finish it.

(836) *bikitoho bāē dā-taʔa-yu la diez rōʔō-hi-rā*
     morning now 3p-wait-PRES ten^o'clock place-EXTENT-LOC
     In the morning now they wait until ten o'clock.

Text 3 Airplane story

This text provides many examples of the variation between *-rape* and *-rapa-ka/-ko/-rā* (past). Notice also that the number/gender suffix (following *-rapa*) does not always agree with the subject in gender and number. When the subject is clearly marked by prefix, or term case marking on a subject noun phrase, the number/gender suffix *-ka* (neuter) seems to simply nominalize the verb phrase or mark it as the dependent clause. The division of the text into sentences has not been certain. It may very well be that the sentence division is wrong and that *-rapa-ka/-ko/-rā* actually occurs mostly in dependent clauses. For example, (841) could be analyzed so as to combine it with the following clause. The resulting gloss would be: 'now, coming to Caño Colorado, we arrived.' Those places where other sentence divisions seem possible will be indicated by alternative glosses in brackets.

(837) *apapuri-pi yi-iʔta-**rapa**-ka i-bāharoka yi-oʔo-ērā baa-yu*
     Apaporis-INSTR 1s-come-PST-n ?-story 1s-write-PURP do-PRES

     bāē
     now
     Now I am going to write the story of my coming from Apaporis.

(838) *yiha-iʔta-rape wiʔia-pi*
     1p-come-PST house-INSTR
     We came from the house.

(839) *yiha-eta-rape wiyawaia-rā*
     1p-arrive-PST airplane-LOC
     We arrived at the airplane.

Appendix

(840) *yiha-hāī-rape*
   1p-board-PST
   We boarded.

(841) *bā̰ḛ̄ yiha-i?ta-rapa-ka oko-hū?ā-yaka-rā*
   now 1p-come-PST-n   water-red-river-LOC
   Now we came to Caño Colorado.

(842) *yiha-eta-rape*
   1p-arrive-PST
   We arrived.

   Or: [Now, coming to Caño Colorado, we arrived.]

(843) *bā̰ḛ̄ to-rā   yiha-ībā-rape*
   now there-LOC 1p-be-PST
   Now we were there.

(844) *gasolidā dā-paa-rapa-ka*
   gasoline 3p-pour-PST-n
   They poured gasoline (in the airplane).

(845) *wei-rapa-ka*
   finish-PST-n
   (They) finished.

(846) *yiha-hāī-rape wiyawaia-rā*
   1p-board-PST airplane-LOC
   We boarded the airplane.

   Or: [When they poured gas and finished, we boarded the airplane.]

(847) *ki-rihiata-rape*
   3ms-start-PST
   He started (the motor.)

(848) *bā̰ḛ̄ yiha-wi-rapa-ka-ha*
   now 1p-fly-PST-n-ADVLZR
   Now we were flying.

(849) *yiha-rui-rape yapu-rã*
1p-land-PST Yapu-LOC
We landed at Yapu.

Or: [Now flying, we landed at Yapu.]

(850) *ĩpa-rã-te   rueta-rape*
two-p-TERM disembark-PST
Two (passengers) disembarked (at Yapu).

(851) *to-rã   põʔĩbãhã-re yiha-ĩã-rape rĩkibã-iʔtaka*
there-LOC people-TERM 1p-see-PST   many-INTS
There we saw lots of people.

(852) *aʔte   yiha-hãĩ-rape*
again 1p-board-PST
Again we boarded (the plane).

(853) *bãẽ aʔte yiha-iʔta-rapa-ka-ha*
now again 1p-come-PST-n-ADVLZR
Now we were coming again.

(854) *yiha-ĩã-rape riaka wehea wiʔia bãẽ*
1p-see-PST   river land house now
We saw rivers, lands, and houses now.

Or: [Now coming again, we saw rivers, lands and houses now.]

(855) *to-rã   bãẽ obãka   yi-re   baa-rape*
there-LOC now sleepiness 1s-TERM do-PST
There now, I got sleepy.

(856) *gloria-re   baa-rapa-ka obãka*
Gloria-TERM do-PST-n   sleepiness
Gloria got sleepy.

(857) *yiha-re baa-bãka yiha-hai-rape*
1p-TERM do-COND 1p-talk-PST
When it did that to us, we talked.

Appendix

(858) *bīraflore yiha-ĩã-rape*
Miraflores 1p-see-PST
We saw Miraflores (a town).

(859) *yiha-oʔ-rape*
1p-pass-PST
We passed (over it).

(860) *karetera yi-ĩã-rape*
road 1s-see-PST
I saw roads.

(861) *paʔwa pusia ãta boyaka dẽʔẽtãta yiha-ĩã-rape*
lake hill rock plains miriti^palm 1p-see-PST
We saw lakes, hills, plains and Miriti palms.

(862) *lobālĩda paʔwa yiha-ĩã-rape*
Lomalinda lake 1p-see-PST
We saw Lomalinda lake.

(863) *pista-rã yiha-rui-rape*
airstrip-LOC 1p-land-PST
We landed on the airstrip.

(864) *aeropuerto-rã yiha-eta-rape*
airport-LOC 1p-arrive-PST
We arrived at the airport.

(865) *yi-bẽ-rape*
1s-get^out-PST
I got out.

(866) *adĩta yiha-re heyẽ-**rapa**-ko*
Anita 1p-TERM greet-PST-3fs
Anita greeted us.

(867) *ĩbã-**rapa**-ko betadĩa*
be-PST-3fs Bethanie
Bethanie was (there).

(868) bōka ībā-**rapa**-ko
Mocha be-PST-fs
Mocha (a dog) was (there).

(869) ehersita-rā-ka ībā-**rapa**-rā
army-p-n be-PST-p
Army (soldiers) were (there).

(870) bāẽ kle-re bōto-pi gloria-re ki-eʔe-waʔ-rape
now Clay-TERM moto-INSTR Gloria-TERM 3ms-get-AWAY-PST

    ki-wiʔia-rā
    3ms-house-LOC
Now Clay took Gloria by moto to his house.

(871) supatirā yi-re ki-eʔe-waʔ-rape
then 1s-TERM 3ms-get-AWAY-PST
Then he took me.

(872) to-rā bāẽ yiha-baʔa-rape
there-LOC now 1p-eat-PST
There now we ate.

(873) yiha-iʔta-rape aʔte yiha-wiʔi-hīka-rā
1p-come-PST again 1p-house-DIM-LOC
Again we came to our little house.

(874) ki-iʔta-rape sa-rā yiha-ībā-rape
3ms-come-PST 3ns-LOC 1p-be-PST
He came to it, we were there.

(875) bikitoho yi-uʔya-koʔo
morning 1s-bathe-PST
I bathed in the morning.

(876) yi-baʔa-turū-koʔo
1s-eat-wake-PST
I ate breakfast.

(877) wei-koʔo-a
finish-PST-n
Finished.

Appendix

(878) *yiha-i?ta-ko?o ofisidā-rā*
1p-come-PST   office-LOC
We came to the office.

Or: [When it was finished, we came to the office.]

(879) *yiha-ībē*
1p-be
We are (there).

(880) *kopakaha bāē yi-ō-rī-be-yu-a   bāē*
finally   now 1s-know-EP-NEG-PRES-n now
Finally now I don't know anymore.

Subject agreement marking on the verb

Table (881) summarizes the methods of marking agreement using number/gender suffixes (column one). Column two illustrates constructions with subject case marked as term or with a subject pronominal prefix. Example clauses are provided to supplement the notation in the chart's summary.

(881) Subject agreement marking summary

	Subject agreement marked	Subject agreement unmarked
NP subject	S V-s	S-re V
Pronoun subject	(Pro) V-s (Pro)	s-V Pro-re V

S (subject NP)
s- (subject pronoun prefix)
V (verb)
Pro (subject pronoun)
-s (subject agreement suffix)
-re (term case marked)

Subject NPs (agreement marked on verb)

(882) *tomas   baʔa-koʔo-ki* (S V-s)
 Thomas eat-PST-3ms
 Thomas ate.

(883) *yaiwēkoa rī-yū-a*   (S V-s)
 dog   run-PRES-n
 The dog runs.

(884) *yaiwēkoa sa-hāā-koʔo-a* (S o-V-s)
 dog   3ns-kill-PST-n
 The dog killed it.

Subject NPs (agreement unmarked on verb)

(885) *toma-re   baʔa-koʔo* (S-re V)
 Thomas-TERM eat-PST
 Thomas ate.

(886) *toma-re   hose-re   īā-koʔo* (S-re O-re V)
 Thomas-TERM José-TERM see-PST
 Thomas saw José.

(887) *toma-re   sa-hāā-koʔo* (S-re o-V)/(O-re s-V)
 Thomas-TERM 3ns-kill-PST
 Thomas killed it/It killed Thomas.

Subject pronouns (agreement marked on verb)

(888) *iʔki baʔa-koʔo-ki* (Pro V-s)
 3ms eat-PST-ms
 He ate.

(889) *aʔ-ri-be-sa-rā-ki   iʔki* (V-s Pro)
 go-EP-NEG-EP-FUT-ms 3ms
 He will not go/not be the one to go.

(890) *yiʔi sa-rupukoʔa baʔa-rā-ki* (Pro O V-s)
 1s   3ns-head   eat-FUT-ms
 I will be the one to eat its head.

Appendix

Subject pronouns (agreement unmarked on verb)

(891) *iʔki-ré   baʔa-koʔo* (**Pro-re** V)
    3ms-TERM eat-PST
    He (the one nearby) ate.

(892) *waʔia ki-baʔakoʔo* (O s-V)
    fish   3ms-eat-PST
    He ate the fish.

(893) *ki-re   ki-ĩã-koʔo* (O-re s-V)
    3ms-TERM 3ms-see-PST
    He saw him.

(894) *sa-ki-baʔakoʔo* (o-s-V)
    3ns-3ms-eat-PST
    He ate it.

References

Barnard, Mike and Robert E. Longacre. 1968. Grammar and lexicon in Dibabawon narrative procedure discourse. Philippines: Summer Institute of Linguistics.

Barnes, Janet. 1984. Evidentials in the Tuyuca verb. IJAL 50(3):255–71.

———. 1990. Classifiers in Tuyuca. In D. Payne (ed.), Amazonian linguistics, 273–92. Austin: The University of Texas Press.

Beekman, John, John Callow, and Mike Kopesec. 1981. The semantic structure of written communication. Dallas: Summer Institute of Linguistics.

Clark, E. 1978. Locationals: Existential, locative, and possessive constructions. In J. Greenberg, C. Ferguson, and E. Moravcsik (eds.), Universals of human language 4: Syntax, 85–121. Stanford: Stanford University Press.

Comrie, Bernard. 1981. Language universals and linguistic typology. Chicago: University of Chicago Press.

Derbyshire, Des. 1982. Arawakan (Brazil) morphosyntax. UND SIL Work Papers 26. Grand Forks: University of North Dakota.

———. 1986. Handbook of Amazonian languages 1. Berlin: Mouton de Gruyter.

Dixon, R. M. W. 1982. Where have all the adjectives gone? and other essays in semantics and syntax. Janua linguarum series maior 107. Berlin: Mouton Publishers.

Fox, B. A. 1987. Anaphora in popular written English narratives. In R. Tomlin (ed.), Typological studies in language: Coherence and grounding in discourse 11:157–74. Philadelphia: John Benjamins Publishing Co.

Frantz, Don. 1979. Grammatical relations in universal grammar. UND SIL workpapers 23. California: Summer Institute of Linguistics.

Gaviria, Sofía Victoria and Luis José Azcárate. 1979. Fonología y lexicología de la lengua tanimuca. (Lecturas en teoria y practica en etnolingüística 1) Bogotá: Depto de Antropología, Universidad de los Andes.

Givón, Talmy. 1980. The binding hierarchy and the typology of complement. Studies in language 4:333–77. Philadelphia: John Benjamins North America Inc.

———. 1983. Topic continuity in discourse: An introduction. In T. Givón (ed.), Topic continuity in discourse: A quantitative cross-language study, 18. Philadelphia: John Benjamins Publishing Co.

———. 1984. Syntax: A functional typological introduction 1:117–25. Philadelphia: John Benjamins Publishing Company.

Hopper, Paul and Sandra Thompson. 1984. The discourse basis for lexical categories in universal grammar. Language 60(4):703–52.

Jones, W. and P. Jones. 1991. Barasana syntax. Arlington: The University of Texas and Summer Institute of Linguistics.

Keenan, E. 1985. Relative clauses. In T. Shopen (ed.), Language typology and syntactic description 2: Complex constructions, 161. Cambridge: Cambridge University Press.

——— and Bernard Comrie. 1977. NP accessibility and universal grammar. Linguistic Inquiry 8:66.

Key, Mary Ritchie. 1979. The grouping of South American Indian languages. Ars linguistica commentationes analyticae criticae 2:120. Tubingen: Gunter Narr Verlag.

Levinsohn, Stephen. 1978. Participant reference in Inga narrative discourse. In J. Hinds (ed.), Current inquiry into language and linguistics. Anaphora in discourse 22. Edmonton, Canada: Linguistic Research Inc.

———. 1980. Relationships between constituents beyond the clause in the Acts of the Apostles. Ph.D. thesis, University of Reading, England.

Lyons, J. 1968. Introduction to theoretical linguistics. London: Cambridge University Press.

Malone, T. to appear. Sound change in the Tucanoan language family.

Maxwell, Mike and N. Morse. to appear. Cubeo grammar.

Metzger, R. 1981. Gramatica popular del Carapana. Bogotá: Instituto Lingüístico de Verano.

References

Payne, David 1990. Some widespread grammatical forms in South American languages. In D. L. Payne (ed.), Amazonian linguistics, 77–8. Austin: The University of Texas Press.

Robayo, Camilo A. 1981. Elementos de morfología de la lengua tanimuka. Lecturas en teoría y práctica en etnolingüística 1. Bogotá: Depto de Antropología, Universidad de los Andes.

Ruhlen, M. 1987. A guide to the world's languages 1. Stanford: Stanford University Press.

Schachter, Paul. 1985. Parts-of-speech systems. In T. Shopen (ed.), Language typology and syntactic description 1: Clause structure. Cambridge: Cambridge University Press.

Schauer, S. and J. Schauer. 1978. Una gramática del Yucuna. Articulos en Lingüística y campos afines. 5:46. Bogotá: Instituto Lingüístico de Verano.

Shibatani, M. 1976. Causativization. In M. Shibatani (ed.), Syntax and semantics, Japanese generative grammar 5. San Francisco: Academic Press.

Strom, Clay. to appear. Syntactic change in the Tucanoan family. ms.

Waugh, L. and M. Monville-Burston. 1986. Aspect and discourse function: The French simple past in newspaper usage. Language 62(4):846–77.

West, B. 1980. Gramática popular del Tucano. Bogotá: Instituto Lingüístico de Verano.

Wise, Mary Ruth. 1990. Valence changing affixes in Maipuran Arawakan languages. In D. L. Payne (ed.), Amazonian linguistics, 103–7. Austin: The University of Texas Press.

Index

A

ablative case 62–63
accessibility hierarchy 156
active 191–95
adjective 11, 23–28, 51, 56, 129
adverb 33–34, 43, 103–10
adverbial clause 40, 107–8
agent 59, 198–201
agreement 71–72, 124, 195
aspect 38, 76–80, 106–7, 195–97
assimilation 22
attitude markers 105–6
auxiliary 38, 72

B

background/foreground 85, 191–97
benefactive 3, 65–66, 120, 157

C

case 8–10, 24, 35, 37, 53–54, 59–67, 152–55
category 7, 11, 25–27, 33, 35, 45, 94, 103, 107, 121–23, 159, 161
causative 92–101
  analytical 92–95
  lexicalized 96–99, 121–23
  morphological 43, 92, 98
  volitional 93–96
classifier 11, 37, 54–57
clause 103, 134, 151–78
clitic 2, 9, 14, 35–36, 154
comparative 6, 26, 177
complement 33, 158–66
compounding 33, 91–92
condition/grounds 172–73, 177–78
conjunction
  coordinating 39, 64–65
  subordinating 40, 167–68, 176–78
contingency 170–71
contra-expectation 80, 82–83, 107, 161, 163, 165, 175, 178
copula 25, 28, 123–24, 146
courtesy
  with imperatives 136–39
  with questions 144

D

declarative 2–3, 34, 40, 90, 115, 121–25, 138, 143, 145–46
definite 24, 27, 36, 51, 60, 126–28, 131–32
deixis 13–15, 129

deletion 12, 159
demonstrative 36, 51–53, 132
derivational 41, 107–10
deverbalization 41–42
directional 18–19, 88–89
discourse 7–8, 41–42, 179–207
ditransitive 32, 94, 118–23

E

epenthesis 15, 17
evidentials 39, 90–91
existential constructions 124–26
experiencer 124–25, 158, 180, 190–91

F

focus 3, 10, 46, 57, 59, 61, 79, 126, 128, 193, 195, 199, 201

G

gender 10–11, 41, 56–57
genitive 5, 47

H

head (relative clause) 151–56
hierarchy
  accessibility 156
  animacy 119, 189–90
  grammatical relations 53, 93–94

I

imperatives 135–39
  direct 135–36
  hortatory 137–38
  indirect 136–37
  negative 137, 139
imperfective 195–97
inanimate 10–11, 30, 45–47, 67, 95, 153, 166, 189, 198, 201
incorporation 100–1
indirect object 93–94, 121–23, 156
infinitive 42

instrument 3, 63–64, 100, 157
intensifier 39, 89–90
intention 72, 81, 165–66, 170
intransitive 31, 94, 99, 112–14, 133

L

length 12, 13, 15
locationals 104, 112–13, 116–17, 126–28
locative case
  general 3, 30, 37, 61–62
  specific 62, 158

M

manner 103–13, 117–18
modifier 4, 25
mood 38, 80–83, 106–7
morpheme 5, 7, 12, 15, 17, 20–21, 27, 36, 41, 49, 136, 147
morphophonemic 21–22

N

nasalization 12–13, 19–21, 77, 98, 107
negation 3, 6–7, 17–19, 40, 137, 139, 142, 145–49, 172
nominalization 7, 10, 41, 148, 151, 176, 194, 198–99
noun 3, 7, 10–11, 23–28, 31, 35–37, 41–42, 64, 127, 148, 151
noun classes 10–11, 45–47, 71, 123, 192–93
noun phrase 2, 4–5, 8, 24, 36, 39, 45, 59, 61–62, 64–66, 71, 74–75, 84, 86, 93, 103, 111, 113–19, 123, 130, 133, 146, 153–54, 156, 162, 177, 179–82, 186, 188, 195
numerals 50–51

O

object 7, 32, 94, 100, 114–23, 157–58
order
  affix 5, 16, 48, 69–70
  clause 168, 172, 177

Index

word 2–7, 32, 51, 53, 94, 111, 113–15, 118–23, 126–28, 131–32, 134, 145–46, 168
OV 2–6, 114–18, 134, 145

P

participant 179–91
  central character 180–81, 183, 186, 190, 202
  major 180, 182–83, 186–89
  minor 180, 182–83, 186–89
  villain 180, 185
participial 41–42
participle 86–88
parts of speech 23–43
patient 31, 59, 94, 99, 125, 180
phoneme 11–12
phonological rules 12–13
possessive 66–67, 130–32, 158
postpositions 4, 37
prefix 5, 35
pronoun 3, 34–36, 60, 129
prototypical 27, 192–93
purpose 164–65, 169–70, 172

Q

quantifiers 37, 48–50, 148
questions 7, 141–44, 149

R

reason/result 173–75
recipient 3, 8, 59, 157
reciprocal 99–100
reflexive 133–34
relative clause 151–58
  definition 151
  internal head 6, 48, 151–56

S

sentence 111–34, 145–46
spatial relator 29
stative 84–85, 191–95
stress 13–19
subject 7, 9, 71, 114, 124–26, 156, 198–99
subordination 151–78
  adverbial clause 134, 167–78
  complementation 158–66
  relative clauses 151–58
suffix 6, 25, 35, 39, 41, 152, 168–75, 195
syllable 17, 21, 24
syntax 7–10, 156

T

tense 38, 72–76, 155
term 10, 59–61, 152
thematic development 201–7
time 104, 112–13, 116–17, 120, 168–69, 176–78
topic 49, 61, 126, 179, 201
transitive 31–32, 94, 114–18
typology 5

V

valence 31, 43, 94, 100, 122
verb 15, 28–33, 38–39, 69–101
  cognition/utterance/sensory 162–64
  manipulative 161–62
  modality 159–61
  motion 164–65
  preventative 165–66
VO 7
volition 93–96
vowel 12
  harmony 33, 98, 107
  length 12
  nasalization 12

www.ingramcontent.com/pod-product-compliance
Lightning Source LLC
Chambersburg PA
CBHW050137240426
43673CB00043B/1708